MUSICIANS FROM A DIFFERENT SHORE

MUSICIANS

from a

DIFFERENT

SHORE

Asians and Asian Americans

in Classical Music

Mari Yoshihara

TEMPLE UNIVERSITY PRESS
Philadelphia

TEMPLE UNIVERSITY PRESS
1601 North Broad Street
Philadelphia PA 19122
www.temple.edu/tempress

Designed by Kate Nichols

♾ The paper used in this publication meets the requirements
of the AmericanNational Standard for Information Sciences—
Permanence of Paper for Printed Library Materials, ANSI Z39.48-1992

Library of Congress Cataloging-in-Publication Data
Yoshihara, Mari, 1968–
Musicians from a different shore : Asians and Asian Americans
in classical music / Mari Yoshihara.
p. cm.
Includes bibliographical references and index.
ISBN 13: 978-1-59213-332-1 (cloth: alk. paper)
ISBN 10: 1-59213-332-0 (cloth: alk. paper)
1. East Asian American musicians—Social conditions.
2. Musicians—East Asia—Social conditions.
3. Music—Social aspects—United States. 4. Music—Social aspects—East Asia.
I. Title.
ML3795.Y67 2007
780.89'95—dc22

2 4 6 8 9 7 5 3 1
2007018929

Contents

Preface | vii

Introduction: A Rising Scale
in Relative Minor | 1

1 | Early Lessons in Globalization | 11

Voices | 49

2 | The Roots and Routes of Asian Musicians | 62

3 | Playing Gender | 100

4 | Class Notes | 131

Voices | 166

5 | A Voice of One's Own | 187

Conclusion: Musicians First | 225

Acknowledgments | 235

Notes | 239

Selected Bibliography | 255

Index | 263

Preface

In many ways, I had a typical urban, middle-class childhood in Japan in the midst of its period of economic growth. I was born in New York City in 1968 and raised in a middle-class neighborhood in Tokyo. The condominium in which I grew up was miniscule even by Tokyo standards, and the Yamaha upright piano my parents bought for me occupied one-third of the total space of my room. I started piano lessons at age three with a teacher in my neighborhood, and when I proved to be a better-than-average student, I was "upgraded" to a teacher who lived a little farther away. Soon afterward, that teacher "transferred" me to her own mentor for more rigorous training at his studio a few train stops away from where we lived. In the time, place, and culture in which I lived, where virtually every middle-class girl took piano lessons, it seemed as if the distance to which one traveled for piano lessons represented one's seriousness about music. I was serious indeed and spent much of my childhood practicing Hanon scales, Czerny études, Bach fugues, and Beethoven and Mozart sonatas for a few hours each day. Around age eight, I also started ear training and sight-reading lessons, and I have had perfect pitch as long as I can remember. All during this period of my life, I never asked myself why I was learning music or whether I even liked playing the piano. Such questions never even occurred to me. Music was not something I had the option of liking or not liking; it was just there for me to do.

Although my mother and I used to think that my seriousness about piano made me special, my piano training was in fact quite typical of my generation of urban, middle-class girls in Japan. After domestic mass production of pianos in the 1960s and 1970s made the upright piano attainable for the middle class, having a piano in the house and sending children—especially girls—to piano lessons became common markers of class status. More than three million households owned a piano in the early 1970s, and every middle-class neighborhood seemed to have its own piano studios.[1] At the same time, Japan's economic development during this period created an extremely tight housing situation, symbolized by the mass construction of uniform condominiums and subsidized housing in urban and suburban areas.

These two phenomena came together in August 1974 in a government-subsidized housing project in a city located about an hour from Tokyo. A 46-year-old unemployed man stabbed two young girls and their mother who lived on the floor below him because he was upset by the constant sound of piano practice. The two girls, four and eight years old, were killed in the 3-*jo* [approximately 5.5 ft x 8.5 ft] room that housed the upright piano the parents had purchased the previous fall. On the sliding door, the man scribbled, "You could at least say sorry, since you're inconveniencing the neighbors."[2] The "Piano Noise Murder Case," as it was famously known, horrified the nation, and many families with children playing the piano—including mine—bought a sound-absorbing damper to put behind the piano and made sure to limit the children's practice in the evening hours.[3]

With so much classical music in my life, my musical sensibility was Western, and piano was my identity. In the music room of my public elementary school, the portraits of Bach, Beethoven, Mozart, and Chopin hung on the wall, but I recall no portraits of Japanese composers. Aside from the pop songs I listened to and some folk songs I learned in school, I was exposed to little Japanese music. My childhood routine of daily piano practice, weekly lessons, and yearly performances also included watching *Meikyoku Arubamu*, a daily five-minute program on NHK (a government-subsidized public television network) that featured famous pieces of classical music and showed beautiful European landscapes on the screen. I also watched the broadcast of the Vienna Philharmonic's New Year's Eve concert and ball every year, and my childhood dream was to some day become a debutante in Vienna and dance to *The Blue Danube* with a tall European gentleman. I never noticed that there was not a single Asian face at the Viennese ball, and

I found no contradictions between my strong identification with European high culture and all the material accoutrements of my life in Tokyo—symbolized by the doilies on top of the television showing the Viennese ball and the wall hangings that did not match—that shouted Asian tacky.

Although I certainly was not aware of it at the time, my musical training was a central part of my gendered middle-class upbringing. In addition to my piano playing, my preoccupations and aspirations were highly gendered. If I was not playing the piano, I was reading, and I identified strongly with the character of Jo in *Little Women*. At the end of each school year, we wrote in the class booklet what we wanted to be when we grew up. The most common answers among girls were "stewardess," "nurse," or "teacher." (The most common answers among boys were "pilot," "doctor," "baseball player," or "company president.") I remember writing "pianist" in some years and "writer" in others. I did not learn until much later that both the music and literature professions were male-dominated. In my naiveté, I believed that a woman with talent (which I assumed I had) could rise to the top in either profession.

My upbringing was also shaped by Japan's place in the growing global economy. Because of my father's job at an import-export company, when I was eleven my family moved back to the United States. We lived in California for two and a half years, where I took piano lessons from a Japanese American teacher and a Russian émigré pianist who together ran a music studio in Palo Alto. In contrast to the rather programmatic training I was used to in Japan, these teachers used a much freer method of piano instruction, giving me the kinds of pieces that Japanese teachers consider beyond twelve-year-olds' level of emotional maturity—Chopin études and scherzi, the Mendelssohn piano concerto, Scriabin études, and so forth. I was both excited and confused about the different ways in which music students, teachers, and audiences related to classical music in the two cultures.

Because I did not speak a word of English when I first moved to California, my social life in the first six months or so there was quite limited, and piano came to occupy an even larger portion of my identity than before. As I went on to junior high school and had to choose electives, my parents thought that music classes were the way to go because, even with my limited English-language skills, I would not be at a disadvantage in those classes. So I took band and started playing the flute. I also took chorus. My piano background helped me quickly become one of the key members in both the band and the chorus, and I played some solo pieces in school concerts. In the meantime, my piano teachers gave me the opportunity to perform in several concerts in the community, and my name appeared in a review in the *San Francisco Chronicle* of one such concert. I gave my first recital at my teachers' studio at age thirteen. In these difficult and confusing years of crossing cultures and languages, having a musical identity helped sustain my sense of self and confidence.

Despite the centrality of music to my life and my identity, in the end I chose not to pursue music professionally. I continued my piano lessons after returning to Japan, but a few years later I decided—a fairly momentous decision for me, given how much I had invested in piano thus far—not to go to a music conservatory. In retrospect, this decision was influenced by my emerging consciousness of my social, cultural, and gendered place as a young woman in Japan. Until then my identity was primarily "the girl who plays the piano well"; yet, on returning to Japan from the United States, I had acquired a new identity as "the girl who speaks English." With my English-language skills and strong academic record, I realized for the first time in my life that there were other life options available to me besides playing the piano. Around the same time, reading Simone de Beauvoir on my own, I also became a budding feminist. I began to understand that a woman seeking an independent life in Japan needed some tool for empowerment, such as a degree from a prestigious—and hence male-dominated—university. I also began to notice that, among my acquaintances, the girls who went to conservatories exuded the type of femininity—symbolized by the velvet dresses and long curly hair displayed in their headshots on their recital flyers—that had no appeal to me whatsoever. My developing political awareness and career ambitions, combined with my utter frustration with Liszt's Paganini Étude that I was working on at the time, led me to say farewell to the conservatory path. I entered the University of Tokyo and majored in American Studies. I then came to the United States to begin graduate work and became an academic.

By the time I started graduate school, piano occupied a relatively small part of my life. However, little did I know on entering American academe that not only would I have zero time for piano playing but also that the academic discourse I was jumping into would forever alter my relationship to my dream of the Viennese ball. As I began my scholarly work on Orientalism, I quietly put my classical musical past away in the closet. A few years into graduate school I did get a spinet and played occasionally, but I compartmentalized my life so that my academic and musical selves were completely separate. In the light of day, I was a liberal intellectual critiquing Western cultural imperialism and Asian complicity in it. In the dark of my closet, I was an avid fan of Rachmaninoff and all the dead white male European composers. I felt a big sense of relief and validation when I learned that Edward Said was an accomplished pianist and also wrote extensively about classical music. But for the most part, I suppressed the musical part of my identity, and few of the friends I made during graduate school and in my first years working in academe knew me as a pianist.

Watching the 2001 broadcast of the Vienna Philharmonic's New Year's Eve concert changed all that. Twenty years after forming my childhood fantasies, I saw *The Blue Danube* now being conducted by Seiji Ozawa. And when the camera turned to the audience, it captured several Japanese men and women sitting gracefully in the balcony. I was stunned to discover that some of my compatriots had realized my childhood fantasies. But more important, it suddenly dawned on me that the middle-class Asian preoccupation with Western classical music was a unique historical and cultural phenomenon that I could analyze using both my personal experience and scholarly training. I had just completed my first book on American Orientalism. Phasing into post-tenure life, I had also bought a digital piano and taken my old music quite literally "out of the closet." As I listened to Strauss waltzes, I made two resolutions for 2002: to return to my music and to write my next book on Asians and classical music.

My background has shaped my approach to this book's topic in several specific ways. I now have a decisively different relationship to classical music than I did before I entered academia. Having acquired a scholarly language and framework to think about the history of East-West relations, I no longer consider the power of Western classical music as deriving solely from the universal appeal of its aesthetic achievements but also acknowledge the role of global history and power relations in spreading classical music beyond the Western world. As a scholar who looks at the historical and structural relations of race, ethnicity, class, and gender in the United States, I see Asians' success in Western classical music not simply as a product of individual effort and talent or a reflection of some essential elements of Asian culture. Instead, I see their accomplishments as shaped by various structural factors that encourage many Asians to pursue this particular art form. I am also aware of many forms of inequality and prejudice that Asians—including classical musicians—face in the United States today, which the Asian musicians themselves are often unaware of or choose not to dwell on. In this sense, my scholarly eyes compel me to pose critical questions and analyze issues that many musicians might not consider relevant to their experience.

When I first began this project, therefore, I thought I would rely on the familiar academic concepts and categories, such as class, race, gender, imperialism, and hegemony, to analyze Asians' investment in classical music. Indeed, those frameworks do play a crucial role in the book, because I believe that one cannot understand the overrepresentation of Asians in classical music without addressing the historical and structural factors of East Asian encounters with Western music. Nor can one understand the experiences of Asian and Asian American musicians in the United States without placing them in the context of U.S. race relations and immigration history, class dynamics, and gender and sexual norms.

However, doing research in which I was simultaneously an insider and an outsider, and thinking through the issues not only as a scholar but also as a musician, I also came to feel the limitations and inadequacies of these analytical frameworks and was compelled to rethink many of my own assumptions and approaches. As I watched Asian musicians dedicate themselves to music despite constant disappointments, frustrations, and self-questioning as they pursued their artistic goals, and as I heard the passion with which they talked about their relationship to music and their audience, I had to question the relevance of those academic categories to what the musicians really do. Categories like race and culture seemed hopelessly abstract in relation to the unbelievably detailed and endless process of music-making done in the solemn, solitary interface between the performer and the composer. On the other hand, the profound and real connections that music—and musicians—create among people of different parts of the world seemed irreducible to categories like race, nation, and imperialism. In many ways, the vocabulary and frameworks I had as a scholar were both too big and too small to talk about the musicians' relationship to music that is at once intensely personal and communal.

Moreover, although I decided to return to piano playing in part because I hoped it would help sharpen my thinking on the project, my own involvement in music actually added to, rather than helped solve, my research dilemma. As I struggled to perfect the details of tone, phrasing, rhythm, and dynamics and to capture the wonders of each piece, I asked myself the same questions I posed my informants: whether my Japanese identity had anything to do with the way I understood, felt, and played Chopin, Rachmaninoff, Debussy, Scriabin, and Barber. Although I hoped that my informants would respond in brilliant sound-bytes to my question, I found it utterly impossible to answer my own question. I could arguably say that the way I tended to phrase certain passages sounded more like a Japanese *enka* [a genre of Japanese popular music akin to ballads, mostly about lost love] than a Polish folk dance or that the mood I created was more like that of a fishing village in northern Japan than Majorca in the rain. A creative process is shaped by one's imagination and expressive vocabulary, and to the extent that a large part of my imagination and expressive vocabulary *was* Japanese, it seemed reasonable to say that my playing was influenced by my Japanese upbringing. But in all honesty, where and how I grew up felt rather irrelevant as I was trying to distinguish the tone color in different voices in the Rachmaninoff D-Major prelude or to get the rhythm right and hesitate properly in "Hesitation-Tango" in Barber's *Souvenirs* suite. My general problems in playing—my inability to wait and enjoy the anticipation, my tendency to prematurely rush to the climax, my inclination to play fast and loud in parts I like, and my failure to distinguish and prioritize between the lines—definitely reflected my personality and behavior patterns, but are those characteristics Japanese? I had spent years doing cultural criticism and thinking about the relationship between the scholar and her subject, but as I worked on my research and my music, I found myself at a loss as to how to negotiate between my critical thinking as a scholar and my personal experience as a musician.

In the course of writing this book, I thus struggled with the intellectual and emotional as well as ethical issues of my project. On the one hand, I often worried that I might be imposing my own academic agenda onto musicians who were not concerned by the same questions I had as a scholar. At times, because of my empathy and admiration for my informants and my desire to represent their perspectives faithfully, I felt the urge to suspend my critique even as I encountered ideas and situations that my scholarly brain found questionable. On the other hand, I am, after all, writing this book as a scholar. It would be intellectually irresponsible for me to simply take everything I saw and heard at face value without subjecting it to critical analysis and contextualizing it in a broader framework. Even in the moments where

I am consciously taking off my academic hat, it is neither possible nor desirable for me to entirely rid myself of my scholarly perspectives.

These are the dilemmas that trouble all scholars, especially ethnographers writing about living people with whom they develop personal relationships. In particular, those who are doing "native anthropology" (i.e., a study of a community of which the scholar is a part) struggle with the often conflicting obligations they have to their profession and the community about which they write.[4] Of course, in the context of this project, I am not a "native anthropologist" in a strict sense, as I left the world of music a while back and am not a professional musician. Yet, as someone who once studied music seriously and also as an Asian person living in the United States, I do have an intimate understanding of both the pleasures and pains of musical pursuit as well as of living with multiple cultural identities in a society in which one is part of the minority. In the end, what impelled me to write this book is my personal investment in classical music just as much as my interest in the questions of identity, race, gender, class, and culture.

What follows then is an account shaped by the productive tension between my musical past and my scholarly present, between my position as an insider and as an outsider, and between my responsibilities as an advocate and as a critic. I try to present both what the musicians themselves see and what they do not see. I attempt to explain the musicians' experiences, ideas, and perspectives in their own terms. At the same time, I discuss some issues in ways that are not typically done by the musicians themselves, not because I know better than they do, but because my scholarly training has enabled me to ask—and even answer—the questions they may not ask. If the remainder of this book gives the reader a glimpse of the extremely rigorous, painful, and rewarding nature of both classical music *and* scholarly analysis, it would make all the travails of my research and writing worthwhile.

Musicians from a Different Shore

Introduction:
A Rising Scale in
Relative Minor

[At Juilliard Pre-College], I got so much stimulation from just being around highly motivated, talented musicians. Of course, there were many Asians. When I started attending Juilliard—I mean, right now, at Juilliard, it's like all Asian. Have you been to the Saturday school [Juilliard Pre-College]? It's unbelievable. But even back then [in the 1970s], the tide was turning. Eastern European and Jewish students were diminishing and Asians were just coming up. And I remember one time I had an ear-training class. There were fourteen of us, and we were all Asians. They all had perfect pitch, and they all wore glasses [laughs]. We were all nerdy Asian kids. It was very nice, because in South Carolina [where he lived at the time], there were so few Asians there, so it was very stimulating and comforting to be with lots of other Asian kids. It was like going to Korean church on Sundays; it's comforting because everyone else is Asian.

—David Kim, concertmaster, Philadelphia Orchestra

[Moving from Maui to New York to attend Juilliard and dealing with a huge culture shock], being around people that played music helped. That was . . . you know what, there's something that bonds people that play music together . . . it really is amazing. There's a connection. And it goes through all cultures. And I think that's the most amazing thing. Because we can have different opinions politically, we can have different opinions culturally . . . when it comes to the way we feel about music it's very similar, and there's this common bond that brings people together really easily. That's the thing I love the most.

—Kurt Muroki, double bassist

Yo-Yo Ma. Seiji Ozawa. Zubin Mehta. Midori. Sarah Chang. Tan Dun. Lang Lang. These musicians are well known not only among classical music fans but also in America's cultural landscape at large. In addition to the star status of these solo performers, conductors, and composers, Asian musicians have gained visibility as members of professional orchestras across the United States. Six of the nine new musicians who joined the New York Philharmonic in 2006 were Asian (all but one of those six were female string players); as a result, approximately one-fifth of the members of the New York Philharmonic are now Asian. Xian Zhang, its associate conductor since 2005, is a Chinese woman. Some of the other top-level American orchestras, such as the Philadelphia Orchestra and Chicago Symphony Orchestra, as well as several regional orchestras, have Asian concertmasters or associate concertmasters. In addition, a large number of Asian professional musicians work as teachers, chamber musicians, accompanists, and freelance performers.

Young musicians from Japan, China, Taiwan, and Korea as well as Asian Americans are regularly among the winners of major international competitions. In the 2002 International Tchaikovsky Competition, well over half of the fifty-five piano contestants and nearly half of the forty-six violin contestants were Asian.[1] Ayako Uehara became the first woman (as well as the first Asian) in the history of this competition to win first prize for the piano; although there was no first prize awarded for the violin, Tamaki Kawakubo of Japan and Chen Xi of China both won second prize. In the 2005 Van Cliburn International Piano Competition, nearly half of the thirty-five contestants were Asian or Asian American.[2] The first prize went to Russian Alexander Kobrin, but nineteen-year-old Joyce Yang of South Korea won the silver medal and two extra jury awards, and Sa Chen of China placed third. The notable number of Asian contestants and winners drew much attention from the media, generating newspaper articles with such headlines as "In the Key of China," "The Now Dynasty," and "Asians Strong Players in Cliburn Competition."[3] The media have captured as well the larger trend of Asians' remarkable success in classical music in recent decades.[4]

Asians comprise less than 5 percent of the total population of the United States, but at prestigious music conservatories, such as Juilliard, Eastman, Curtis, and the New England Conservatory, they make up a disproportionately high percentage of the student body. At the Juilliard School, in the

2003–04 academic year, approximately 30 percent of the 834 students were Asian.[5] Among these Asians, East Asians clearly dominated: both among international students and non-citizen permanent U.S. residents, the largest contingent came from Korea, Canada, Taiwan, China, and Japan, followed by those from Israel and Russia.[6] At the Eastman School of Music, between 70 and 80 percent of the school's piano students are Asians.[7] At the Curtis Institute of Music—a conservatory with one of the most competitive admission processes because it offers full funding to all its students—of the fifteen piano students in 2004–05, nine were from China and one was from South Korea.[8] These figures indicate that Asians—and specifically East Asians—constitute a considerable presence in a world in which other non-European groups remain largely invisible.[9]

The success of East Asians in classical music might seem unremarkable in the context of their general socioeconomic attainment in the United States. After all, their overrepresentation in higher education and in many professional fields has given them the designation as the "model minority" in the postwar decades. Yet, consider that classical music is usually regarded as a form of quintessential white European culture and that Asians' exposure to Western music and musical instruments began barely a century ago. Although some Asians studied music in Europe in the prewar decades, it was only in the 1960s that a significant number of Asians came to the United States to study music. Within a single generation, musicians from Japan, followed by those from South Korea, mainland China, Hong Kong, and Taiwan, as well as second- and third-generation Asian Americans, quickly made their presence known to American—and world—audiences. The great majority of Asian musicians play what are often considered to be the most "prestigious" instruments—piano, violin, and cello, as well as voice—that offer opportunities for solo careers; there are far fewer Asian woodwind, brass, or percussion players.

Often hailed as icons of Asian and Asian American success, these classical musicians occupy a particular space in the racial and cultural map of contemporary America. Because classical music is associated with Western high culture and because the performance of classical music requires many years of disciplined training, Asians' success in this field is often thought to exemplify their assimilation into Euroamerican culture. Through their industrious commitment to years of rigorous training and their families' investment of time and money, these musicians become part of the model minority: those who rise in the existing social structure through hard work and attain success in Western culture without posing a direct challenge to the economic and political status quo. Because they embrace and excel at what is seen as a form of European high culture, Asian and Asian American musicians are not seen as part of a collective movement based on their race or ethnicity. In this sense, classical music functions differently from such musical genres as jazz, blues, folk, or hip hop that immediately evoke racial or class meanings.

Although the prominence of Asian classical musicians is thus often seen as a reflection of their successful transcendence of racial and cultural boundaries, Asian musicians are racially marked in ways that white musicians are not. For instance, many people who have some familiarity with the world of classical music have the perception that Asians comprise a much higher percentage of musicians in America than they actually do. Almost all the people whom I have talked with about this project have made comments such as, "Oh, yes, the majority of students at Juilliard are Asian," or "Asians are taking over American orchestras." Yet in fact the percentage of Asians at Juilliard is roughly 30 percent, far from comprising the majority; according to the 2003–04 Orchestra Statistical Report, "Asian Americans and Pacific Islanders" comprised approximately 5 percent of all musicians, a figure that is roughly consistent with their proportion of the overall population of the United States.[10] The percentage of Asians with decision-making power in the world of music—conductors/music directors of orchestras, administrators of orchestras and other music organizations, faculty and administrators in conservatories, and staff and executives in management agencies—is far lower. According to the 2004 Compensation Survey conducted by the American Symphony Orchestra League, approximately 2 percent of employees of participating orchestras were Asian.[11] The vast majority of trustees on the boards of prestigious arts institutions are non-Hispanic white men and women, most of whom are wealthy donors to the organizations they serve, and they are likely to recruit other members of their social circle onto the board.[12] A 2004 New York Times article reported the shockingly small number of minorities, including Asians, on the boards of directors of New York City's world-famous cultural institutions, such as Carnegie Hall and Lincoln Center for the Performing Arts.[13] Therefore, although Asians' success in classical music is certainly undeniable, they are hardly dominating or taking over the world of classical music. Such an exaggerated perception of Asian dominance in classical music suggests that Asian musicians are racially marked.

Even today, the media almost always use an ethnic or racial category to refer to Asian musicians, as in "Korean violinist," "young Chinese pianist," or "Asian soprano."[14] The very coverage of the wave of "Asian" musicians itself indicates the significance of their race to the discussion. However, even a cursory look at several of the most prominent Asians in classical music today—Yo-Yo Ma, Seiji Ozawa, Mitsuko Uchida, Kyung-Wha Chung, Tan Dun, Midori, Sarah Chang, Lang Lang, and Kent Nagano, to name a few—shows a great diversity not only in their ethnicity and nationality but also their upbringing, cultural identity, and respective relationship to Asia, the United States, and Europe. Although they all have Asian ancestry, the meanings of their Asian-ness vary greatly from one musician to another. Lumping these musicians under the rubric Asian has less to do with their origins, upbringings, or sense of identity than with the perception of mainstream Euroamerican society, which has historically ignored the differences among diverse Asian peoples as well as the difference between Asian nationals and Asians in diaspora.

Moreover, whether praising or criticizing Asians in classical music, often a connection is drawn between their Asian upbringing and their performance of classical music. On the one hand, the success of Asian classical musicians is often attributed to the work ethic, commitment to education, family values, and other traits that are presumably specific to Asian culture. There is little objective basis for such claims, however. Not only is it impossible to quantify such values and compare them across racial or ethnic lines, but also in the United States, so much of one's educational, cultural, and economic attainment is conditioned by the availability of opportunities and resources, which are unevenly distributed across class and racial lines. Attributing Asian and Asian American success in classical music to Asian culture or values reduces the issue to the matter of fixed cultural essence presumably shared by a racial group while eliding issues of history and social structure.

On the other hand, the notion that "music is universal" only seems to go so far in describing Asians' relationship to classical music. As I discuss in detail in Chapter 5, some musicians and critics—both Asian and non-Asian—believe that Westerners and Asians perform and relate to Western music in different ways: that there is something essentially Germanic about

Beethoven, French about Debussy, or Russian about Rachmaninoff that a Chinese pianist has difficulty capturing on some "innate" level. The debates and experiences around issues of cultural authenticity suggest that the concept of the universality of music needs to be analyzed with more nuance and scrutiny.

This book is a historical, cultural, and ethnographic study of Asians and Asian Americans who pursue Western classical music in the United States. How did Asians come to form such a presence in the world of classical music, especially in the United States? How are the experiences of Asian musicians different from those of other musicians? In what ways is—or is not—racial and cultural identity relevant to music-making? To what extent does music really transcend racial, national, and cultural boundaries? By exploring these questions, the book makes four main points.

First, Asians' ascendancy in classical music was shaped by the history of Western imperialism in the nineteenth century, the push for modernization in East Asia from the late-nineteenth to mid-twentieth century, and the process of globalization in the late twentieth century. Precisely because of its Western origin and its association with modernity and high culture, classical music has served an important social and cultural function for Asians. Classical music training has become a form of cultural capital that promises upward social mobility and a place in the Western and global world. Although the economic realities of classical music generally betray such promises, the lure of entry into the realm of high culture and upper-middle class society has led many Asian and Asian American families to make an enormous investment in their children's pursuit of classical music.

Second, the flow of classical music was by no means a unidirectional one from West to East. Rather, Asian governments, elite intellectuals, and individual musicians and their audiences created their own meanings out of Western music and used it for their own, often conflicting goals. In the process, classical music has come to mean far more than a musical form that is specifically European or Western. Asians have created meanings of classical music in ways that could not have been predicted by those who originally introduced it to East Asia in the nineteenth century.

Third, although the association with class and Western modernity has driven Asians' investment in Western music, another set of values independent of material concerns has been an equally, if not more, important part of the field of classical music. Classical musicians, Asians or not, continue to proudly cherish their anti-commercialist, anti-materialist, art-for-art's-sake ideals; their embrace of universal humanism; and their faith in the transcendent power of art. In many ways it is the sense of group identity based on those shared universalist values that has enabled the crossing of racial and ethnic boundaries and the entry and ascendancy of Asians in the field.

Finally, for Asian and Asian American musicians, classical music is the medium through which they experience the social meanings of their racial, gender, sexual, or class identities. In other words, the musicians come to understand what it means to be who they are *through* their pursuit of classical music. Sometimes the practice of classical music reinforces existing stereotypical notions—including the musicians' own ideas—about social categories, such as race, gender, sexuality, and class. At other times, the pursuit of classical music enables the musicians to rethink and redefine those categories, allowing them to live beyond the identities prescribed by dominant society.

It is important here to comment on my use of the terms "Asian" and "Asian American" in this book. I often use the term "Asian" when discussing specifically East Asian experiences, not because I equate the two but because both the reality and perception support such an equation in the field of classical music. Indeed, the vast majority of Asians in classical music are East Asians: those who are ethnically Japanese, Chinese, or Korean. Although the ethnic Chinese musicians I interviewed for this book included those from Hong Kong and Taiwan as well as mainland China, my discussion of Korea does not include North Korean experiences because of a scarcity of information sources, and all my Korean informants are of South Korean origin. Although a few stories of Southeast Asians appear in this book, I did not interview any South Asian musicians for this study. In sum, the overwhelming majority of my informants are East Asians. As Chapter 1 discusses, the dominance of East Asians in classical music is a result of the particular ways in which Western music was introduced to China, Japan, and Korea and the specific history of colonial dynamics in East Asia.

The ethnic origins of my informants are thus rather specific, yet those Asians are quite diverse in other ways. The musicians discussed in this book include Asian Americans who were born and raised in the United States; Asian-born musicians who came to the United States specifically to study music; professional Asian musicians who came to the United States to advance their careers; children of Asian parents whose careers and lives cross national boundaries; Asian musicians who have lived in parts of the world other than Asia and the United States, such as Oceania, Europe, or Latin America, and thus have multiple cultural identities; and those of mixed, part-Asian ethnic heritage. Chapter 2 discusses in detail the important distinctions in the paths through which these musicians came to the United States and in their sense of ethnic, national, and cultural identity.

Let me comment here on another issue of terminology. Although I specify "Asian" or "Asian American" when the distinction is important to the particular discussion, in many places I simply use the word "Asian." I do so not because I subsume Asian Americans under the category Asian but because it is often the musicians' *perceived* racial identity as Asians that shapes their experience, rather than the particularities of their ethnic, national, or cultural identification.

The book opens with a historical review of the place of Western music in Japan, China, and Korea. I explain why so many Asians have invested so much in mastering Western music and discuss how Asians have used the music for their own goals. Tracing the beginnings of the "reverse flow" of Asian musicians to the West, I also examine the remarkable success of the Suzuki Method—a program for music instruction designed by Japanese violinist and pedagogue Shinichi Suzuki—in the United States.

Against this historical background, the remainder of the book presents an account of the lives, works, and ideas of these Asian musicians in America based on my ethnographic fieldwork. Over fourteen months in 2003–04, I conducted in-depth interviews with approximately seventy musicians in and around New York City, including professional performers working as soloists, orchestra members, university and conservatory faculty, and freelance performers, as well as composers working on commissions. I tried to talk with a wide array of musicians in different types of jobs and playing different instruments. I also interviewed undergraduate and graduate students at the Juilliard School, Manhattan School of Music, Mannes School of Music, and New York University. In addition, I had informal conversations with teachers, managers, and scholars. As engaging and revealing as every interview was, I could not include all of the stories. I selected the informants and stories to illustrate the diversity of the musicians' backgrounds, situations, and ideas rather than to represent typical points of view.

As valuable as interviews are, they are also limited as ethnographic data in that they are isolated from the informants' everyday lives and are inevitably shaped by the setting and dynamics of the interview. To gain a broader understanding of the lives of classical musicians, I also conducted other forms of ethnographic research. I attended master classes in which my informants performed. I observed private lessons and coaching sessions in which my informants were students and teachers. I sat in on rehearsals for auditions and performances. I watched musicians practice. I observed a recording session for a commercially released CD. I attended approximately one hundred concerts in which my informants performed, in venues ranging from Avery Fisher Hall at Lincoln Center and Carnegie Hall to a black church in Harlem and a concert for an audience of ten in a private home in New Jersey. And probably most extensively and most importantly, I hung out with many of the musicians—in bars and cafés on the Upper West Side, restaurants in Chinatown or St. Mark's Place, concert halls in Midtown, practice rooms on the fourth floor of Juilliard, musicians' apartments on the Upper West Side or Washington Heights, and taxis, cars, and subways between these sites. In this process, I developed close personal relationships with many musicians, who became not only my valuable informants but also my precious friends and confidants.

In an attempt at participant observation, I also practiced quite a bit of music myself. I took a piano performance class at the Juilliard evening division, and in addition to playing in the class every week, I performed in several concerts. I took private lessons from one of my informants for a period of time, and I took lessons and master classes from a few others. I also entered (and completely bombed) an amateur piano competition. Although I do not compare my relationship to music to that of the professional musicians in this study, I believe that my knowledge and practice of classical music have shaped my thinking in crucial ways.

New York is in many ways America's cultural capital. It draws many talented and ambitious musicians from around the world, and it is where top-level classical music activities are most concentrated. The uniqueness of New York—the diversity of its population, its cosmopolitan culture, the large number of musicians and musical events in town—distinguishes the experiences of Asian musicians in this city from those of the majority of Asian musicians living in other parts of the United States. Therefore, I tried to obtain a more balanced view of America's musical and cultural scene by conducting telephone interviews with musicians in other parts of the country or in-person interviews with musicians who came to Hawai'i where I currently live. I have also conducted ethnographic research in Hawai'i and Japan—interviewing musicians, observing lessons, attending workshops, going to performances, and, again, hanging out with musicians. I have continued my own piano playing as well, taking lessons regularly with a pianist who is also my informant and friend and occasionally performing at home for a group of friends.

Drawing on this fieldwork, the chapters address different dimensions of Asian and Asian American musicians' lives, work, and identity. Chapter 2 explores the meaning of Asian identity for Asian and Asian American classical musicians. It first gives an overview of the roots and routes of Asian musicians in the United States—where they come from, how they came to the United States, and how they became musicians—which reveals the great diversity of Asian musicians. The chapter then analyzes the various meanings of Asian identity in the musicians' lives and how the pursuit of classical music helps them live through and beyond those prescribed identities. Chapter 3 examines the gender and sexual dynamics in the field of classical music and their impact on Asian musicians. It both analyzes the dominant gender and sexual norms that shape and constrain musicians' sense of identity in Asia and the United States and shows how Asian musicians—men and women—navigate these dynamics as they pursue their artistic goals. Chapter 4 examines the socioeconomic aspects of classical music by analyzing the class origins of Asian musicians and the economic conditions of the classical music profession. It also discusses the ways in which the musicians themselves make sense of the meaning of their "class" as musicians. Chapter 5 explores how racial and/or cultural identity is relevant—or not—to musical understanding and expression. I examine the diverse ways in which Asian and Asian American musicians think about that relevance and discuss the significance of their ideas to the concept of authenticity. The chapter thus addresses the question, "Is classical music universal?"

Two sets of "Voices," which are excerpts of selected interviews with my informants, are found in this book. These interviews relate loosely to the themes discussed in the chapters that precede or follow them; I present these excerpts to give a tactile sense of the musicians' lives and ideas and my interaction with them without forcing them into the specific arguments I make in the chapters. I hope that they convey the rich and diverse tones, colors, rhythms, and phrases of the musicians' voices.

1

Early Lessons in
Globalization

Perhaps the best-known portrayal of Western classical music in Asia is the film, *From Mao to Mozart: Isaac Stern in China,* which won the Oscar for best documentary in 1980. The film chronicles the visit by Isaac Stern, the world-renowned Jewish American violinist, to China in 1979, only a few years after the dismantling of the Cultural Revolution. During his month-long trip to China, Stern taught numerous master classes, visited conservatories, worked with orchestras, and gave public performances. The film begins with Stern's own words as he arrives in China: "We [Stern and his accompanist David Golub] are both very interested . . . in how the Chinese musician reacts to Western music; why they have a feeling for Western music." Stern's warm engagement with China's young musicians—some as young as ten—conveys not only the communicative skills of the master performer and teacher but also the power of music to cross cultures and languages. The scenes of master classes and coaching sessions portray Stern humorously teaching the Chinese students to play with emotion and lyricism rather than merely seeking technical proficiency. The film also documents the devastating effect of the Cultural Revolution on Chinese musicians who were persecuted for practicing "imperialist Western culture."[1]

One of the most intriguing moments of the film occurs in the dialogue between Stern and Li Delun, conductor for the Central Philharmonic in

Beijing. Li proposes that the greatness of Mozart had to do with the era in which he lived, which was a time of transition from a feudal to a modern, industrial society. After listening attentively, Stern responds by saying, "Well, I'm not sure that one could argue that the genius of Mozart had anything in particular to do with the development of social or economic stage of life at that time." Thus, whereas Li sees music as a product of a socio-historical context, Stern suggests that the greatness of art lies in the pure aesthetic elements created by the composer's individual genius, independent of external social factors. The two musicians listen to one another with great respect and collegiality, yet the conversation reveals the different meanings that music has for these musicians from two extremely different societies.

Is music a product of economic structures, or is it a purely aesthetic form independent of external factors? Although *From Mao to Mozart* raises this question early on, it never provides a direct answer. Rather, by illustrating the complex and multiple meanings of Western music in China, the film shows that the two seemingly dichotomous views of music are in fact not incompatible but rather play equally important parts in the musicians' lives and ideas as well as in the music itself. The film thus helps the viewer see the meanings of music and the nature of cultural encounters in more complex ways than in simple binary distinctions between West and East or between art and politics.

On one level, the film takes a structural approach in that it shows how the historical and political context shaped the meaning of classical music. The context is the Cultural Revolution, told through the story of violinist Tan Shuzhen, who was placed under house arrest for fourteen months in the Shanghai Conservatory where he taught. The impact of the Cultural Revolution is also glimpsed through the Chinese musicians' response to Stern's question about why the children under age ten play at such a remarkable level, yet those in their late teens are far less impressive: during the years of the Cultural Revolution, the conservatories were closed and instruction in Western music was prohibited, hampering the development for a whole decade of an entire generation of musicians. In this sense, the film shows the role of the state in defining the meaning of music and shaping the course of musical life.

The film also addresses the role of culture and history in musical understanding and expression. During the scene of the rehearsal with the Central Philharmonic, Stern narrates, "[The Chinese musicians'] approach to Western classical music was somewhat limited. They were not accustomed to playing with passion and the variety of color. They had an old-fashioned, technical approach toward the manner in which they played their instruments, but almost an instant understanding and reaction to the given musical stimulus once they were shown what might be done. They had not had the experience of living with Western music for hundreds of years as we have."

Here Stern sets up an "us vs. them" dichotomy between the Chinese musicians and the Western musicians and audiences of the film. According to this logic, Chinese musicians were divorced from the lived culture that produced Western music and therefore lacked an emotional understanding of the music. In contrast, Stern implies, those from Western cultures have an organic relationship to, and a natural understanding of, classical music that comes from their culture. Therefore, even though in the conversation about Mozart discussed earlier Stern advocated a purely aesthetic position and implied that great art transcends social structures, here he also suggests that musical understanding indeed has cultural specificity and a connection to social context.

Yet the film draws other connections between culture and classical music. By showing Stern's amazement at the drive, focus, and organization of teachers and students in the training given gymnasts, ping-pong players, or Beijing opera performers, the film suggests that Chinese people's discipline, dedication, and focus play an important role in their achievements in Western classical music. In other words, the film shows a connection between the cultural traits of the Chinese and their practice of—and accomplishments in—classical music.

On yet another level, the film echoes Stern's message about the transcendent power of music that is not reducible to social explanations. Through the scenes of individual musicians' playing, it movingly depicts the depth and sincerity of their engagement with music. Even to the viewer who is not necessarily familiar with classical music, it is evident that the young boys and girls performing for Stern are not only remarkable in their technique but are also playing with an extraordinary emotional intensity, as if their lives were at stake. (Some of the young musicians featured in the film later became internationally acclaimed performers, such as cellist Jian Wang, who was ten years old at the time of Stern's visit.) Furthermore, by capturing the expressions of the musicians and audiences during master classes, rehearsals, and performances—at times extremely serious, at other times purely rapt, and yet at other times just expressing enjoyment—the film also illustrates the communication that music allows across boundaries of culture, language, politics, and history.

From Mao to Mozart's historical perspective centers on the Cultural Revolution, and it does not provide a full account of China's—and Asia's—encounter with Western music that preceded this dramatic period. Yet, Western music was introduced to China, Japan, and Korea more than a century before Stern's visit, and Asian governments, intellectuals, musicians, and audiences had created and debated the complex and multiple meanings that classical music had for their nations and cultures throughout the late nineteenth to mid-twentieth century. China's Cultural Revolution was certainly an extreme case of such a process, yet it was by no means the first time in the history of Asia that Asians inscribed political meanings to Western music.

Furthermore, as a documentary about a world-renowned violinist's visit to China, the film understandably focuses on Stern's role as the master who frees the Chinese musicians' emotions and expressions that had been suppressed by political and cultural norms and then teaches the students about the true meaning behind the music.[2] The history of Western music in Asia, however, is not merely about heroic Western masters bringing music to Asians. Rather, it involves multi-layered and multi-directional flows of people, institutions, ideas, and creative genius between the West and Asia. Although key individuals guided and shaped these flows, their roles were more complex than that of a Western master, and the process was not a unidirectional one from the West to the East.

This chapter gives a broad overview of the history of Western music in Japan, China, and Korea—the three countries that have produced the largest number of Asian musicians working in the field of classical music. Through long shots panning broad historical periods and a couple of close-ups at particular instances, the chapter highlights several main points. First, the introduction of Western music in Japan, China, and Korea occurred in the context of Western imperialism and the push for modernization by Asian governments and intellectuals. Second, although the history of Western music in Asia was intricately tied to imperialism, its introduction was not a unidirectional process of importation and imposition from the West. It was also shaped by global politics, including the Russian Revolution, Japanese colonialism in Asia, Chinese and Korean nationalism, war, and revolution in Asia. Third, Asian governments, civil institutions, and cultural leaders attempted to integrate Western music into their own national and cultural goals, making the process far more complex than a simple and uncritical adoption of a foreign art form. Western music was often used as a tool of Asian nationalism in its pursuit of parity with—and struggle against—the West. Fourth, the democratization and popularization of classical music among the Asian middle class in the second half of the twentieth century were vital to building the practitioner and consumer base for classical music in these countries. The convergence of social, cultural, and commercial goals nurtured the widespread notion of classical music as a form of cultural capital among the middle class. Finally, the "reverse flow" of Asian musicians, musical instruments, and instruction methods from Asia to the West beginning in the 1960s points to new historical contexts and modes of musical and cultural exchange, at once challenging and reinforcing established notions of music, culture, geography, and race. Thus, Western classical music in Asia has been composed of many voices—voices that sometimes worked in harmony and at other times were dissonant, often developing the original motive in unexpected directions.

Western Music Comes to East Asia

Western classical music's introduction into Asia—particularly the East Asian countries of Japan, China, and Korea—is an intrinsic part of East-West encounters in the second half of the nineteenth century. Western music came to these three countries in strikingly similar ways through three key institutions: the military, churches, and schools. These institutions were intimately tied to Western imperialism and these countries' embrace of modernization.

In Japan, ever since the arrival of Commodore Matthew Perry in 1853 and the subsequent opening of the nation's doors to diplomacy and trade with the Western powers, political and military leaders had orchestrated a process of studying and adopting Western tools for modernizing the country. Building a Western-style military was an important element of that modernization process. Through their encounters with, and observation of, Western armies, the Japanese concluded that military bands contributed significantly to maintaining discipline and raising morale in the military, and so they eagerly formed their own. The Satsuma clan formed Japan's first brass band in 1869, and the national military band was officially founded two years later. These bands introduced to Japan not only band music itself but also the foundational elements of Western music, including orchestral instruments and piano, Western singing style, and the public concert.[3] Similarly, in China after the Opium War, several Chinese leaders believed in the power of music to motivate, discipline, and coordinate troops in Western armies and called for a reform of China's own music. Two of China's most powerful generals, Zhang Zhidong and Yuan Shikai, undertook military reforms during this period, which included the introduction of Western music into China's political-military culture. Particularly after China's defeat in the Sino-Japanese War in 1895, its leaders aggressively pushed reforms in government and education, including the creation of the Western military band. Yuan Shikai's military band was established in 1898, and subsequently several Western-style military bands were formed and trained in various cities.[4]

Likewise, in Korea, the first known Western musical establishment was the military band. At the end of the nineteenth century, as European, American, and Russian battleships were at anchor in Jemulpo Harbor, the bright costumes and loud, fast-paced music of the military bands parading in the area impressed the Koreans, who then formed their first Western-style military band in 1881. In 1901 German musician Franz Eckert was hired as a conductor and teacher, and the band held regular rehearsals and performances in Pagoda Park in Seoul, which soon became identified as the center of Western music in Korea.[5] Thus, in Japan, China, and Korea the association of Western music with military strength, discipline, and modernity—rather than a purely aesthetic interest in the music—was an important driver of the Asian adoption of Western music.

Christian missionaries formed the second key channel for Western music in Asia. Jesuit missionaries such as Mateo Ricci presented the clavichord to the Chinese Emperor in the late sixteenth century and gave lessons in Western music in the Imperial Palace in Beijing. After Protestant missionaries arrived in China in 1805, organ music and choral singing became a key component of Protestant church services across the country. Working primarily among the poor in rural areas, the missionaries rapidly increased the number of Chinese exposed to European music. By 1877, sixty-three different hymn books were circulating in China.[6] Protestant hymns were also introduced to Korea in the late nineteenth century with the arrival of missionaries, Horace G. Underwood and Henry G. Appenzeller.[7] Similarly, in Japan, Protestant missionaries introduced the Christian hymn and hymnal, the Western concept of vocal tone, part singing, sight reading, and the organ, all of which contributed to the development of congregational singing and the popular singing of Western melodies.[8]

In all three countries, the mission schools became another crucial vehicle for Western music education. In China, for instance, the number of students at Protestant mission schools in the country grew from 17,000 in 1899 to 169,707 in 1915. In these schools, singing, often accompanied by the piano, was used widely for devotional and educational purposes.[9] With their clear melodies, solid harmony, and predictable structure, Protestant hymns were an easy tool for training schoolchildren in European music and acculturating them into the Christian tradition.

Basic musical training in the mission schools was accompanied by musical education in more general, including secular, education. The governments of Japan, China, and Korea considered music to be an important element of modern education and eagerly implemented ways to incorporate Western music into school curricula. One product of this effort, common across the three countries, was the "school song" movement, which helped popularize and indigenize Western music in the form of art songs and popular songs taught in elementary schools. In the 1880s, Shūji Izawa, a teacher who had studied in Massachusetts, compiled songbooks for Japanese schoolchildren. Some songs combined Western tunes with original Japanese texts, some newly written Japanese songs used the Western scale, and other traditional Japanese songs were harmonized in the Western tonal system. Izawa's songbooks were used nationally in elementary schools. As various musical traditions associated with specific social settings or institutions (such as the imperial court, Buddhist or Shinto ceremonies, or popular theater) were considered inappropriate for children, the Western-style songs were seen as a means to bring music into primary education.[10] China, after its defeat in the Sino-Japanese War, looked to these Japanese school songs as part of elementary education. In the early years of the twentieth century, Chinese students and intellectuals living in Japan, such as Zeng Zhimin, Shen Xingong, and Li Shutong, studied the school songs and, after returning to China, launched a school song movement of their own, largely by borrowing Japanese songs—most of which were themselves borrowed from the West—

and setting them to new lyrics.[11] Similar adaptations occurred in Korea, where *ch'anggas*, or Korean songs that evolved from Protestant hymns, were used widely in school curricula. In 1910, the Korean government published *A Collection of Ch'anggas for Elementary Education,* and newly composed art songs and popular songs modeled after ch'anggas proliferated in the subsequent decades.[12]

Not only did these East Asian nations adopt Western music in elementary school curricula but they also established institutions for advanced musical training. Japan's Meiji government (1868–1912) established the Music Investigation Committee to explore ways to incorporate Western music into Japanese education; this committee later became the Tokyo Music School and subsequently the Music Department of the Tokyo University of Fine Arts and Music, the most prestigious institution for arts education in the nation.[13] In 1910, Ehwa Women's College (later Ehwa Women's University) in Seoul became the first Korean university to house a department of Western music and has served as one of the most important training grounds for Korean musicians to this day. Two years later, the Chosun Institute of Classical Music was founded as the first Western-style music institute. Other educational milestones followed: the School of Music of the Seoul National University in 1946 and the Korean National University of the Arts, the first conservatory-style musical institution in Korea, in 1993.[14] China established its first conservatory of music in 1927 in Shanghai, a city that enjoyed a rich musical life because of the significant presence of foreign musicians, many of whom were members of the Shanghai Municipal Orchestra. With the founding of the People's Republic of China in 1949, the Central Conservatory of Music was established in Beijing and under the management of the Ministry of Culture became one of the flagship institutions for training the nation's most talented musicians.[15]

Thus, these institutions for music education developed in East Asia as official and unofficial branches of Western power and were orchestrated and promoted by Asian governments. Both Western imperialism and the pursuit of Western-style modernity by the Asian states shaped the development of Western-style music in East Asia. However, the introduction of Western music into East Asia was not a unidirectional move from the West to the East but was influenced by global politics and power relations within East Asia.

Japan's rise to power and its growing military and economic expansion in Asia made it a colonizing power in this period. China and Korea, which modeled their efforts to modernize their educational systems after Japan, developed their own school song movements inspired by the Japanese. Yet, school songs were not the only byproducts of this colonial dynamic in East Asia. In China, a nationalist movement grew to oppose the Western powers in China, culminating in the May 4th Movement of 1919. Subsequently, Chinese students enrolled in universities in Europe, the United States, and Japan. Japan's relative geographical proximity and its rapid growth as an industrial and democratic nation made it a particularly appealing destination for many Chinese students. Among the students going to Japan were musicians, such as Xiao Youmei. Part of the May 4th generation of intellectuals, Xiao studied music and education in Tokyo and Leipzig, and after his return to China in 1921, he dedicated himself to reforming music education and creating a new form of "national music" that combined Chinese melodies with Western harmony and musical forms.[16] In Korea as well, the pioneers of Western music were those who went to Japan to study. After Japan's annexation of Korea in 1910, serious music students began to go to Japan to study. Young-Whan Kim was the first Korean musician to study abroad, and after returning from Japan in 1918, he began his teaching career at what is now Yonsei University.[17]

Although Japan's colonial power in China and Korea thus propelled Western music education in these countries, the Chinese and Koreans did not merely follow the paths of their colonizer in their pursuit of Western music. In fact, as Japan's aggression became increasingly apparent in the 1930s, Western-style music became an important tool for nationalist resistance *against* the Japanese. After Japan bombed Shanghai in 1932, a movement for creating revolutionary music emerged in the city. Through their affiliations with Communist Party-related organizations, the proponents of the movement—such as composer Nie Er—composed unaccompanied songs to be sung in the streets by the masses, motivating resistance to Japan or sympathy with the plight of the poor.[18] In the words of Sheila Melvin and Jindong Cai, "Music, to them, was more than the beautiful art and sometime tool of social change and nation-building promoted by men like Xiao Youmei; instead, it was 'a weapon for liberating the masses' which it was their obligation to wield."[19] The proliferation of these revolutionary songs generated debates among the movement's leaders regarding the artistic significance of these songs beyond their use as political propaganda. Although the critical assessment of the songs varied considerably, it was undeniable that Chinese musicians were motivated more by political exigencies to produce music that engaged the masses than practicing Western music as a purely aesthetic pursuit. Western-style music in Asia thus took on unintended political, social, and cultural meanings as it was assimilated into national life in Asia.

The presence of Russian exiles in China also had a significant impact on the development of Western music in Asia. Many Russian Jews, who fled to Manchuria to escape the Czarist government's increasingly anti-Semitic policies, and White Russians, who remained loyal to the Czar and were forced to flee their country after the Russian Revolution in 1917, first moved to Harbin in northeastern China. There, these Russians created a rich musical life that produced the First Harbin Music Academy, a symphony orchestra, and a string quartet. After the Japanese invasion of Manchuria in 1931, thousands of these Russian exiles fled to Shanghai; many settled in the French Concession, where they contributed to the rich Western musical culture of the city, performing in hotels and dance halls and giving lessons in many instruments. Beginning in 1938, a group of European Jews fleeing the Nazis joined these Russians. By 1941, approximately 18,000 Jewish refugees—including 267 professional artists—found haven in Shanghai, which required neither visa nor passport to enter the city. In this community of exiles, music was a livelihood as well as an entertainment. Among the professional musicians in Shanghai were those who had been acclaimed performers before being forced to flee Europe, and they created a vibrant musical life during the time of political uncertainty and duress.[20] The role that these exiles played in the creation of a musical culture in China exemplifies the multi-layered flows of people and culture that made up the growth of Western music in Asia and illustrates that not all the players in the process had imperialist designs.

During the periods of intensifying nationalism, war, and revolution in the twentieth century, Western music performed a unique role as Asians pursued parity with or resisted the Western powers by establishing autonomous political and cultural systems. Paradoxically, Asians used Western music in their attempt to create a distinct national and cultural identity.

In Japan, rising militarism and imperialist ambitions in the 1930s led to new definitions of cultural nationalism and changing ideas and policies regarding Western music. Until the 1920s Japanese audiences listened eagerly to performances of Western compositions. However, by the 1930s they increasingly demanded that Japanese musicians perform Japanese compositions. This strong nationalism melded with the proletarian movement of the 1930s that called for music that reached the masses. In 1930, a prominent alto, Fumiko Yotsuya, wrote in a newspaper, "In music schools, we have spent the last several years studying exclusively foreign songs in foreign languages as if we are a people without our own language. I cannot determine for sure what path I should follow from here on. But I am determined to step into the masses with all my heart. I will sing folk tunes. I will perform in talkie films. I will dedicate my youthful energy and try everything until I know what my path is."[21]

As the 1930s went on, that call for proletarianism quickly shifted to militarism. Under the banner of "the establishment of national music," political, military, and cultural leaders advocated the "cleansing" of Japan's musical culture of undesirable foreign influences. In 1933, a leading music journal published an article propagandizing, "We must fight the United States and Britain with all of our national force. It is a shame that amidst our music world there are still some ignorant souls who worship foreign conductors, especially the Jews, or who show no qualms about performing pieces like [Rimsky-Korsakov's] *Russian Easter Overture*."[22] In the same year, another music journal included an article titled "The War with the United States and Britain in Musical Culture." The author adamantly called for the purging of "corrupt" American and British influences on Japanese music:

> Religious music, especially hymns brought by Protestants, and theatrical music such as film music have allowed the corruption [of Japan's musical culture] by the invasion of American and British music into our country. . . . Today we must resolutely rid such elements from our culture. Such influences have prevented and distorted the adequate and healthy development of Japan's musical culture. . . . [In order to fight the United States and Britain,] we must make sure that our music does not have even a slight style or flavor of American music, as that would unconsciously allow harmful, impure elements that hamper the solid growth of the musicality of the Japanese people nourished since the ancient times. . . . We must remember that strengthening the healthy musical culture of contemporary Japan, just as German musical culture which produced Bach, Mozart, and Beethoven, is the only way to defeat American and British music.[23]

Musical traditions were categorized in strictly—and rather arbitrary—national and ethnic terms, and a series of policies regulated the performances and sales of recordings of Western music. By 1934, the government heavily censored music books and recordings, banned performances by foreigners except those from Germany and Italy, and permitted only those concerts considered useful for the war effort. After the outbreak of the Sino-Japanese War in 1937, foreign music, except for classical music of their allies, was banned entirely. Japanese musicians—performers and composers alike—either actively collaborated with the government policies or silenced themselves musically and politically.[24]

Although Chinese musicians endured great difficulties during the war with Japan, the most dramatic chapter of Western music in China was the Cultural Revolution, launched by Mao Zedong and his wife Jiang Qing in 1966 to recover control of the Communist Party after the disaster of the Great Leap Forward of 1958–62. The Cultural Revolution's mission to destroy old customs, habits, culture, and thinking of the "exploiting class" led to public attacks and violence against intellectuals who allegedly practiced "feudal" thinking or had a background that could be called "bourgeois," such as having a Western education. Musicians became easy targets for these charges. Western musical instruments and musical scores were confiscated and burned. Musicians were attacked, imprisoned, and forced to work as manual laborers. Those determined to practice music did so in hiding, many miles away from villages, in the middle of the night after a day of physical labor. Some professors at the Shanghai Conservatory and their family members who were subjected to the Red Guard's unfounded allegations, cruelty, and abuse resorted to suicide. Within the first few years of the Cultural Revolution, seventeen conservatory professors, spouses, and students had taken their own lives. Others died during imprisonment or forced labor. Those who criticized the policy of art in service to politics were attacked, sentenced to perform physical labor in rural areas, or imprisoned. This was the fate of He Luting, the president of the Shanghai Conservatory, and violinist Tan Shuzhen. Composer Wang Xilin, imprisoned and abused for objecting to the Communist Party, broke down under mental and physical torture. Lu Hongen, a timpanist for the Shanghai Symphony, spoke out frankly about music and other subjects and was shot in the head for having torn into pieces a copy of *Quotations from Chairman Mao,* or the "Little Red Book." Central Conservatory President Ma Sicong fled China, first crossing the sea to Hong Kong and finally gaining asylum in the United States.[25] This decade-long persecution of musicians and the consequent interruption in musical training had a devastating impact on the development of Western music in China, as portrayed in *From Mao to Mozart*.

As these sketches of the introduction, appropriation, and control of Western music in East Asia demonstrate, Asians welcomed Western music as a signifier of Western modernity, and governments and intellectuals eagerly sought ways to adopt it into their cultural system. At the same time, Asians used Western music in their nation- and empire-building efforts. This process of engagement, appropriation, and meaning-making can be seen at work in the creation of Japan's first diva and in the Japanese responses to Puccini's opera *Madama Butterfly*.

The Flight of the Japanese Butterfly

In the Meiji (1868–1912) and Taishō (1912–1926) periods, Japan pursued modernity in many forms and sought recognition from its Western peers in part by adopting Western arts and culture. At the same time, rapid social change brought about a growing disenchantment with the West, and both the state and the intellectuals reconstructed and reinforced various forms of Japanese "tradition."[26] In this cultural climate, Puccini's popular opera *Madama Butterfly* became an important stage on which Japan was presented to the Western world through the figure of the heroine, Cio-Cio-San.

During this time, by far the most important figure to represent Japan through *Madama Butterfly* was Tamaki Miura (1884–1946). As the only Japanese singer to attain international acclaim in the prewar period, Miura made a name for herself as the "Japanese Butterfly" and had celebrity status in Japan.[27] One can safely say that it was *Butterfly* that gave her access to the international scene that she would not have had otherwise.

Born in Tokyo in 1884, Miura came of age when the original *Madama Butterfly* was being written and produced in Europe and the United States. As a young woman, she enrolled in the new Tokyo School of Music against her family's wishes. She rode her bicycle—a symbol of the "modern girl"—to school every day and became famous as a "Bicycle Beauty" among her peers, her suitors, and later the press. She performed in the first staging of Western opera by a Japanese cast, which established her reputation as a singer. She married Zen'ichi Fujii, a military physician, in 1900, but eight years later, she created a major scandal by divorcing him. She soon caused another sensation by running off to Singapore with her new lover Masatarō Miura, also a physician.

Returning briefly to Japan in 1913, the couple married but soon left Japan for their respective studies in Germany. So began Miura's international career. Although their studies were interrupted by the outbreak of World War I, she made a successful debut in London in 1915 in the role of Cio-Cio-San. After this performance, she became the best-known Japanese singer in the international opera scene and toured extensively around the world performing *Butterfly*. Her husband completed his studies and returned to Japan, but she continued her tour alone and did not reunite with her husband until 1922. After a brief sojourn during which she performed across Japan, she again left the country—despite her family's attempt to stop her—to do tours in the United States. After hearing the news of her husband's death while she was in Honolulu in 1929, she declared: "With the death of my husband who was waiting for my return, there was no longer any point in my rushing to Japan. The best tribute to my husband was to continue to sing as a prima donna and give as much pleasure as possible to the people of the world. And thus from Honolulu I went back to the United States and continued to sing *Madama Butterfly*."[28] Miura finally returned to Japan in 1932, after which she made numerous performances both on stage and on the air. After she and her mother moved to the countryside during the war, her health deteriorated and she died in May 1946.

The American audience's response to Miura was heavily tinged with Orientalist perceptions of Japanese womanhood. American audiences saw Miura's performance of Cio-Cio-San as "natural" and "innate" simply because of her race and ethnicity. Theater critics used the same exoticist and Orientalist terms to describe the *character* of Cio-Cio-San as to describe Miura the *performer*. American reviews referred repeatedly to Miura as "the dainty little Japanese singer," reinforcing the image of diminutive and fragile Cio-Cio-San with comments such as the following:

Tamaki Miura was the "real thing." So dainty, so Japanese, was she that we were reminded of a cute, quaint little doll, wound up to act and sing for several hours, then, after being carefully dusted to be put back on the shelf at Vantine's. . . . She pattered about on those funny little feet of hers and gave some pretty imitations of an Occidental prima donna; but she remained invincibly Nipponese.[29]

Western Orientalist fantasies of Japanese femininity that gave birth to the character of Cio-Cio-San were thus projected onto Miura, who, in fact, was a quite untraditional Japanese woman.

In her real life, Miura was far from the dainty, self-sacrificing creature that she impersonated on stage. Through the choices she made in her personal life, she flouted the Japanese ideal of womanhood of a "good wife, wise mother (ryōsai kenbo)" propagated by the state. In many ways, Miura signified instead what the Japanese media of the period depicted as the "Modern Girl (moga)."[30] Already a celebrity before leaving Japan, Miura appeared in the media as a woman of the new age, and she happily took on the role, publicly commenting on her views about women and femininity.

Not only did Miura hold—and live out—an unconventional and modern view of womanhood but she was also remarkably savvy about the creation and performance of her role on stage. Miura's published commentaries about Butterfly reflect her understanding of the Orientalist nature of the Butterfly narrative, even before she launched her international career. In 1912, she edited and published a collection, Sekai no Opera [The Opera of the World], which introduced the plots of seventy-some operas to Japanese readers.[31] She made this bold commentary in the section introducing Butterfly: "Seen from our Japanese eyes, the Japanese culture and customs that appear in this opera are not merely extremely strange but rather infuriating. However, judging in terms of its musical value, it seems understandable that the piece received unprecedented acclaim in Europe and America."[32] In her description of the first act, she remarked further: "This first act is almost thoroughly absurd to the Japanese, and one can see this as an unfiltered expression of the fantasies of the foreigners who have no understanding of Japan."[33]

Although she thus clearly understood Butterfly's distorted representation of Japanese culture and the Orientalism of the Western audience, Miura still performed her role in ways intended by the opera's creators and expected by its non-Japanese audience. In fact, once she began performing outside Japan, Miura quite consciously and skillfully enacted the character of Cio-Cio-San to appeal to her Western audiences. Her own account reveals her thinking in this process:

After all, this story was first written by a foreigner based on his imagination; and then a foreign genius composed the music out of his own head by incorporating melodies of Japanese music here and there. Therefore, no matter how hard I try to perform in an authentically Japanese fashion, such a performance would not fit neatly with the opera as a whole. One has to harmonize Japanese emotions and manners into the opera.[34]

Miura thus made costume adjustments, such as tying the sashes flatly rather than in a round, Japanese style so that she would not appear hunchbacked to the Western audience. She also convinced the director to add the exchange of *sake* during the wedding ceremony in Act One to introduce the Western audience to this exotic Japanese custom.

In addition to crafting Cio-Cio-San's character, Miura also voluntarily performed the role of the typical Japanese woman created by Western Orientalism. On her tour in Europe and the United States she not only performed in *Butterfly* but also often played the heroine in other Orientalist operas—such as Messager's *Madame Chrysanthème,* Jones's *The Geisha,* Mascagni's *Iris,* and Franchetti's *Namiko-san*—all of which cast the diva in the stereotypical female Japanese role of the geisha.[35] Miura seemed to have accepted such casting, however, as the quickest route to an international audience. In fact, Miura seemed to gain proficiency in mastering the ways to please her Western audience as her international tour progressed. She typically dressed in a kimono when appearing in front of a Western audience, even though by that time Japanese women of her social status commonly wore Western clothing. Her recital programs usually mixed Western classical songs by Mozart, Schubert, Mendelssohn, and others with traditional or folk Japanese songs such as "Sakura" and "Kuruka kuruka to," and closed with "Un bel di," the most famous aria from *Butterfly.*[36]

Yet, Miura did not simply pander to Western tastes; she also attempted actively—and selectively—to make her performance authentic. She complained when the costume staff, ignorant of Asian cultures, dressed Japanese characters in Chinese clothes.[37] She was deeply dissatisfied by the inaccuracies that marred the stage sets, props, and makeup in the productions around the world.[38] She did her best to take control over her performance amidst such surroundings: for example, she incorporated the movements of traditional Japanese dance into her performance and sought instructions on

TAMAKI MIURA

(*Tamaki Miura, Chicago Opera Co.*; anonymous photographer, gelatin
silver print photograph, ca. 1918–1926; courtesy Robert Lancefield)

her choreography from the wife of a Japanese actor.[39] She boasted of having
met Rosa Long, the sister of John Luther Long, who wrote the original short
story for *Butterfly*.[40] She also boasted that during her trip to Italy in 1920
she met Puccini, who welcomed her with much enthusiasm.[41] Furthermore,
she was highly concerned with the emotional rendition of her character
and studied ways to convey "the virtues of a chaste and affectionate Japanese woman" to Western audiences.[42] In the negotiation between Japan's
self-image and Western expectations, Miura had to contend not only with
Western Orientalism but also with a Japanese public ambivalent about her

international success and her place in Japanese society. Precisely because of her international visibility, Japanese society was invested in Miura's performance—less in the role of Cio-Cio-San than in that of a "proper" Japanese woman befitting the nation's role in the world. At a time when Japan was trying to prove its equal status with Western nations, the representations of Japanese women abroad had a particularly potent meaning for the nation.[43] In this context, Japanese singers' accomplishment in the world of opera was a highly effective symbol of Japan's entry among the ranks of the Western powers. The fact that a Japanese singer could now perform in this Western high art form symbolized Japan's legitimate position in Western civilization. Yet, for opera to serve Japan's nation- and empire-building objectives, the Japanese prima donna herself needed to act in ways that were appropriate for the modern Japanese nation.[44] The government thus attempted a series of "reforms" of the Japanese theater and controlled the overseas travel of Japanese performers, especially women.

Many Japanese eagerly praised Miura's accomplishment and hailed its significance for the nation. Shūichi Takaori, who conducted the first performance of *Butterfly* in Japan, reviewed Miura's performance in a production in St. Paul, Minnesota, for a leading music journal in Japan. Given how critical he was of Miura's performance skills, it is significant that Takaori nonetheless wholeheartedly praised her accomplishment and saw its significance for Japan's national pride:

> It is a great pleasure for our nation's music world that *Madama Butterfly* and other Japanese opera are performed on the same Western stage where the top professionals of the real scene appear. . . . It is truly praiseworthy that Mrs. Miura stood up to the top singers of the world and performed in the way she did. In this sense, I as a Japanese cannot help but shout a great "banzai" for Japan and for our nation's music.[45]

The Japanese media hailed Miura as the one who exposed Japan's cultural achievement to the larger world. After her first return to Japan in 1922, one critic in a mainstream national newspaper exclaimed as follows:

> Welcome the homecoming of Ms. Miura Tamaki—the genius, the extraordinary talent of the music world! Show respect to the only

world-class artist our country has produced! . . . We are indebted to Ms. Tamaki, who introduced Japanese culture to the world, who brought us the sympathy of innumerable people in many countries . . .[46]

Miura's success was thus seen as the nation's success. In performing in Western opera and playing the role of a Japanese woman created by Western Orientalism, Miura became the carrier of *Japanese* culture to the world. Japan's assertion of its national identity and power was not only compatible with but very much depended on its eager adoption and successful performance of Western culture.

However, because she represented Japan to the world both on and off stage, Miura was subjected to intense national scrutiny, even before she launched her international career. Japanese audiences judged Miura not only on her artistic achievements but also on her performance of prescribed gender roles. In venues ranging from serious music journals to tabloid newspapers and magazines, the Japanese avidly debated Miura's womanhood in relation to her artistic career. Both the mainstream newspapers and the tabloid press eagerly reported her divorce from her first husband in 1909,[47] provoking public debate on the question of "the woman artist." Some sympathetically argued that women endowed with special artistic talent should devote themselves to their pursuit rather than being confined to domestic life.[48] Others criticized the divorcée for not properly performing the role of a woman. One writer expressed this particularly strong view in a prestigious music journal:

> I would like to say a word to Ms. Tamaki. Which do you think is more important, music or your husband? Do you believe that you are a great enough genius to become a musician at the expense of morality? What is your understanding of the sanctity of music? . . . Your art is no longer sacred . . . tainted art cannot be in the service of the world. . . . Once a woman has wedded a husband, she should help her husband and manage the household and never dream of leaving that family. . . . I am sure that you have responsibilities and obligations to the music world. Yet those cannot be so great that you need to fulfill them by leaving your husband. How do you intend to teach others when you don't value young women's chastity? Can you remain a music teacher in this way? . . . I am afraid that this inci-

dent of yours [the divorce] will have an effect on the world of music and ultimately corrupt Western music. . . . Ms. Tamaki, you have already become a person of immorality. I grieve for the music world, and I lament for Ms. Tamaki.[49]

According to this logic, Miura's failure to perform the proper role of a woman also meant her failure to perform her role as a singer for the nation. The Japanese concern over Miura's gender and sexuality was further heightened once Miura became an international figure. News reports often used sensational vocabulary to dramatize her husband's presumed agony and her family's efforts to tie her down to domestic life. Miura did not return when her husband earned his doctorate in 1923. Throughout her tour in the United States in the following decade, the media continued to publish articles about her awaiting husband. She did not return even when she received the news of her husband's death. When she finally did step on the soil of her home country in 1932, newspapers portrayed her as a disingenuous performer prone to eye-catching theatricality. According to the reports, she visited her husband's grave, embraced the tombstone, cried out loud, and sang. The language used in the reports highlighted the theatrical nature of her demeanor and mentioned that the town's residents were astonished by such melodramatic behavior and flamboyant manners.[50] One college student even wrote a letter to the editor of a newspaper that Miura's behavior was a shame to the nation, which was published under the heading, "Sleazy Old Maid a National Humiliation.[51] Such portrayals of Miura point to the Japanese public's confusion and dismay at her refusal to play the role of a proper Japanese woman. However, Miura could not have cared less about such concerns. Whether the Japanese public saw her as a symbol of national pride or of national humiliation, she saw herself as serving her nation. She continued to play the diva both at home and abroad.

However, as the Pacific War escalated and the Japanese government enforced a series of sanctions against Western music, urging the creation and performance of Japanese music, Miura joined the war effort and agreed not to perform *Butterfly* or any other Western music.[52] She wrote a patriotic article shunning the blind adoption of Western music and calling for the appreciation and performance of Japanese music.[53] After the war ended, despite her declining health she performed in several recitals, singing both Japanese and Western songs; she performed at a concert for the occupying

American officers in January 1946. Shortly before her death, she was baptized, just as was Cio-Cio-San; John G. Chapman, a reverend for Douglas MacArthur's General Headquarters, gave her the sacrament.

Although Miura's career as a Japanese Butterfly illustrates her navigation between Western Orientalism and Japanese patriarchy and nationalism, the creation of the Japanese Butterfly was influenced by larger influences than Miura's performance style alone. In the early Shōwa period when Japan's growing militarism and imperialism reflected its desire to break from the West and to be a leader and model for Asia, Japan's male cultural elites had high stakes in creating and presenting a "proper" image of Japan to both their Western audiences and Asian neighbors. In several ways, they engaged and appropriated *Butterfly* toward this goal.

The most notable event in this effort was the 1930 production of *Butterfly* at the Kabuki-za Theater in Tokyo. This four-day performance featured Kōsaku Yamada, the foremost Japanese composer of the period, as director and conductor, and it used the libretto translated by Keizō Horiuchi. Satoko Matsudaira (1896–1931), a graduate of the Tokyo School of Music, played Cio-Cio-San. What was distinctive about this production was the great deal of liberty the Japanese producers took in creating their own *Butterfly*. Translator Horiuchi's own account reflects the Japanese sensitivity to the insulting Orientalism of the original opera: "Even Westerners must find it absurd that these characters with *chonmage* [top-knot] appear onstage—one cannot tell whether the setting is supposed to look like Japan or China—in shuffling steps, put their hands on the ground, and bow up and down."[54] Even before the actual performance, the media discussed the significance of this production in upholding Japan's dignity. One newspaper article praised the producers' struggle "to eliminate the national humiliation generated by the quasi-Nippon performances of this opera traditionally done by the Westerners."[55]

Horiuchi and Yamada made various changes and adaptations to correct what they saw as the inaccuracies and absurdities of the original opera. On a most basic level, they "authenticated" the performance by casting Japanese singers in Japanese roles and Caucasian singers in American roles. Horiuchi translated the libretto so that the dialogues among the American characters were in English. Because Lieutenant Pinkerton was not supposed to know any Japanese, all the conversations and songs involving Pinkerton were done in English, but because Consul Sharpless had lived in Japan for a long time, when he talked with Japanese characters he did so in Japanese. On a more substantial level, Horiuchi and Yamada raised Cio-Cio-San's age to twenty-two, because they thought the plot (in which Cio-Cio-San falls in love and marries Pinkerton against her family's wishes and gives birth to his child) was implausible given the heroine's original age. Furthermore, they transformed the character Goro, who in the original was, according to Horiuchi, a "highly unpleasant fellow who serves as a vulgar broker and treats women as commodities and engages in various sleazy activities," into an "intelligent translator." Because they felt that Goro acted crudely in taking advantage of Cio-Cio-San, they made him a gentleman. As for Count Yamadori, he was changed to be an import-export businessman as befitting the plot in which he was on friendly terms with the American consul.

In addition to these character transformations, the producers changed the plot as well. Viewing Pinkerton and Cio-Cio-San's wedding in Act One as "utterly infuriating," they deleted the entire wedding scene. In Act Two, they thought the scene in which Cio-Cio-San spreads flower petals on the floor was ridiculous, so they had her put flowers in a vase instead.

Horiuchi and Yamada even tinkered with Puccini's music. Feeling that the occasional faux-Japanese tunes sounded absurd, Yamada changed some of Puccini's melodies and tempi to make them more "natural."[56] In this way, Horiuchi and Yamada appropriated *Butterfly* to assert Japanese control over its self-representation.

This unique production evoked mixed reactions from the Japanese audience. Although many praised Horiuchi and Yamada's efforts to authenticate the opera's setting and story, several critics questioned some of their decisions. One reviewer commented,

> There are two questionable points about this production. One is that Butterfly and other Japanese characters were so realistic both in their costume and in their acting that the exotic flavor of the original is almost entirely eliminated. Of course, it is understood that in the case of this particular opera, what is exotic in the West is not at all exotic in Japan. Nonetheless, since one of the strengths of this opera is in its exoticism, is it appropriate to direct the piece in ways that lose that element? . . .[57]

Thus, the Japanese audience imposed complex and competing demands on *Butterfly*. On the one hand, sensitive to the Orientalism of the opera's narrative and its Western performances, the Japanese wanted to take control over how the nation was represented to the world. At a time when Japan's place in world affairs was becoming increasingly visible with the expansion of its military and economic power, the Japanese called for "authentic" portrayals of Japan—and Asia—on the international stage. On the other hand, at the same time, Japan was eagerly learning and adopting Western art forms and also wanted to follow, achieve, and maintain another kind of "authenticity"—authenticity to Western high culture that opera exemplified.

Classical Music for the Middle Class and the "Reverse Flow" from Asia to the West

Whereas from the late nineteenth to the mid-twentieth century, Asian governments and intellectuals took initiative and control over the adoption and use of "Western" music, in Japan after World War II, South Korea after the Korean War, and China after the Cultural Revolution, Western music left the hands of the state and became a mainstay of middle-class life in East Asia. The growth of domestic manufacturing of musical instruments, the development of music pedagogy and a wider availability of private instruction, and the popular acceptance of musical training as a form of cultural capital spurred adoption of Western music by the middle classes. Middle-class sociocultural aspirations combined with commercial interests of the growing music industry and social ideals for democratic citizenry to transform classical music from the pursuit of the privileged elite to an art form practiced by the middle class.

Among all the musical instruments, the piano played a particularly central role in symbolizing modernity and class. Only elites owned pianos in early Meiji Japan, but gradually a new middle class comprised of bureaucrats, professionals, and entrepreneurs managed to acquire them. Yet, even as late as the 1920s, a new, domestically produced upright piano cost six to eight times the average monthly income of a middle-class worker.[58] However, in postwar Japan, technological innovations, particularly at two major manufacturers, Yamaha and Kawai, increased piano production dramatically. In merely one decade from 1954 to 1963, Japan's piano output grew tenfold from 10,000 to 109,699. In 1968, Yamaha alone produced 240,000 pianos, followed by Kawai's 50,000.[59] Just two years later, Japan surpassed the United States and became the number one producer of pianos.[60]

Piano manufacturing in Korea and China followed a similar pattern. In Korea, Young Chang and Samick began operations in the years immediately following the Korean War, and in less than three decades, by 1985, Korea had become the world's third largest producer of pianos after Japan and the United States.[61] China's "piano fever" created such a high demand that factories could not begin to fill the orders. According to Melvin and Cai, "Getting a piano was a matter of waiting for years or using back-door connections and bribes. Some people even bought pianos for investment purposes only, certain that both demand and price would continue to rise so that owning a piano was 'better than putting their money in the bank.'"[62] Piano production in China increased more than 100 percent between 1991–95 and 1996–2000. Today, Guanzhou's Pearl River piano factory is second in the world only to Yamaha, and China also excels at producing other musical instruments, such as the violin.[63]

In all these countries, expanded production made upright pianos accessible to the middle class, but increased availability alone cannot explain why the piano became a symbol of the urban middle-class lifestyle. A Japanese government report attributed the increasing demand for musical instruments in Japan in the late 1950s and early 1960s to five factors: the introduction of instrumental training in music education; the proliferation of radios and televisions, which resulted in the growing popularity of music; increased leisure time and changing notions of recreation; manufacturers' efforts to increase demand; and the growth of personal income.[64] In advertisements, manufacturers deftly linked the piano to class status by featuring famous actresses associated with sophistication.[65] Such strategies were clearly effective, and for middle-class families, a piano displayed in the living room came to signify their rising fortunes just as did other new household purchases, such as a car, color television set, and air conditioner. As traditional Japanese music increasingly came to be seen as arcane, Western music quickly gained symbolic power as a marker of middle-class status. These trends in Japan from the late 1950s through the 1970s took hold in Korea and China in the 1980s onward.

Advertising images alone, however, were not enough to sustain demand for musical instruments. Because musical instruments, especially the piano, are not commodities that ordinary households replace on a regular basis, sales would soon saturate the market. The musical instrument industry addressed this problem in part through its launching of music schools to expand the piano-playing population. Although public schools provided basic music education, they did not offer private instruction in instrumental performance; in contrast, conservatories focused on advanced training for aspiring professional musicians. Instrument manufacturers such as Yamaha and Kawai responded to this education gap by enlisting prominent musicians to design a pedagogical method and music schools that provided private and group lessons. Collaborating with Yamaha sales dealers in local neighborhoods and offering lessons at stores or local kindergartens, the Yamaha Music School provided reasonably priced lessons not only in piano and organ playing but also in ear training, sight reading, and theory. Within Japan, the school experienced incredible growth—from 500 teachers, 700 schools, and 20,000 students in 1959 to 2,800 teachers, 5,000 schools, and 250,000 students just six years later. Propelled by the success of Yamaha, its rival Kawai opened its Kawai Music School in 1956.[66] The proliferation of these programs throughout the country enabled the growth of the nation's music industry and expanded the reach of classical music training to the middle class during this period.

In Korea, similar music lessons became available through numerous private music academies, or *ûmak hakwôn,* across the country. Offering basic instruction to neighborhood children, these academies are a springboard for serious students who go on to take private lessons from more prestigious teachers affiliated with conservatories.[67] In China as well, music training centers and schools have sprung up across the country. Some are run by famous musicians, such as the Liu Shikun Piano Arts School, which has its headquarters in Hong Kong and branches all over the country. In 1998, China introduced a graded test system to standardize teaching and to measure students' progress, which has become popular among parents eager to quantify their children's accomplishments.[68]

The "middle-classing" of classical music in Asia through the expansion of instrument manufacturing and the growth of music training in Asia soon led to the reverse flow of musical instruments, musicians, and music training from Asia to the West. During much of the 1950s, Japan's piano makers could not compete with top-level American manufacturers, such as Steinway, Baldwin, or Wurlitzer, in terms of either quality or quantity. Intent on increasing its U.S. market share, Yamaha International Corporation opened in Los Angeles in 1960 and quickly became known for its technical innovations, carefully targeted marketing, and impeccable customer care. In 1962, the company won the bid for all piano purchases by the Los Angeles school district, and soon to follow were the San Francisco school district, Stanford University, and the Hilton Hotel in New York.[69] Korean and Chinese piano manufacturers followed suit, expanding their shares of the international piano market. Along with Japan's Yamaha and Kawai, Korea's Young Chang and Samick have become two of the largest and most automated piano producers in the world and also have joint ventures in China and Indonesia. Seven Chinese manufacturers also export pianos to the United States, and some, including Pearl River Piano Group, Beijing Piano Company, and Dong Bei Piano Company, produce pianos for dealers and producers in the United States.[70] The total output of pianos produced in these countries, combined with the joint ventures and investments of these Asian manufacturers in other Asian markets, makes East Asia the heart of today's piano industry.

It was not only the instruments that were exported from Asia to the West during this period. By the late 1950s, Asian musicians began to attract the world's attention, winning major international competitions and performing around the world. In 1959, Seiji Ozawa won the International Competition of Orchestra Conductors in Besançon, France, and in the following year he earned the Koussevitsky Prize at the Tanglewood Music Center in Massachusetts. After Leonard Bernstein took him under his wing, Ozawa became an assistant conductor for the New York Philharmonic in 1961. He then served as the music director for the Toronto Symphony and San Francisco Symphony and, for three decades, as the music director for the Boston Symphony Orchestra. Ozawa's brilliant international career gave an enormous boost to the nation's morale in the decade when Japan was returning to the world stage. At the same time, a larger wave of Japanese musicians were making their presence known in the West. In 1960, the NHK Symphony Orchestra, Japan's first professional orchestra established in 1926, toured the world with a sixteen-year-old pianist Hiroko Nakamura. In subsequent years, several Japanese musicians won major international competitions, setting in motion a steady flow onto the world stage.

The Koreans and the Chinese soon followed the Japanese musicians onto the international scene. Members of the Chung family—cellist Myung-Wha Chung, violinist Kyung-Wha Chung, and conductor and pianist Myung-Whung Chung—have had successful international careers after moving to the United States to study at Juilliard and winning major international competitions. As I discuss in later chapters, a generation of Chinese composers who grew up during the Cultural Revolution came to the United States to study during the 1980s, paving the way for successive musicians—composers as well as performers—to develop careers in the West.

Methods of music instruction were also exported from Asia to the West. In fact, music schools and instructional methods such as the Yamaha Music School and the Suzuki Method may represent Asia's most significant impact on the classical music scene, as they reached hundreds of thousands of students worldwide. The first Yamaha Music School, which opened in the United States in 1965, began with only sixty students. The reasonable tuition ($10 per month) and the accessibility of the method to students with no musical background proved to be a major draw for American families, and within a year, Yamaha Music Schools enrolled 3,000 students in 100 locations nationwide.[71] The Yamaha Music School also opened in the United Kingdom in 1976, making a significant impact on the European scene as well. Yet, the Suzuki Method had an even greater impact on instrumental training in the United States and elsewhere. A close look at the origins of the Suzuki Method and the process of its globalization illuminates the multiple meanings of the reverse flow of Western music from Asia to the West.

Globalization of the Suzuki Method

When President Jimmy Carter visited Japan in 1979, he stepped out of Air Force One with his wife Rosalynn and his daughter Amy, who was carrying a violin case. Three days later, in a town meeting in Shimoda, the site of Commodore Perry's arrival 125 years earlier, he warmed up to Japanese citizens by saying that Amy was learning to play the violin through the Suzuki Method.[72] This small exchange showed that the Suzuki Method had already become a very widespread and respected institution in the United States and around the world. In fact, several years after Carter's visit, *Time* magazine's special issue on Japan featured Suzuki as one of the most important people in contemporary Japan.[73] Akio Mizuno, one of the proponents of the Suzuki Method, was not exaggerating when he claimed, "The most well-known Japanese name in America today—not corporate names like Sony or Honda but name of an individual—is Shinichi Suzuki."[74]

The Suzuki Method, a highly successful method of teaching young children to play musical instruments, was originally designed for violin and later adapted to other instruments, such as piano, cello, and flute. Developed by Japanese violinist and pedagogue Shinichi Suzuki, it is practiced today by more than 400,000 students in thirty-four countries around the world. Although its objective is not necessarily to train professional musicians, many internationally acclaimed performers, such as violinists Sarah Chang, Jennifer Koh, and Kyoko Takezawa, learned to play using the Suzuki Method.

Shinichi Suzuki was born in Nagoya, Japan, in 1898. His father came from a *samurai* family that had taken up the trade of *shamisen* (traditional Japanese string instrument) making. However, after seeing the violin owned by an instructor in a teachers college, his father studied the mechanics of the instrument and became one of the first violin manufacturers in Japan. Suzuki's family also included a Zen Buddhist monk. Suzuki thus grew up in a family that eagerly studied Western music and culture while also upholding Japanese traditions and values.

Suzuki studied violin in Japan for some years before going to Germany in 1920 where he became highly self-conscious about his lack of German-language skills. Returning to Japan to perform and to teach after a decade of study in Germany, he developed a method for teaching the instrument modeled after the way children learn language—thus calling it "the mother tongue approach."

The Method's basic principles reflect this approach, recommending an early start in children's musical education, beginning as young as age two, and regular exposure to music. Emphasizing parental involvement, especially the mother's role, Suzuki's design has the mother begin lessons before her child so she can stimulate the child's interest and guide his or her daily practice. It stresses imitation of recordings and repetition as the basis of learning. Students memorize all the pieces studied and use no score until their basic technique is established. Finally, the Method incorporates group lessons and performances as an integral part of the learning process. Based on these principles, all students of the Suzuki Method follow the same sequence of materials, using ten volumes of music—ranging from "Twinkle, Twinkle, Little Star" to violin music by Vivaldi, Bach, and Handel—carefully selected and/or arranged by Suzuki according to skill level. Because of these standardized materials, all Suzuki students have a common repertoire that they can play together in ensembles without rehearsals.

Suzuki's philosophy was clearly shaped by his beliefs about nationalism and democracy in the context of 1940s Japan. In 1941, when Japan was entering a total war with the United States, Suzuki argued that all children would become individuals with great, useful talents if their abilities were nurtured through a proper method. Rather than making a general claim about child development, Suzuki connected his ideas to the making of a "great Japanese citizen." He argued that training children's abilities in the same manner that children learn a language was a sure way to "create citizens that truly excel in the world." He wrote, "Japan must have a firm belief and develop its own method of education in order to educate ideal individuals as Japanese citizens. Unless educators have a strong conviction, the Japanese will forever remain a people who will merely follow the paths of foreign nations."[75]

Although Suzuki was not an overtly political man and rarely discussed the war and its impact directly, he adapted his educational principles to the postwar context in several ways. Most important, his ideas about the education of Japanese citizenry then explicitly took on the language of individualism that was more latent during the war years. Lamenting what he saw as the flawed educational system that led to the nation's defeat, Suzuki criticized the emphasis in Japanese schooling on mass uniformity for hampering the development of its citizens' abilities.[76] His pedagogy focused on nurturing the innate talent of every child through early guidance, daily immersion, and belief in the child's abilities. He firmly believed in the capacity of every child and stressed nurture over nature, and his principles were adamantly democratic and egalitarian. In this sense, the Suzuki Method was conceived as a program for developing democratic citizenry rather than simply a method for music instruction.[77]

Suzuki's philosophy meshed with the cultural aspirations of the Japanese, particularly among the middle class, in the postwar decades. During the war years, various forms of Western culture, including music, were suppressed in Japan; after the war, the new generation of Japanese avidly slaked their thirst for things Western. In this cultural climate, the Suzuki Method made Western music accessible for the masses. Because Suzuki believed that musical sensitivity and skill are not inherited but nurtured by the environment, and because the Suzuki Method provided a concrete, step-by-step process for all parents and children to acquire musical skills regardless of background, it offered a particularly welcome way for the Japanese with little or no prior exposure to Western music to study the violin. For a large number of Japanese citizens in the postwar decades, learning Western music became a way of acquiring a piece of Western culture and desired cultural capital.

The Suzuki Method also expressed the gender ideals of postwar Japan. In the years immediately after the war, Suzuki developed and articulated his ideas about the importance of the mother's role in her child's education and in Japan's future: "All mothers of Japan, please begin an early education so that your children will become Japanese citizens who can realize their abilities to the fullest." He had an ambivalent reaction to the new political environment of postwar Japan in which women first gained suffrage under the U.S. Occupation: "Fortunately, women have now gained the right to vote, and women lawmakers have been elected. Under these circumstances, political movements can be made by women as well. However, I believe that more important than such political movements is for mothers throughout Japan to embark upon a movement to bring talent education and character development to their children."[78] By making mothers central in children's learning, the Suzuki Method defined women's place as the home. It assumed that the mother had the time not only to attend the child's lessons but also to learn the instrument herself and supervise the child's daily practice. The centrality of the mother's role in the Suzuki Method and the preponderance of female Suzuki instructors supported middle-class gender assumptions.

Suzuki's belief in individualism and democracy, his emphasis on the mother's role as defined in bourgeois domestic terms, and the choice of Western music as a tool for human development were also quite in accord with dominant American ideologies of the postwar decades, which enabled his method to take root in American soil. Considered by some to be uniquely Japanese, the Suzuki method is indeed quite culturally hybrid, if not even American.

The globalization of the Suzuki Method started in May 1958, when Kenji Mochizuki, then a graduate student of theology at Oberlin College, showed violin professor Clifford Cook a film of Suzuki's young students performing in a concert. The short (5 min, 40 sec) film was taped at the Grand Concert of Suzuki students held at the Tokyo Metropolitan Sports Hall in 1955. Cook was overwhelmed by the spectacle of nearly a thousand children performing Bach's *Concerto for Two Violins* with perfect form, harmony, and tone. He immediately urged Mochizuki to show the film to the members of the Ohio String Teachers Association at its conference held shortly thereafter. American string teachers became intrigued with the results of Suzuki's method and began to visit Japan to learn more about the program.[79]

In 1964, Suzuki brought ten students, ranging in age from five to thirteen, to the United States. The "Suzuki Children" toured all over the United States for three weeks and performed in such venues as the Juilliard School and Carnegie Hall for packed audiences. The U.S. tour of the "Suzuki Children," selected each year by Suzuki himself based on recordings sent by students from all over Japan, took place annually for thirty years until 1994. The children's performances, promoted under the phrase "East Meets West," were instrumental in the global spread of the Suzuki Method.[80] The children deeply impressed renowned violin teachers such as Dorothy DeLay and Ivan Galamian. After seeing the performances of the Suzuki Children, many American violinists decided to study the Method, and many went to Matsumoto to study directly with Suzuki. These trained musicians then taught more instructors all over the United States, quickly expanding the Method and thereby revolutionizing string instruction.

The timing of Suzuki's overseas expansion is significant. The first U.S. tour of the Suzuki Children took place in 1964, the year in which the Japanese government liberalized its policy for Japanese travel overseas. Along with the Tokyo Olympics held in October of the same year, the liberalization of foreign travel signaled to many Japanese the re-entry of Japan into the world arena, nearly two decades after its defeat in World War II. The Suzuki Children's U.S. tour epitomized this re-entry particularly well because it demonstrated that Japanese children were performing Western music with Western instruments on a level much higher than an average American violin student.

The spread of the Suzuki Method through these cross-Pacific exchanges had an immense impact on string instruction in the United States. Many American violinists assert that the Suzuki Method played a crucial role in overcoming the shortage and poor quality of string instruction in the United States. Yet, praise for the Method was not universal.

The portrayals of the Suzuki Method reveal the changing American attitude toward Japan. At first, Americans enthused over the spectacle of young musicians trained in the Method. In 1966, when the Method was just beginning to spread in the United States and when Japan's economic penetration into the global market was in its early stage, a *New York Times* reporter praised the Suzuki Children's New York performance for its "naturalness" despite occasional technical imperfections:

> One of the nicest things about the demonstration was that the children played like children. There was no strain, no pretense, no pressure for perfection.
>
> Isako Fukazawa, for example, is only 8, and when she played Mr. Suzuki's arrangement of Corelli's "La Folia," one could believe it.
>
> In a sense, her accomplishment was astonishing, but there was something about it, apart from the little imperfections, that made it seem quite natural and healthy. This was the good feeling one had about all the solo and group performances of the afternoon.[81]

In stark contrast, the review of a concert of students of the Suzuki Method in 1984 focuses on technical perfection and the lack of naturalness in the children's playing:

> However, while nobody expects profundity from pre-schoolers, the collective playing was automatic. More disturbingly, some solo performances by senior members of the ensemble—pianists and violinists old enough to know better—were technically assured but absolutely devoid of germinal musical insight.
>
> All of which makes one suspect that the Suzuki method is to music making as parrot chatter is to oratory. This listener, for one, would rather hear a fumbled, halting rendition of the Brahms lullaby or "To a Wild Rose" that a child has cherished, wrestled with and made his own than empty precocity on the stage of Carnegie Hall.[82]

Words such as "collective," "automatic," "parrot chatter," and "empty precocity" reflect the way in which many Americans came to view the Method in the decade when Japan's technology and industry were seen as quickly eroding the American economy. Such a depiction also anticipates the stereotype of Asian musicians as technically proficient but artistically inexpressive, the stereotype that emerged with the "model minority" discourse about Asian Americans and prevails to this day.

A cultural essentialism inflects discussions of the Suzuki Method in the United States. The most common American understanding of the Suzuki Method is as a regime of imitation and repetition. A 1959 article in *Time* explains that "Suzuki's method is simple sound repetition."[83] More specialized discussions of the Method in *Music Educators Journal* also focus on the importance of repetition and imitation in children's learning to hear and understand the correct sound.[84] Although these elements are certainly part of the basic principles of the Method and for many observers account for its remarkable success, the associations of imitation and repetition with Japanese culture deploy and reinforce notions of specifically "Japanese" systems of education, namely the emphasis on standardized rote learning. Critics of the Suzuki Method consider rote learning to be a great obstacle to nourishing students' individuality and artistry.

Among the harshest critics of the Suzuki Method is Ronald Cavaye, a British pianist who taught in Japan during the 1980s. Cavaye argues that children's ability to imitate a recording merely shows their acquisition of skills in mechanically copying a model but does not reflect a comprehension or interpretation of the piece as a work of art, and that having thousands of children playing a piece in unison simply shows that they have been trained to be a unified machine but does not demonstrate an ability to create art.[85] Such characterizations construct the performance of Western music as an individualized artistic process that is distinct from Japanese traditions.

Such a binary construction of Western individualism and Japanese conformity is shared even by Suzuki teachers. Lois Peak, an education specialist who studied the Suzuki Method through participant observation, explains Suzuki's emphasis on learning by ear by pointing out that "the traditional Japanese classical music was also primarily an oral tradition in which students learned to play by ear." Peak underscores the "Japanese-ness" of such a tradition by highlighting its difference from the "Western artistic tradition" in which "'creativity' or the ability to develop a uniquely individual rendition of even very well-known works is one of the most important goals of the artistic process" and "[c]onscious imitation of even artistically superior models is believed to be inimical to the development of such creativity."[86]

The inscription of Japanese-ness onto the Suzuki Method is also seen in the way in which American representations focus on the Method's elements of group learning and performance. Although group lessons and performances are only two of Suzuki's many ways to provide children with encouragement and support, they receive disproportionate attention in popular accounts of the Method in the United States. Many media reports on the Suzuki Method include a photograph of young Japanese children lined up on stage, often in identical outfits, playing the violin, usually "Twinkle, Twinkle, Little Star."[87] Even favorable accounts say that these children "are far from robots,"[88] an odd form of praise that highlights the association between the group performance and the standardized production of unindividualized masses.

These characterizations took on more ominous tones when combined with the discourse of the "yellow peril" that was revitalized in the period of Japan's economic penetration into the U.S. market from the 1960s onward. A 1967 *Time* article discussed the Suzuki Method with a title no other than "Instrumentalists: Invasion from the Orient." The article begins as follows: "Until recently, the idea of Orientals performing Western music seemed about as freakish as Heifetz playing the one-string ichigenkin. Now all that has changed. In the past few years, American and European concert halls have experienced something close to a full-scale invasion by talented Korean and Japanese musicians."[89] The use of the word "invasion" to talk about young fiddlers playing "Twinkle, Twinkle, Little Star" gives a distinctly racial meaning not only to the Suzuki Method itself but also to the musicians and musical practices.

As disturbing as such racialized language might be as an expression of Western Orientalism and prejudice, it is echoed in the comments of the Japanese practitioners and proponents of the Suzuki Method who also firmly believe in, and take pride in, the Method's "Japanese-ness." Japanese proponents often draw a connection between the Method's principles and traditional Japanese culture, values, and ways of learning. When asked about the significance of the Japanese origin of the Suzuki Method, several Japanese leaders of the Method comment on Suzuki's family background and his exposure not only to traditional Japanese music and instruments but also to Buddhist philosophy and Confucian thought.[90] For example, according to Kōji Toyoda, current president of the Talent Education Research Institute (headquarters of the Suzuki Method), Suzuki's emphasis on learning by ear derives from the long-held Japanese idea that numerous repetitions naturally lead to comprehension: just as young Buddhist monks are trained to repeat chants even if they do not understand their meanings, in Japan children are often taught through copying and repeating adults. Although such a practice tends to be seen as a meaningless mechanical exercise in the West, the practitioners of the Suzuki Method find immense value in training children's ear, concentration, and musicality in this way. Thus, Suzuki edited a collection of 100 *haiku* by well-known poet Kobayashi Issa, and reciting those poems is an important part of each lesson even with children too young to understand the meaning of each poem.[91]

The Japanese-ness or Asian-ness of Suzuki's principles is also expressed, according to the Method's proponents, in the way students are taught to love and respect others in a manner rooted in Confucian morals. Toshio Takahashi, who designed the Suzuki Method for the flute, says that Suzuki's insistence that the student and the teacher formally bow to each other at the beginning of each lesson reflects his Confucian philosophy: "A student is not told to bow to the teacher because the teacher is a greater being. A bow is instead an expression of mutual respect, based on the notion that all living beings are equals. Manners are all about social order, and young musicians must learn to respect others in society. [Cellist Pablo] Casals said music would save the world, but Confucius said the same thing many centuries before Casals."[92] Suzuki teachers in Japan and the United States strictly observe Suzuki's emphasis on proper respect and manners, and even in places such as New York or Honolulu, most Suzuki teachers and students follow established protocols—such as bowing—at the beginning and end of each lesson.

Thus, ideas about cultural and musical differences between the East and the West—as well as about the Method's universal applicability—are held mutually on both sides of the Pacific. As they embrace, perform, and teach Western music, Japanese practitioners of the Method do not necessarily see what is Japanese and what is Western in binary terms. Their proud insistence on what they see as the Japanese elements of the Method indicate that they feel no need to be Western to perform Western music. Yet, their seeming comfort with the ways in which the Method has spread around the world also shows that the Japanese-ness of the Method, although certainly significant, is not an essential factor in the Method's larger goal of nurturing character through music.

The globalization of the Suzuki Method has produced new exchanges and meanings for classical music. Suzuki's egalitarian belief in every child's ability to perform and the principle of "nurture over nature" have taken root and blossomed in settings dramatically different from his original context in Japan. The most notable example is the work of Roberta Guaspari-Tza-varas in East Harlem, New York. Growing up in a working-class family in Rome, New York, Guaspari took violin lessons through the public school system and went on to earn music and music education degrees from the State University of New York at Fredonia and Boston University. Financially and emotionally devastated after her husband left her with two small sons, Guaspari moved to New York City in 1980 and started teaching violin to public school students in one of the toughest neighborhoods in New York. Her dedication to the violin program provided a creative outlet for children who would not otherwise have been exposed to music. When budget cuts eliminated her teaching position in 1991, she founded a non-profit organization, the Opus 118 Music Center, to continue teaching in East Harlem and enlisted the support of prominent musicians, such as Isaac Stern, Itzhak Perlman, and Midori. Opus 118 provides violin instruction for hundreds of students between the ages of five and twelve, the vast majority of whom are African American and Latino and cannot afford violin lessons or their own violin. Guaspari-Tzavaras's extraordinary success in providing motivation, discipline, and joy through music for these children inspired the documentary film, *Small Wonders,* in 1995 and the 1999 Miramax feature film, *Music of the Heart,* starring Meryl Streep in the role of Guaspari.[93]

Few examples demonstrate the success of the Suzuki Method in crossing cultural and social boundaries better than Guaspari's work. Although neither of the two films makes specific references to the Suzuki Method, the pieces children play in the film—from Suzuki's "Twinkle Variations" and "Andantino," Vivaldi's Sonata, to Bach's *Concerto for Two Violins*—as well as the philosophy with which Guaspari teaches children announce that she is a practitioner of the Suzuki Method. According to the Japanese translator of Guaspari's memoir, her visit to a Suzuki violin class in Hawai'i had a profound influence on her philosophy and attitude toward music education.[94] Visiting Japan for the opening of the feature film in 2000, Guaspari recollected her attendance in the First International Suzuki Teachers' Conference in 1975. She entered the hall carrying her infant son, worrying that he might start crying in the middle of the workshop, and Mr. Suzuki immediately pointed to her and said, "You and the baby, now is the crucial moment, the baby's education has already started!"[95] As European music was passed onto a Japanese violinist whose pedagogy was then carried on by an Italian-American woman teaching African American and Latino children in East

Harlem, Suzuki's beliefs in every child's ability, his principle of "nurture over nature," and his faith in the power of music in endowing agency to children have crossed the boundaries of culture, race, and class.

Conclusion

The history of Western music in East Asia has been composed of many voices. In the early stage of classical music's introduction to Japan, China, and Korea, its association with modernity, Westernization, and hence national progress was at the heart of the eagerness with which Asian nations adopted the music into their own educational and cultural institutions. Direct government involvement and leadership facilitated the systematic institutionalization of Western music education in these countries. Yet, the later history of Asian engagement with classical music has been far from a simple continuation or variation of this opening theme. Although the association with modernity has remained an important factor in Asians' interest in classical music, as Asians gained more agency in defining the meanings of the music for themselves and using it for their own goals, they translated the original motive into many different forms. Interestingly, in the nation- and empire-building period in East Asia, Asian intellectuals and governments used Western music as a tool for promoting Asian, rather than simply Western, cultural values and political objectives. Especially during war and revolution, Asians invested distinct political meanings into classical music, and musicians practicing classical music were treated as arbiters of imperialism or nationalism, or sometimes both.

The government and the intellectual and cultural elite controlled the ways in which Western music was practiced by their citizens until the mid-twentieth century. However, in Japan after World War II, South Korea after the Korean War, and China after the Cultural Revolution, classical music became a much more broad-based pursuit of the middle class. The image of classical music as a form of elite culture, as well as its association with modernity and the West, certainly continued to shape Asians' enthusiasm for the music, thus making it an important marker of status and taste. With increased access to musical instruments and musical training, classical music became a much more popular practice through which people with little or no background in Western culture could come to own a piece of symbolic and cultural capital and claim a class identity. The reverse flow of music, musical instruments, and musicians from Asia to the West from the 1960s onward further underscored the process of democratization and popularization of classical music.

Just as the composer and the conductor alone cannot create music without the performers, the intent of the government or the music business cannot be executed without the musicians who play music and the audiences who listen to it. While the musicians are certainly part of the larger historical and social context in which they live, and their lives and work are shaped by the demands, expectations, and responses of their audiences, on the deepest level the musicians engage music in ways that often defy external circumstances. As can be seen in the life of Tamaki Miura, the flowering of the Suzuki Method on the American soil, or the intensity with which a ten-year-old cellist performed for Isaac Stern in post-Cultural Revolution China, Asian musicians have embraced classical music on their own terms and, in the process of creating their own voice through the music, have made it deeply moving and meaningful for their audiences, both in and outside their cultures. The subsequent chapters illustrate how Asian and Asian American musicians in the United States today have both inherited and transformed the legacies of this history of East Asian encounters with Western music.

VOICES

*S*ince 1999, David Kim has been the concertmaster for the Philadelphia Orchestra, one of the most prestigious orchestras in the United States and the world. Born in Carbondale, Illinois, of Korean parents, he began studying the violin at age three under what he describes below as "an Olympic-style" regimen. At age twelve he appeared with Itzhak Perlman as the subject of "Prodigy," a WNEW-TV production in New York, and has been featured since on CBS, NBC, and PBS. He studied with Dorothy DeLay at Juilliard and was a classmate of internationally acclaimed violinist, Cho-Liang Lin.

 I interviewed Kim in the concertmaster's dressing room at Carnegie Hall just before the Philadelphia Orchestra's concert there in January 2004. Although his upbringing perfectly fits the pattern of Asian families investing heavily in the child's music training, his story is unique in its candidness about the evolution of his career and his goals—from striving for a solo career to becoming a very successful orchestral musician. He talked about what many musicians might consider a huge disappointment as "the greatest thing that happened to me." He was extremely cordial and generous—he was one of the few musicians who called me directly on the phone after receiving my request for an interview. As we began talking, we were amused to find that all of the places that he has lived in before Philadelphia—Carbondale, Illinois; Columbia, South Carolina; and Kingston, Rhode Island—are places where I have been to visit close friends. A very engaging conversationalist, he was very interested in me and my project, and throughout our interview, he frequently interjected my name as he was trying to make a point.

DK: My mother was among the first generation of Koreans to enter classical music, along with Kyung-Wha Chung and other big names. She was a very accomplished pianist and was very famous in her native Korea, and she went through all her education in South Korea and she did her master's degree at Southern Illinois University. She did her doctorate at Eastman School of Music at Rochester, and she was the first Korean woman to receive a doctorate in music outside of Korea ever. So she obviously knew all about music and had the love and drive. And then, when in her early twenties I was accidental pregnancy [laughs]. Even so, she had this dream that she wanted her son to become a famous violinist. She had that determination very early, even before I was born. So when I turned three, she started teaching me very intensively, practicing every day, no days off. It was like Olympic training. I was practicing three or four hours a day by the time I was six years old. And then when I was eight, I went to take an audition with my teacher Dorothy DeLay and started studying with her. I mean, the stories are endless. [My mother] wanted to make sure that I had perfect pitch, so every day she would train me with the piano, she just was . . . I think she was one of the pioneers in the pushy Asian mother genre [laughs]. Really. There was no such thing as bedtime until I practiced five or six hours every day. . . . When I was ten, we moved to South Carolina because both my parents got jobs at the University of South Carolina, and from there, I was flying every other week by myself to study at Juilliard. It was incredible, the dedication. . . . So, I'll just give you a few more examples. My father wanted to have more children, but my mother said no, it would be too much distraction. My parents sacrificed everything, because it was very expensive to fly me every other week, year after year, and Ms. DeLay, my teacher, and my mother formed an alliance and worked hard and pushed me.

MY: Many kids come to resent that sort of thing, but obviously you didn't.

DK: Sure. Of course I didn't like all the practicing. But because my mother sacrificed everything for the sake of my music, our life was completely about my music. Even in the morning, at breakfast, we'd listen to twentieth-century opera, or Palestrina . . . it was just complete immersion in music. And I must say that when I started studying with Ms. DeLay, she was so stimulating and warm and giving and wonderful that from that point on, I did it more because of my love for Ms. DeLay and I wanted to please her rather than because my parents pushed me. I never had the choice that many kids have of quitting after a certain point. I never had that choice. I think deep down I understood that this was my destiny, that this was going to be my life's work . . .

[At Juilliard], I got so much stimulation from just being around highly motivated, talented musicians. Of course, there were many Asians. When I started attending Juilliard—I mean, right now, at Juilliard, it's like all Asian. Have you been to the Saturday school [Juilliard Pre-College]? It's unbelievable. But even back then [in the 1970s], the tide was turning. Eastern European and Jewish students were diminishing and Asians were just coming up. And I remember one time I had an ear-training class. There were fourteen of us, and we were all Asians. They all had perfect pitch, and they all wore glasses [laughs]. We were all nerdy Asian kids. It was very nice, because in South Carolina, there were so few Asians there, so it was very stimulating and comforting to be with lots of other Asian kids. It was like going to Korean church on Sundays; it's comforting because everyone else is Asian.

MY: Was your career goal always to be in an orchestra?

DK: Oh, no, it was never. In fact, until I was about 31 or 32, if you would ask me if I wanted to be a concertmaster I would never have said yes. I never thought of settling for something less than a big-time solo career. And part of that was that I was brainwashed by everyone around me that my becoming the next Itzhak Perlman was a foregone conclusion. My whole life. Part of it was my ego, which also fully expected that I would achieve the highest levels. But then, even though I got really close . . . I got so close at times . . . I had really wonderful concert days, I performed all over the world! But it wasn't really at the same level as the A-level soloists, the Cho-Liang Lins and Midoris and people like that. So although I got very, very close in my late twenties and early thirties, it suddenly started to diminish. I was suddenly playing in towns like Carbondale, Illinois, or Beaufort, South Carolina, in much smaller gigs, and the fees were dropping, and I was starting to have to scramble in order to make enough concerts to really call myself a soloist. And finally I had an epiphany when I was thirty-three. It was not going to happen. You can try and hit your head against the wall, and it's just not going to happen. It finally hit me that I was not good enough. I didn't have the necessary . . . I didn't have the ingredients that they were looking for, they being the big managers or conductors that I played for all the time . . . the special ingredients you need to have a top-level career. So overnight, literally, I decided to join an orchestra. Part of it was financial. My wife was working for a large accounting firm and was supporting me for ten years, commuting into New York, and I just felt like . . . She has her BA, she was working so hard, supporting us, as I went to play in Elkhart, Indiana, to make 500 bucks in five days. She was very loving and understanding as I was chasing that dream until the end. And when I finally said, "OK, that's it," it was so liberating! To finally not have that pressure. And I think she was relieved.

But then, jumping way ahead, now that I'm here, in this wonderful position, I realize that, the people who have solo careers are a certain kind of person. And I wouldn't trade places with any of them even for a million dollars or ten million dollars. . . . I love my life being in this incredible institution. It's just such an honor to be a member of an orchestra like the Philadelphia Orchestra or Chicago Symphony. There are so many orchestras in the world, and it's such a privilege to be a member of any of it. But I'm most fortunate to be a concertmaster of the Philadelphia Orchestra, one of the greatest orchestras in the history of Western music, and so now I realize that what I'm doing now is so much more rewarding, at least to me. And I get to stay most of the time, with my two little daughters, I get to be home with them. It's just the greatest thing that ever happened to me. I just wish that I had had the stupid epiphany five years earlier [laughs] instead of traveling all over the place. But I probably wouldn't have been able to achieve this level without all that experience.

Cellist Lifen Anthony grew up in China during the Cultural Revolution. Despite much harassment by the Red Guard, her family encouraged her brother and her to study music, and her father learned to make cellos so that they could play. In 1974, at age 11, she entered the conservatory as the Cultural Revolution was waning and the conservatories were reopened. She experienced the rigorous discipline of the conservatory life for ten years. After graduating, she taught in China for a few years while her brother went to Japan to study. While visiting her brother in Tokyo, she auditioned for a symphony in Yamagata Prefecture and got a position and later became the principal cellist. She then lived in Japan for seventeen years, and in addition to playing for the symphony, she played in a trio with her brother and had four successful concerts in Japan.

She now lives in Hawai'i with her American husband whom she met in Yamagata. She was tired of playing for the orchestra, and her husband, a native New Yorker, wanted to return to the United States. They spent several years looking for a place to live in the United States, when one day they just hopped on an airplane to Hawai'i and decided to move there. Not knowing anyone in the islands, she went to a Honolulu Symphony concert and introduced herself to some musicians backstage. Reflecting on her bold move, she laughed as she talked about how "crazy" her husband's and her decision to move to Hawai'i was and how "un-Japanese" her way of making friends has been. After only one year of living in the islands, she is already a very popular and successful teacher with

more than fifty students. She still performs in Japan regularly with her brother,
and she also substitutes for the Honolulu Symphony. Her two daughters, ages
eleven and thirteen at the time of our interview, are also talented musicians. I
interviewed her at her home in Honolulu.

LA: I grew up in the north of China. At the time, China was very shut
down in classical music because of the Cultural Revolution. And of course
our family had lots of problems with the Red Guards, the usual story, right?
My father just wanted us to study Western music and leave China. My father
was not a musician, but he studied architecture in Shanghai. He didn't fin-
ish his schooling . . . because he thought that if he finished [his degree], our
family would be in trouble because we would be sent to the countryside. So
he went to work as a regular factory worker. But he was so smart and could
do anything. He could make everything by hand, like a bicycle or a radio.
He mastered all the factory work really fast. When I was about eight years
old, all the conservatory teachers were sent to the countryside to work in the
field, and that place [where the teachers worked] was close to our house. So
one of my father's friends had connection with a conservatory teacher, and
my father said, "I want my daughter to study cello." And then his friend
said, "Well, where are you going to get a cello?" So they went to talk to the
conservatory teacher, who said, "Well, I think you can make a cello." My
father didn't think so, but the teacher let him open his cello, and my father
copied it and made a cello.

MY: Wow! So your first instrument was one made by your father.

LA: Yeah. And we got into trouble because the Red Guard came to our
house and saw the cello. My father got into big trouble. But anyway, when
I was eleven years old, I think it was in 1974, they decided to reopen the
Conservatory, and the first audition was in 1974. And the audition was very
hard, because I think in my year there were twenty students to be selected
from all of China. I got in and started studying at the Conservatory for ten
years.

MY: And what was the training like?

LA: We were trained like soldiers in the army [laughs]. Get up at five
o'clock in the morning, run, and come back and play scales for two hours.
At 7:30 we would go to eat breakfast. Our food was very good, because
Mao's nephew was the mayor of our city, so he had special power and we
were lucky to get good food. But the training was just crazy. We were not

allowed to play Western music, so they made us play Chinese music, which was quite difficult, because a lot of Chinese music is fast. We played a lot of scales in the morning, and then after breakfast, we all start practicing until 11:30. Each student had a practice room with a piano and each room had a small window so the teachers could watch us. And then we eat at 11:30, take a nap, and after that we have regular classes, like ear training, Chinese history, and so forth. Then we go eat around 5:30, and afterwards we go play our concertos. Yeah, it was quite a life. . . . Teachers would punish me if I didn't practice well, she would make me sit outside under the sun or the snow. But you know, when you don't know anything else, you just do your best with what you have, you know. [laughs]. . . . So when I came to America, and I thought it was so great for American kids because they have a much better life than Chinese kids. You can't tell American kids to practice for eight hours. They can't do it. But the Chinese, the parents will say, "Do it, it's good for you. Do it." And the kids would do it. So back then, I didn't know that it was hard, but I'm not sure if my kids can do it because they were born in Japan in a different situation.

MY: And the kinds of music you played must have changed a lot, right?

LA: Changed a lot. Even though the Red Guard said, "Don't play Western music," the conservatory teachers had played a lot of Russian music, so we used a lot of Russian textbooks. And even though we were not supposed to, we did play Western music. We played Western études. In the end, I think our training balanced out. Each person played one Chinese piece, and Western étude, concerto, and Bach. Which is really not bad.

[After graduating, she and her brother lived in Japan and played for the Yamagata Symphony for many years.]

MY: When you got to Japan, did you find that the playing was very different from what you were trained in?

LA: Very different. The basic personality is very different, and personality comes out in playing. So generally, Japanese is more dark, and Chinese is too bright. I was lucky because my teacher was Japanese, so when I got to Japan it wasn't too bad. I think now the Chinese are getting much better, but back then, even when we just played sixteenth notes, Chinese and Japanese sounded completely different. . . . I just figured out that Americans are in between [laughs]. Often when I play a concert, I play a Chinese piece and a Japanese piece . . .

MY: So you were in Japan for a very long time.

LA: Yes. I can't really think I'm Chinese or Japanese. I am a Japanese citizen now. But it was very hard for me to work for a Japanese orchestra. And then with some luck I became a principal [cellist for the orchestra], and that was even harder, because I was a Chinese woman, not a [Japanese] man, sitting in a very important chair, and that made life really hard. Now, I think it was good, because I learned how to deal with being pushed around. Are you Japanese? [MY: Yes.] You grew up in Japan? [MY: Yeah.] So you know how it is, right? [laughs] It's really hard, especially artists. Everyone has *hen na jishin* [strange sense of confidence]. Of course everybody believes they're the best. Plus the society is the men's society. I believe Japanese women are really good, much stronger and smarter [than men], but they always have to be one step behind, or at least act that way. But I am not Japanese, so I can't act like that, and that made things hard.

MY: Did you feel that people in Japan were hostile to you because you were from China?

LA: Yes. Especially the conductor. [MY: Oh, really? Like what kinds of things did you encounter?] Like at every rehearsal, he would blame everything on me. If he can't keep a regular tempo, and I'm following him, he would blame it on me, because he didn't have confidence [in his own conducting] and was depending on me to keep the tempo. But I understood later that if he were a good conductor, he wouldn't have to depend on anyone. At first, I didn't understand [what was going on]. Because in Japan, you cannot really talk to people. I have some friends in the orchestra, but the way people become friends [in Japan] is also very different from the way the Chinese make friends. So even with friends, you can't really talk much about your problems. If you do, they will put you down. Maybe that means they're not real friends, I don't know. I have lots of nice friends outside the orchestra, so I cannot say that it's all Japanese people who are that way. But working there in the orchestra, it was really difficult . . .

MY: Looking back, do you think that having spent that much time in Japan was good for your musicianship?

LA: Yes. The Japanese are very *komakai* [detailed]. I think the Chinese are the opposite. So in this way I think I learned a lot from playing in the orchestra. . . . I had never played for an orchestra, so I learned a lot from working for an orchestra in Japan about being professional . . .

*F*lutist Toshio Takahashi is one of the first disciples of pedagogue Shinichi *Suzuki. Takahashi studied music with Suzuki in his hometown of Matsumoto as he was exploring ways to develop as a musician. Suzuki then entrusted Takahashi to design the Suzuki Method for the flute. Takahashi also played a key role in the globalization of the Suzuki Method, as he introduced it to American teachers and also accompanied the U.S. tours of the Suzuki Children for many years. He is now one of the principal teachers and administrators of the Suzuki Method.*

One of the favorite stories Takahashi likes to tell is the encounter he had with a businessman who sat next to him on an airplane when he was on a business trip to the United States in 2003. The Japanese gentleman sitting next to him was the executive of a floppy disk manufacturer. When Takahashi told him about his work, the man—who apparently knew much about the Suzuki Method—was very excited and told Takahashi about the significance of the Suzuki Method for Japan. According to this Japanese businessman, the Suzuki Method is "the only software Japan has exported to the world." Because the Japanese are skilled at copying others, the man said, they have learned to produce hardware that originated in the West, have improved it, and have exported it abroad, but the Japanese had never exported software. The man ecstatically said to Takahashi, "The Suzuki Method is the first software that Japan brought to the world. You are doing a historically important job." Takahashi told me this story during our interview at the headquarters of the Suzuki Method in Matsumoto, Japan. Takahashi's narrative shows the intense yearning for classical music on the part of the young man in postwar Japan and the determination and dedication with which he studied music. As I did not use a tape recorder during this interview, the following narrative is reconstructed from my notes.

[In the 1950s,] I was studying to be an English translator and working at the Imperial Hotel in Tokyo. One day, while meandering in the crowded streets of Takada-no-baba district, I passed by a music shop and heard a flute performance broadcast on NHK radio. I had never heard—or seen—the flute being played before, let alone the particular piece of music. But I was completely blown away by the sound. So I walked into the store and asked the owner what it was that I just heard. The store owner told me that it was Doppler's *Hungarian Pastoral Fantasy for Flute and Piano*, performed by [world-renowned flutist] Marcel Moyse. Right then and there, I decided that I wanted to become a flutist. The store owner showed me the flutes they had in stock. The cheapest one cost 7,000 yen. Of course, as a poor student, I didn't have that kind of money. I told him that I would work and save money and come back to buy the flute six months later.

For six months, it was all work and no play, but I had only saved 5,000 yen. Seeing my determination, my father presented me with the remaining 2,000 yen. I rushed to the store and bought the flute. I started practicing on my own. In those days, there was no teacher or a manual, so I learned just by listening endlessly to Moyse's recordings. It was very hard, but for six months, I had built up all this anticipation, so being able to practice was a pure joy for me. During the week, I could only practice for a few hours a day because I was working, but I practiced for twelve hours a day on weekends. After a year, I had learned the *Hungarian Pastoral Fantasy* and started playing in ensembles with students at the Tokyo University of Fine Arts. At the time, I thought of music as sacred, so I did not want to earn money through music. So I made a living through other jobs and practiced at night.

After a few years, I became ill from too much practicing and went to live with my parents in Matsumoto. While I was in Matsumoto, I studied with Mr. Suzuki. He had no background in the flute, but he gave me musical suggestions on the entire flute repertoire. When I was twenty-eight, I went to the United States to find and study with Moyse. I had heard that Moyse was living in Vermont. So I went to Vermont and found him. And I studied with Moyse for three years and returned to Japan.

After I gave a performance in Matsumoto, Mr. Suzuki asked me to edit Suzuki music for the flute. I spent the next three years selecting the music, and Zen-on Publishing agreed to publish it in 1971. In 1978, I took Suzuki flute students to the summer institute held at the University of Wisconsin. After this trip, Suzuki flute quickly spread in the United States. It now has about 200 teachers and several thousand students across the country.

Violinist Kyoko Takezawa is one of the most talented violinists of this generation. She began studying the violin at the age of three through the Suzuki Method in her hometown in Aichi Prefecture in Japan. At age seven, she was selected as one of the Suzuki Children to tour around the United States. She entered the high-school division of the Toho School of Music in Tokyo and in her junior year won the Japan Music Competition. She met the prominent peda-

*gogue Dorothy DeLay when she came to give master classes at her school, and
at age seventeen she went to the Aspen Music Festival to study with DeLay. She
subsequently left for New York to study at Juilliard, and while she was a student
there she won first prize at the International Violin Competition in Indianapolis, which launched her concertizing career.*

*She has performed with numerous orchestras and conductors around the
world. She is also a prolific recording artist with BMG's RCA Victor Red Seal
label. She says that she is most comfortable playing the type of music that feels
grounded in the earth, such as Bartók. Whereas she has mostly performed the
repertoire from the Romantic period to the twentieth century, she says she hopes
to expand her expressivity so that she can become a violinist who can express
not only the strength but also the delicacy and subtlety of music. At the time of
our interview at Mozart Café on the Upper West Side of Manhattan, she was
pregnant with her daughter due to be born in a month. She told me that she was
getting tips on how to juggle performances and childrearing from other Japanese
musicians whom I had interviewed who have children.*

MY: You started the violin with the Suzuki Method, right?

KT: Yes. There are no musicians in my family, but both my parents liked
classical music. I had two cousins who were a little older than me, and they
were studying violin with the Suzuki Method, so I was exposed to the tone
of the instrument. So I naturally began to want to play the violin, like a
child wants a toy, and that's how I started. My parents bought me a violin
for my third birthday. I grew up in Aichi, where the Suzuki Method is very
vibrant. So my parents found a teacher who is a friend of Mr. Suzuki. . . .
When we went to observe the lessons, seeing the children having a lot of fun
with the instrument seemed to inspire my mother. But because my parents
had no musical background, they weren't thinking at all about a musical
career for me. I started with the Suzuki Method because it was there, close
to me . . .

I didn't know until I left Japan that Suzuki Method was so global.
Because I had toured in the United States as a child, I had some sense
that Suzuki was big in the United States, but I have been surprised to find
the Suzuki Method even in European cities where not that many people
visit . . .

The teacher I studied with was someone who stressed the spiritual
dimension of playing music. This is true for the Suzuki Method in general,

KYOKO TAKEZAWA
(Photograph by J. Henry Fair)

but things like bowing to the teacher at the beginning of the lesson were very important. That's how we were trained to nurture concentration, and beyond things like technique, we were taught the mental aspect of creating music. Especially my teacher was very insistent about developing one's own tone and training one's ear. . . . Also, performing with other children on a regular basis made it fun, and it drew me to music more and more. Then, when Mr. Suzuki listened to one of my tapes, I was selected to play solo at the summer school in Matsumoto. Then when I was in first grade, I was chosen as a member of the Suzuki Children to tour the United States.

MY: You were that young when you first toured the United States?

KT: Yes, but I wasn't the youngest in the group. I think the youngest was three or four years old. . . . For about forty days during the fall, we took time off from school and traveled around the United States and gave about twelve performances. For me, because I grew up in a small town in Aichi, going to a foreign country was really a big deal. . . . At first I was worried, but once we began the tour, I had a really good time. Of course, part of the fun was that I was visiting a foreign country for the first time, but beyond that, we played in great venues like the Carnegie Hall in New York, and every performance was sold out. It may have been partly the novelty of little children performing, but in any case, if we played well, the audience responded with a lot of enthusiasm. So that was the first time I experienced performing in front of a large audience and getting a response from them. That was when I learned what it's like to have the audience be moved by my playing. Even as a little child, I was very struck by that experience. I decided that if I can do this sort of thing, I would like to continue playing the violin. It also gave me a new goal and motivation for practicing more.

MY: When you went to Juilliard, did you find that the training there was very different from what you had had in Japan?

KT: Yes. First and foremost, it was Ms. DeLay's teaching. Until then, when I was studying at Toho, I had taken lessons from teachers from Europe, but for the most part, I was the kind of student who diligently did what the teacher told me to do. Generally speaking, the lessons I had had until then were the ones where I learned the "proper" way of playing certain pieces. On the other hand, in the case of Ms. DeLay, she had many drawers in her head, and she was able to instantly understand what each student had and needed. And when she taught students, instead of telling us how we need to play, she would first ask us how we thought about a particular phrase on the score, and then she would show how we could express what we wanted to express by giving us concrete ideas about technique. So, first, there was a freedom on the part of students to choose how we wanted to play, and she emphasized our own ideas about how we wanted to play. Of course, if our ideas were far off from the conventions of music, she would steer us in the right direction, but most importantly, she valued what the students wanted to express and how we wanted to express them. Until then, even when I did have things I wanted to express, I didn't really know how to express them, and I hadn't really thought about all the things I needed to do to express them. I was more or less copying what I was told to do. So, coming to Juilliard, I was very impressed by how all the students had a lot to say musically . . .

MY: In your work as a musician, in what ways are you made conscious of your identity as a Japanese or an Asian?

KT: When I was living and studying in Japan, I didn't really think about my being Japanese, I was just doing what I liked to do. But when I came to the United States and went to Juilliard, I was shocked to find that more than half of the students were Asian. It was a big surprise for me. But New York is a very cosmopolitan place, so I never really felt that I was discriminated against because of where I'm from. But once I started performing and got a management [agency], I came to realize that [people think about me as an Asian]. Especially around the time when I started concertizing, in major competitions there were lots of Asians who won the top prizes. The number of Asians in classical music, especially women, was quite noticeable. I think it's especially the case in violin. So when I was being interviewed, I was often asked why there were so many Asian violinists [laughs]. That's when I began to realize that people think about it. I don't really know why there are so many Asians, but in the case of violin, I think that the fact that the Suzuki Method was developed in Japan about fifty years ago and that the population of violin students grew significantly was certainly a factor. Among the people who are having successful careers right now, there are many people who started with the Suzuki Method . . .

I don't feel this so much in the United States, but in Europe, people often have preconceived notions about Asian musicians who win major competitions. There is a stereotype of Asian musicians as technically very reliable, and that may be why they are good at competitions, but that aspect is very much on people's mind. And other things like musicality is often considered lacking in Asian musicians. So in Europe, it is difficult to promote Asian musicians. At the same time, I feel that there is some grain of truth to the stereotype. When I am teaching in Japan, I find that few students have things that they really want to express, and few students have a very strong character. I think this has to do with the education system in Japan. So when I perform abroad, there is a part of me that is consciously trying to break away from those stereotypes of Asian musicians.

2

Roots and Routes of Asian Musicians

Many musicians think of themselves as musicians first before contemplating other categories of identity such as race or ethnicity. Indeed, when asked about what their racial and ethnic identity means to them, many informants replied that "musician" is their "race" or "people." For instance, when I asked violist Junah Chung about his Korean identity, he reflected,

[When I go back to Korea maybe once every two years] I really don't feel very Korean. . . . I don't think like a Korean, and I feel like a foreigner. And it's funny because I look at all these Koreans there, and I still feel like I'm looking at foreigners. I don't feel like I'm looking at my own people. But in America, I don't particularly feel American, either. So I've felt like I don't really fit in American society, and I don't feel accepted by Koreans, either. . . . *I feel that artists and musicians are my people. That's where I feel my identity. And I also feel that I can relate and identify the easiest with artists.*[1] [emphasis mine]

Violinist Jennifer Koh had a similar response to the same question:

Amongst the musicians that I work with . . . and we're all different races, I mean, the pianist that I always work with is Japanese

American, there are the Israelis, Indians, and there's a whole gamut of races . . . and there's this sense that throughout everything you're a musician first, and I think that's true for almost everybody that's really passionate about music. You know, people ask you what your religion is. It's music. Who are you? Above all else, you are at all times a musician.[2]

What links these two comments is the shared sense that being a musician is a more meaningful category of identity than racial or ethnic identity. In our conversations, Asian musicians tended to use "musician" as a primary category of identity and often downplayed race as a category relevant to their everyday lives.

Asian musicians downplay—and almost disavow—race as a primary category of identity for several reasons. In many cases, their musical identity develops much earlier than their racial identity. Most classical musicians begin their musical training at a very young age. Pianists and violinists start as early as age three, and those who reach a professional level generally begin serious training well before age ten. Students of large instruments, such as the double bass and harp, and of instruments that require that the player has reached a certain level of physical growth—such as woodwinds and brass, as well as voice—usually start training somewhat later, in their early teens; however, many have already studied another instrument, such as piano or violin. Serious students who pursue a musical career usually have been practicing for at least three or four hours daily since childhood and as much as eight or ten hours, and sometimes more, while preparing for competitions or auditions.

Asian American musicians—whether 1.5, second, third, or fourth generation—also have developed a strong sense of identity as musicians well before they become aware of the social meanings placed on their racial identity. As a result, they experience and understand their identity as Asian *through* their lives as musicians, as I discuss later. This is even more true for Asian-born musicians who come to the United States to study or work as musicians. Having grown up in Asia, where their Asian-ness is a given, they become defined as Asians only when they enter America's racialized society. Their racial identity thus comes into question well after their lives as musicians have become a central aspect of who they are.

Another reason for Asian musicians' de-emphasis of race is the generally depoliticized nature of the world of classical music. Although the internal dynamics of the classical music world and its self-positioning vis-à-vis mainstream culture and society are not free of politics, musicians share the belief that classical music is a pure, autonomous art form—"absolute music"—that stands outside and above the sphere of politics. Such a belief is particularly manifest in music conservatories where, as ethnomusicologists Bruno Nettl and Henry Kingsbury have illustrated, the training nurtures those very beliefs in a culture akin to that of a religious institution.[3] Although the conservatory curriculum includes courses on music history, those courses often lack analytical rigor and rarely nourish critical thinking about music's social or political functions or musicians' roles in society. The absence of a liberal arts education outside of music and the lack of exposure to the political activities that take place on many university campuses compound this disengagement. Active explorations of racial identity or discussions about history or current affairs are usually not part of conservatory students' educational experience. In fact, this disengagement was the very reason why the more intellectual and politically engaged among my informants became disillusioned with their conservatory training. Although many Asian students do, as I demonstrate later, develop a nuanced and complex understanding of racial identity through their own experiences and encounters, they do not obtain from their musical training a politicized language through which to articulate their ideas.

In addition, many Asian musicians consider race to be relatively unimportant in their lives because they believe that there is little racism in the world of classical music. Most of my informants had no direct experience of racism and denied that there was much racism in the field, citing as evidence the large number of Asians who are successfully pursuing careers in classical music. Indeed, most American orchestras audition musicians behind a screen precisely to avoid race- or gender-based discrimination in hiring decisions. Therefore, orchestral musicians generally assert that only performance is relevant to the hiring process and that they have never experienced discrimination in their workplace. Many freelance performers and teachers generally share this belief.

Yet, perhaps the most important reason why "Asian" is not the most salient category of identification for many of these musicians is that their individual experiences of Asian-ness are quite different from each other and do not form a coherent identity that unites the group. Looking at the backgrounds of the most famous musicians, one can even question whether they should all be grouped under the category of Asian.

For example, conductor Seiji Ozawa is a Japanese national born in Manchuria in 1935 and raised in Tokyo. His international career began when he won the Besançon Competition in 1959, and he has gone on to hold major leadership positions, including director of the Boston Symphony for several decades. Yet, he also maintains strong ties to Japan and clearly identifies as a Japanese national. Cellist Yo-Yo Ma was born in 1955 to Chinese parents living in Paris and during his early childhood moved to New York, where he spent his formative years. He pursued a liberal arts education at Harvard University in addition to conservatory training at Juilliard. He identifies as Asian American. Composer Tan Dun, born in 1957, grew up in China amidst the Cultural Revolution and trained in Beijing opera. He was among the first group of music students from China to study composition at Columbia University in the early 1980s. Conductor Kent Nagano, a third-generation Japanese American, was born in Berkeley, California, in 1951, grew up in rural California, and became deeply involved in social movements during his college years in the 1970s. Violinist Sarah Chang is a second-generation Korean American born in 1980 and raised in Philadelphia by parents who are also classical musicians trained in the United States.

Asian and Asian American scholars and activists have long tried to demonstrate that, despite Euroamerican culture's tendency to lump all Asians and Asian Americans together, Asians—both in Asia and in the United States—are an extremely diverse group. They have shown that, whereas Asians do share certain phenotypical characteristics and cultural heritage as well as the common history of subjection to Western imperialism and various forms of race-based exclusion and discrimination in the United States, Asians divide along ethnicity, nationality, religion, language, class, gender, and sexual orientation. For Asian Americans, generation and geographical location are also very important categories of identity.

Just as important as ethnicity, nationality, class, gender, and sexual orientation in shaping the identity of Asian and Asian American musicians are their very different modes of entry into the United States. Determined by specific historical, socioeconomic, and cultural conditions of the late twentieth century, these routes of entry in turn shape the musicians' relationship to race, ethnicity, and nation. It is important therefore to map out the roots and routes of Asian musicians.

Roots and Routes of
Asian Musicians in America

Asian Americans

Many Asian musicians in the United States did not "arrive" in the United States, but rather are Asian Americans born and raised in this country. Although it is difficult to determine what proportion of Asian musicians were born in the United States, one can use enrollment statistics at the Juilliard School to speculate on the ethnic and racial composition of the U.S. classical music world. Of the 834 students at the Juilliard School in 2003–04, 146 were U.S. citizens or permanent residents of Asian descent, and 121 were international students from Asia ("non-resident aliens").[4] In other words, in the student body at the Juilliard School, a little more than half of Asian students fall within the category of "Asian American." In relying on these statistics, one caveat is that the distinction between Asian American and Asian is based on citizenship status, and such legal and bureaucratic demarcations often do not reflect accurately the actual experiences and identities of many Asians and Asian Americans today.

Within the limited pool of Asian American musicians whom I interviewed, most are second generation (i.e., American-born children of Asian-born immigrant parents) or so-called 1.5 generation—those who were born in Asia and emigrated at a young age with their parents and, although they are technically first-generation immigrants, are closer to second-generation immigrants in terms of identity. As I discuss in Chapter 4, most come from professional, middle-class families who emigrated to the United States after the 1965 Immigration Act gave preferences to those professionals with skills in demand, such as physicians, scientists, and engineers. Thus, most have been raised by educated parents in middle-class environments, often in the suburbs of large cities, such as New York, Chicago, or Los Angeles, or in university towns across the United States.

Although the backgrounds of these Asian Americans are similar, their experience of growing up in America and their sense of identity as Asian American vary considerably. Some claim that they never experienced racism while growing up and have never been particularly conscious of their Asian-ness. Others say that they always were aware of their difference from others and, by the time they reached adulthood, had developed a strong consciousness as being part of a minority. Some feel completely American, others would never call themselves American, and still others feel neither completely American nor completely Asian.

Andrew Le is a Vietnamese American pianist who grew up in Michigan. He was in the doctoral program at Juilliard at the time of our interview. When asked about his racial and ethnic identity, Le responded that, even though he did not know any other Vietnamese American in the field of classical music, he had never been particularly conscious of his racial or ethnic identity. The only incident that reminded him of his Asian identity took place in his early childhood. He wanted to swim in the pool of a friend in the neighborhood, but his friend's parents would not allow him to do so because Andrew was Asian. He said, "I feel so Americanized since I grew up here that sometimes I wake up and I look in the mirror and I find myself surprised to see an Asian person . . . (laughs) . . . yeah . . . I really don't think about [my Asian identity] very much. . . . I really don't."[5] For Asian American musicians like Le, who did not grow up with a strong sense of Asian-ness or of being a minority, their identity as Asian is incidental both to their work as a classical musician and to their lives in general.

In contrast, internationally acclaimed violinist Sarah Chang grew up with a strong sense of her Korean background and asserts that her Korean identity was always very much a part of who she was. Her father is a violinist who came to the United States to study with Dorothy DeLay at Juilliard. Her mother is a composer who came to study at the University of Pennsylvania. Chang was born and raised in Philadelphia, but her parents insisted on speaking Korean at home and made sure that their children learned to read and write Korean. In my telephone interview, she told me that her father in particular is "extremely Korean" and was set on keeping Korean customs at home and that her brother was sent to Korea for a year at age twelve. Although she has had less first-hand experience of Korean culture, she goes to Korea about once a year to perform and to spend time with her relatives. She also performed at the White House when the Korean president visited the United States.[6] For Chang, her Korean identity has been very much a part of both her familial upbringing and her professional life.

Like Chang, violinist Conway Kuo considers his ethnic background to be a large part of his identity. Kuo is a member of the New York City Ballet Orchestra and the New York City Opera, and he also plays in other gigs in the New York area. Raised in New Jersey by parents who emigrated from

Taiwan, he thinks of himself as American, but claims that "there are also distinct parts of [him]self that are Chinese." Many aspects of his life could be stereotypically characterized as Chinese; for example, his parents were frugal and instilled in him a strong work ethic and respect for authority, which he considers an important part of who he is. However, in our interview he also acknowledged that his identity reflects a particular kind of Chinese-ness distinct from that of people from China: "Though I'm very influenced by Chinese culture, when I'm with people from China, I feel a bit out of my element." Many of his friends are Asian Americans, both by circumstance and by choice. At work, he finds that most people close to his age are Asian, and thus he naturally tends to hang out with other Asians. At the same time, he is aware that cultural identity is not synonymous with racial identity. He said that there are specific elements of upbringing and cultural knowledge that second-generation Asian Americans have in common and that he felt most comfortable with those who share such a background.[7] His ethnic and racial identity is thus specific to second-generation Asian Americans and distinct from Asian nationals.

Although Asian American musicians relate in different ways to cultural elements they identify as Asian, on the whole, most are not active in Asian American organizations or engaged in exploring political or cultural issues related to their Asian identity. Many are simply too busy practicing and performing to have time for such activities. Having spent as much as eight or ten hours every day practicing since early childhood and having placed a priority on music almost all their lives, these musicians tend to be removed not only from Asian American activism but also from any issues not directly connected to their lives as musicians. As described earlier, most spend their college years in generally depoliticized conservatory settings and thus are not exposed to the kinds of political discourses and activism that many Asian American youths encounter for the first time when they go to college. In addition, because many of these conservatories or universities have a high percentage of Asian and Asian American students, they rarely experience racially-based marginalization and do not feel compelled to organize around their racial identity. In contrast to many college campuses with significant Asian American student populations, music conservatories usually do not have Asian American student organizations. At Juilliard, for instance, the only identity-based student organization involving Asians is the Korean Christian student group.

In other words, Asian Americans in the world of classical music do not share any coherent Asian American identity, nor do they feel the need to organize around such an identity. For them, the category "Asian American" is mostly a descriptive one, rather than an identity that they actively claim for political, social, or cultural purposes, as it is for many other Asian Americans.

International Students

Extrapolating from recent enrollment figures at the Juilliard School, nearly half of Asian musicians in the United States are non-resident aliens. These musicians arrive in the United States in several different ways. Probably the largest contingent of Asian-born musicians come to the United States as "international students" to study music, mostly at the college or graduate level. These students have had rigorous musical training in their home country, usually at a conservatory, such as the Toho School of Music in Tokyo or the Central Conservatory of Music in Beijing. Some have had some graduate-level training in their home country as well. These students audition for a U.S. conservatory, and on being admitted, many earn scholarships or other forms of funding to support their studies.

Many of these students first considered the prospect of studying abroad when they took a master class by a visiting foreign faculty member at their school, attended summer music festivals such as Aspen or Tanglewood, or began to feel dissatisfied with the training they were receiving in their home country. Others were "discovered," often when they won a major competition, by some teacher or potential sponsor who encouraged them to study abroad. Those who choose to come to the United States mostly do so because of their—or their teacher's—personal contact with a teacher in America. Some arrive in the United States after a few years of study in another country, often in Europe.

Violinist Hiroko Yajima is one of the pioneer Asian musicians who came to study in the United States in the 1960s. She grew up in Tokyo and started taking violin lessons at age five. She studied at the Toho Gakuen Music High School under Hideo Saitō, who trained many prominent musicians, including Seiji Ozawa. While in high school, she toured in the United States for the first time with her school orchestra and performed at the 1965 New York World's Fair. When she was a high-school junior, she won a major competition, and a recording of her performance in the semi-finals was sent to Juilliard without her knowledge. The teacher who listened to the tape invited her to come to Juilliard and offered her a scholarship. A Fulbright scholarship covered the remaining expenses for her study at Juilliard. She worked under prominent violinists and teachers Ivan Galamian and Dorothy DeLay, and her peers included such extraordinary violinists as Pinchas Zukerman and Itzak Perlman. She also began studying with Felix Galimir after attending the Marlboro Music Festival in 1966 and later became a member of the Galimir String Quartet. She won the Young Concert Artists competition in 1967. A few years later, she married violinist Samuel Rhodes and has stayed in New York throughout her career. She is currently on the faculty of the Mannes School of Music where she chairs the string department.[8] Yajima's career trajectory is typical in that classical music allowed her to enter the United States and establish herself in American society through professional, familial, and social networks.

Pioneers such as Yajima blazed a path for the next generation of Japanese musicians who came to study in the United States. Trombonist Kōichirō Yamamoto grew up in a musical family—his father is a trombonist, his mother a violinist, and his two sisters are a pianist and violist, respectively—but he had little interest in music until he started playing the trombone in junior high school. As soon as he started playing, however, he knew he wanted to be a professional musician, and he went to the high-school division of the Tokyo Conservatory of Music. Most of his peers who left Japan around this time went to Germany or France, but because of his chance encounter with a Hungarian teacher, as well as Hungary's low cost of living and the fact that his sister was living there at the time, he left Japan after high school and studied in Hungary for three years. During that time, the New York Philharmonic toured Hungary, and Yamamoto met the orchestra's principal trombonist, Joseph Alessi, who is also on the Juilliard faculty. Alessi encouraged Yamamoto to audition for Juilliard, and in 1994 Yamamoto moved to New York to become one of three trombone students there. At age twenty-five, Yamamoto joined the Metropolitan Opera Orchestra, becoming the first Japanese brass player in a major U.S. orchestra.[9] After nine seasons with the Metropolitan Opera Orchestra, he took the position of principal trombonist for the Seattle Symphony in 2005.

Although the first wave of music students to the United States were Japanese, now students from Korea, China, and Taiwan outnumber the Japanese.

Cellist I-Bei Lin came from Taiwan to California when she was sixteen. She had studied piano and cello in the government-sponsored experimental program for talented musicians in Taiwan and started winning national competitions as she became more serious about cello. Her parents did not feel she could get the best instruction in Western instruments in Taiwan and hoped to send her to Paris, but did not have enough funds to do so. In the meantime, one of her classmates, a horn player, performed at a festival in the United States and impressed a teacher at a music school in California, who then arranged scholarships for Taiwanese students. Lin was one of four scholarship recipients, winning for the cello, and she moved to California to study music. She then went on to study at the Eastman School of Music and Northwestern University. She is currently on the faculty at the Department of Music at the University of Hawai'i, and she also performs in solo recitals and chamber ensembles in Hawai'i, the continental United States, and Asia.[10]

Like Lin, Chinese violinist Duoming Ba came to the United States as a teenager. She started to play the violin at age four after her father responded to a newspaper ad for violin lessons. She took group lessons for the first year and a half, and after switching to private lessons she began to play more seriously and to enter competitions. She went on to study at the Central Conservatory of Music in Beijing, and while performing as a soloist with the school orchestra, a Singaporean businessman and his wife who saw her performance offered to sponsor her study abroad. The businessman's brother in Chicago offered to become her legal guardian, and so she moved to Chicago at age seventeen where she attended a local high school. She found it difficult to improve her violin playing while learning to speak English and keeping up with her academic work in high school. Because her violin teachers were on the faculty at the Oberlin Conservatory, she enrolled in Oberlin without finishing high school. For the first two years at Oberlin, she lived with her teachers and six other students (including students from Japan, Korea, and Israel), learning to speak English, playing many new pieces, and developing musically. Ba was then accepted into the Curtis Institute of Music, where she studied for two more years. Around that time, she began to realize that she was not going to have a career as a soloist but that she needed a job to stay in the United States. She obtained a position with the New Jersey Symphony and started working while completing her studies at Curtis. After two years at the New Jersey Symphony, she passed the audition for the New York Philharmonic where she has been a member since 2003.[11]

These students, most of whom were born and raised in their home country until their late teens or early adulthood, are challenged by their lack of English-language skills and various forms of culture shock when they come to the United States. For many international students, the stress of the intense and competitive atmosphere of the conservatory setting is exacerbated by their sense of isolation and the absence of family and close friends. Several informants shared stories of friends or fellow students who had suffered nervous breakdowns; some committed suicide. Many students from Asia, especially those from China, also struggle to support themselves financially during and after their school years. Even though many international students receive scholarships to cover tuition and some living expenses, few can live comfortably solely on financial aid, and many students work to pay the bills. Working not only cuts into their practice time but also causes a great deal of stress and anxiety about their future prospects.

These students' career paths beyond school are shaped in large measure by their legal and financial status. Every international student comes to the United States on a student visa. Some have government or private scholarships that require them to return to their country after completing their study in the United States, but those who want to remain in the United States after they graduate have to shape their career in a way that allows them to do so. Those who do not land an orchestra or teaching job that would earn them a work visa or a green card have to find other means of remaining in the United States. Some choose to become naturalized U.S. citizens, others shift their career paths, and many pay thousands of dollars to lawyers to obtain a visa or a green card and wait for many years for the paperwork to be processed.

Immigrant Geniuses

A third group of Asian musicians comprises those whose families emigrated to the United States specifically so they could study music, often when they were very young. Although there are no data about how many musicians come to the United States through this route, these musicians form a distinct contingent in such prestigious conservatories as Juilliard Pre-College.

Perhaps one of the most high-profile examples of such an "immigrant genius" is the violinist Midori. Born in 1971 in Osaka, Japan, Midori Gotō started playing the violin under the instruction of her mother Setsu and made her concert debut at age six. Two years later, a family friend sent a recording of Midori's performance of a Bach sonata and Paganini and Saint-Saëns concerti to Dorothy DeLay, who was so astonished by her playing that she invited Midori to the Aspen Music Festival to study with her. At Aspen, Midori's performance of a Bartók concerto deeply moved virtuoso violinist Pinchas Zukerman, who became a close friend and mentor. Midori earned a place in DeLay's studio at Juilliard Pre-College, and she and Setsu, then a single mother, moved to New York City in 1982. That year, at age eleven, she made a surprise debut at the New York Philharmonic's New Year's Eve Concert conducted by Zubin Mehta, which launched her concertizing career. In 1986, she made her legendary debut at Tanglewood with the Boston Symphony Orchestra, where she played Leonard Bernstein's *Serenade* with Bernstein conducting. In the middle of the fifth movement, after the E string broke on her violin, she quickly exchanged the instrument with the concertmaster and continued playing without missing a beat. The E string then broke again, and she took the associate concertmaster's violin. Although Midori's own instrument was smaller than the borrowed full-sized violins, she was completely unfazed, and when she finished the piece, the audience and the orchestra erupted in applause and Bernstein fell on his knees. The following day, the *New York Times* reported the incident on the front page under the headline, "Girl, 14, Conquers Tanglewood with 3 Violins."[12]

Performing as a young teen with major orchestras around the world, Midori became an icon of the child prodigy.[13] Many media stories reported on the intensity of her mother Setsu's investment in Midori's career.[14] When Midori was struggling to make the transition from child prodigy to adult musician and to find her own voice both in music and in her life, Setsu was rumored to exercise such excessive control over Midori's life that she drove her to a mental breakdown and an eating disorder. Whether such accounts are true or not, the story of Midori and Setsu is a classic example of parental sacrifice and commitment to the child's music training and career. Even when the child becomes a superstar like Midori, the life of the family of an immigrant genius is not easy in the United States, as the parents have to maneuver the legal system and the labor market to earn a visa or green card to stay in the United States. As I discuss in Chapter 4, these families often experience downward mobility and incur considerable expenses that the child's career in classical music cannot recoup.

HAN-NA CHANG
(Courtesy of the artist)

In recent years Koreans have been most represented among these immigrant geniuses. One well-known example is cellist Han-Na Chang. Born in Suwon, Korea, in 1982 as an only child, she started piano at age three and switched to cello three years later. After studying with a cellist in a local orchestra in Korea for several years, her parents—her mother is a composer and her father is a marketing research manager—thought she needed more rigorous training. The family moved to the United States when she was ten years old so that she could study at Juilliard Pre-College. In 1994, at age eleven, she won first prize at the Rostropovich International Cello Competition, which launched her concertizing career.

These success stories have encouraged waves of immigrants to come to the United States to pursue the dream of their children becoming the ne. prodigy. But dreams alone do not drive this form of immigration; structural factors facilitate it as well. A growing number of educated, urban, professional members of the middle class in Asia live in an increasingly globalized world that carries a legacy of Western, and particularly American, hegemony in Asia. They are increasingly exposed to a flow of information and culture from the West; they hear top-level performances of classical music, whether through touring performers, broadcasts, or recordings, which strengthen their yearnings for musical training in the West. They both understand the value of Western education and culture in the global market and possess the economic and cultural capital that enable the pursuit of such training in the United States. The large immigrant community in the United States, which grew after the 1965 Immigration Act dramatically increased the number of immigrant professionals from such countries as Korea and China, also facilitates the immigration of those with transnational family and social ties.

Migrant Professionals

Some Asian-born musicians complete their formal training in their home country (or sometimes a third country) and come to the United States as practicing musicians seeking to expand their professional horizons.

Marimbist Makoto Nakura is one such professional musician who has chosen to make New York his home. Nakura was born in Kobe, Japan, in 1964. When he heard the marimba for the first time as a third grader, he began taking lessons and soon knew he wanted to be a professional marimbist. After graduating from the Musashino Academia Musicae in Tokyo, he studied in London for a year. In contrast to his experience as a student in Tokyo, he felt that music students in London were treated as professional performers, and his year there opened up entirely new ways of thinking and performing. In 1994, he became the first marimbist to win the Young Concert Artists Competition in New York and joined the roster of a management agency that provides booking, promotion, and career guidance. Since his debut recital in New York and Washington in 1995, he has toured in forty states in the United States and performed widely in Japan and other parts of the world. He stayed in Japan for two years after his debut, but moved to New York in 1997. He believes that this move expanded the scope of his work by enabling encounters and collaborations with composers and performers and that living in a diverse environment forces him to constantly ask himself who he is and what he does, providing inspiration and drive for his music.[15]

Asian musicians who come to the United States as adults generally have a very different sense of racial and cultural identity than those who cross national and cultural borders at a younger age. Despite their often ambivalent feelings toward their home country and its music scene, most belong to professional and social networks that enable them to continue working in their home country even after moving to the United States. In many cases, the experience of living and working in the United States also enhances their credentials in their home country, increasing their opportunities for performing, teaching, or composing there.

Yet, musicians who come to the United States as adults also face some disadvantages. Many arrive without affiliations with U.S. schools or other institutions that would put them on a standard track for professional development. Once in America, they have to build their own networks and find opportunities for performances and collaborations. Winning a major competition helps them obtain management and performance opportunities, but musicians without networks or professional know-how struggle to create a niche in the American music scene, where Asian musicians are by no means a novelty. A few possess or quickly acquire the off-stage skills needed to gain ongoing work opportunities, but a great many return to their country after failing to stand out in the throng of talented musicians who gather in America.

Transnational Offspring

Some Asian musicians come to the United States as children of transnational professionals or businesspeople and end up making the United States their primary home. Most received early music training in their home country or elsewhere and pursue more advanced training and career opportunities in the United States. In many ways, they are very similar to the 1.5-generation Asian Americans discussed earlier. However, they and their families continue to maintain close ties to the home country, often moving back and forth between the United States and Asia, and so rather than seeing themselves as Asian American or as primarily American, they maintain a strong sense of national identity. Creating their own niche in the transnational movements of capital, labor, and culture, they develop a complex and fluid sense of belonging simultaneously to different political, economic, and cultural entities; they skillfully maneuver their different forms of citizenship vis-à-vis multiple nation-states, as anthropologist Aihwa Ong illustrated with the concept of "flexible citizenship."[16] These transnational offspring demonstrate that the considerable presence of Asian musicians in the classical music scene is very much a product of global flows of capital and labor since the late twentieth century.

Korean pianist Soyeon Lee comes from a transnational family and continues to straddle national borders. Born in Korea in 1979, she began taking piano lessons at age four, but piano was always something she did for fun, and never having had a piano at home, practicing was not an everyday project for her. She moved to the United States at age nine because her father was studying for a PhD in political science in West Virginia. When she was fourteen, her father finished his PhD, and the family prepared to move back to Korea. However, her parents began to worry about her readjustment to Korean life. Around the same time, she entered a piano competition in Texas and met a teacher at the Interlochen Arts Academy in Michigan who encouraged her to study there. And so when her family returned to Korea, she went to Interlochen for her senior year of high school. She then attended Juilliard where she received a bachelor's, master's, and an Artist Diploma.

With her complete fluency in English, Americanized manners and charm, and the sense of confidence she exudes on stage, Soyeon appears, at least on the surface, very American. Yet she has a very different sense of identity from many Korean American students. Her sister, Soeun Lee, is a pop singer in Korea, and because her family lives there, she continues to have a strong connection to that country. "I've never considered myself American," she said in our interview. "I still now consider myself Korean. I have a very strong love for my country. I don't have a strong love for the people in it, necessarily, but I do have a strong love for my roots." At Juilliard, she felt uncomfortable with fellow Korean students, who hung out in cliques—"Koreans who just came from Korea hang out together; Koreans from LA hang out together"—and experienced an identity crisis during her first years there. She devoted all of her energy to piano, earning a full scholarship for her master's and doctoral program. She also won the William Petschek Award, one of the highest honors given by Juilliard to a pianist with exceptional potential and gave a debut recital at Alice Tully Hall in

Lincoln Center in 2004. She has also won major international competitions and has toured Spain, as well as many cities across the United States.[17]

The transnational life trajectories of these musicians are, on the one hand, a product of a specific historical period and the structural factors that have shaped cross-Pacific migrations in the late twentieth century—for example, the investment of Asian capital in the American market; increasing financial and other resources that draw intellectuals to American universities; and the growing technology enabling cross-Pacific communication and mobility and that allows transnational middle-class professionals to hold onto their familial, social, and professional ties in their home country while taking advantage of the increasing flow of capital, labor, knowledge, and culture across national borders. The fact that Western music was "given" to these individuals from such backgrounds shows the class-specific nature of the practice of Western music, as I discuss in Chapter 4. On the other hand, transnational musicians like Lee have chosen to make the United States their primary home and Western classical music their principal means of fashioning and expressing themselves as they negotiate competing identities and affinities. Their life paths and choices exemplify the conditions, privileges, and challenges of transnational identities in the age of globalization.

"Hybrid" Asians

Some Asian musicians based in the United States possess multicultural identities that show the varied faces of the Asian diaspora and the highly diverse ways of being Asian in the age of globalization. Their lives reflect the fact that the categories, Asian and Western, are more complex than geographically bound, coherent, and discrete entities. They also call our attention to the situated nature of racial and ethnic identities that are experienced and articulated differently according to social context.

One such hybrid Asian is pianist Ju-Ying Song, who was born in Taiwan but soon embarked on a multicultural journey. Her grandmother was a well-known pianist and piano teacher, and her mother was one of the first Asian pianists to attend Juilliard in the early 1960s. Her father, a theologian, moved the family to Geneva when she was nine months old. She received all of her education there, speaking French until she finished high school, at which she was the only Asian student. At age four, she began taking piano lessons with her mother, and when she was nine, she studied at a conservatory. Having developed a strong interest in science, she came to the United States to do her undergraduate degree in microbiology and music at Stanford, from which she graduated in 1991. After spending a semester in England, she decided to study music more seriously and went to Juilliard to focus all of her energy on music. Currently Song teaches at the Mannes School of Music in addition to performing around the world.

In our interview, she reflected that, despite her recent arrival and multifaceted cultural background, at Stanford she was instantly categorized as Asian American, which was just as foreign to her as any other category of identification. Moreover, having grown up in a family of talented musicians, classical music was a cultural norm for her, and her relationship to classical music was different from that of most Asians, Americans, or Asian Americans.[18] Thus, Song's experience of her Asian identity was shaped by her upbringing in Europe, race relations and multicultural discourse in the United States, and her professional training in classical music.

Like Song, violinist Ignace Jang's identity was also shaped by Asian, European, and American culture. Born in 1969 in Grenoble, France, to Korean parents who had gone there to study, Jang and his older siblings grew up speaking French as their first language. Jang says that his parents were most concerned about integrating their children into the country of residence and so placed a high priority on their French education. After moving to Paris and studying at the Paris Conservatory of Music for five years, Jang met a professor at Indiana University, and with a scholarship from the French government, he moved to the United States to study in Indiana. After graduation, he took a position with the Denver Symphony for five years; he then became the concertmaster for the Honolulu Symphony and moved to Hawai'i.

Jang told me that living in Hawai'i, "where cultures blend more easily than on the [U.S.] mainland," has made him feel much more Korean than ever before and more Korean than his siblings, who have never lived outside France. When living in France, Indiana, and Colorado, he never thought he would date an Asian woman; coming to Hawai'i changed his feelings, and he is now married to an Asian American woman from Hawai'i. Yet, he is still "not sure if [he feels] that Korean," he prefers French food to Korean food, and he speaks little Korean.[19]

Pianist Henry Wong Doe also has a hybrid background. His grandfather moved from China to New Zealand as an immigrant worker, leaving his wife and children in Guangzhou. Henry's father went to visit him when the New Zealand government granted visitation rights to the families of immigrants and was unable to return to China when World War II started. He then became a pharmacist and went to live in Japan to work for an American pharmacist in Tokyo, where he met his wife. She had grown up in Tokyo, where her parents taught music. She was also a singer, and all her siblings were musically trained, although the war kept her from obtaining formal music training. Henry's parents then moved to Auckland, New Zealand, where Henry was born and raised. He started taking piano lessons at age five. When he entered his first competition in Hamamatsu, Japan, at age twenty-one, he was exposed to other forms of training and felt the need to get out of New Zealand. He came to the United States to pursue a master's degree at Indiana University and then went on to earn his doctorate at Juilliard.[20] His sense of identity therefore spans several corners of the world, including China, Japan, New Zealand, and the United States, and which of those elements are most important varies depending on social circumstances.

Many musicians of mixed racial and ethnic backgrounds are children of the first generation of Asian musicians who came to study in the United States or of Asian professionals who came to the United States since the 1960s and then married an American or a European. For instance, Alan Gilbert, who serves as the chief conductor for the Royal Stockholm Philharmonic Orchestra and the music director for the Santa Fe Opera, is the son of violinists Michael Gilbert and Yoko Takebe, both of whom play for the New York Philharmonic. Takebe, a contemporary of Seiji Ozawa, studied under Hideo Saitō at the Toho School of Music and came to study at Juilliard under Ivan Galamian. The mother of composer and violist Kenji Bunch is a comparative literature professor who came from Japan to the United States to do graduate work in the 1960s. She married an American political scientist and settled in Portland, Oregon, where Bunch and his brother were born and raised. Violinist Anne Akiko Meyers; sisters Jennifer and Laura Frautschi, both of whom are violinists; and cellist Kristina Reiko Cooper are among the most successful musicians in recent years who come from mixed Japanese and American parentage. The fact that most of these part-Asian musicians have a Japanese mother reflects the history of the reverse flow, in which Japanese students were the first generation of Asians to study and settle in the United States.

These mixed-race Asian musicians have diverse ways of identifying with or claiming the Asian part of their background, and some might even argue against categorizing them as Asian musicians. However, the use of their Japanese middle names—some have chosen to use their Japanese name after a certain point in their career—and the ways in which their attractive appearance is often used in marketing illustrate that, at least for some musicians, being ethnic functions favorably in today's market, as I discuss in later chapters.

Understanding Difference Through Music

As these diverse profiles make clear, there are many routes by which Asian musicians enter the music scene in America and even more diverse ways of what being Asian means. The category of Asian in the United States is highly fluid and even contested, and Asian musicians do not necessarily identify with other Asians from quite different backgrounds and experiences simply on the basis of race. Yet, independent of their own sense of identity, they are racialized as Asians—in other words, they are grouped together under a racial category that carries value-laden meanings. This section explores how Asian and Asian American musicians shape and articulate their own Asian identity *through* classical music.

Pianist Thomas Yee, a Chinese Canadian born in Newfoundland in 1973, earned his doctorate from the Eastman School of Music and currently teaches at the University of Hawai'i. Since his arrival in Hawai'i in 2002, Yee has been one of the most active and respected performers in the classical music scene there, giving solo recitals, playing a concerto with the Honolulu Symphony, performing with numerous chamber ensembles, and accompanying instrumentalists and singers, in addition to teaching at the university and giving private lessons.

During our interview at his studio at the University of Hawai'i, Yee recalled that since his early childhood he had celebrity status because he won all the local piano competitions and performed at school concerts. As a Chinese in an all-white environment, he always knew he stood out, and he asserted that he was never discriminated against: "Growing up, standing out was a definite advantage." Excelling at the piano made people look up to him even though he was a member of a minority. He remembered that, when he went to piano competitions, "all the other contestants were Caucasian girls accompanied by soccer moms." In his recollection, these mothers would take one look at him—a Chinese boy physically much smaller than all the girls at the competition—and throw up their hands, knowing that all their daughters could hope for was second place. He recalled that one girl, on finding out that she had to play the same piece immediately after him, vomited. Before another competition even started, a young child asked for his autograph. He also recalled that his brother and sister, who were in their twenties at the time, were known in the community as "Thomas Yee's brother and sister." According to him, "They wanted to have some sort of an identity, and didn't have it. I had that always as a young kid." These recollections show that during his early years the stereotype of an Asian prodigy was very much operative, which Yee's career went on to support.

For Yee, being Asian and being an outstanding pianist went together in forming his identity and sense of self-esteem. He exclaimed,

[I was thinking,] "It is *cool* to be Asian. Being different, being minority, is *in*! It is *huge*!" And we're talking about mid-1980s, too . . . and I said to myself, "You know what? *I* get the respect I deserve." I don't know if it was because I was Asian. I think it was more of what I did, and that I was successful, that earned the respect. So that was a really cool thing for me. I didn't wish I was white. I didn't wanna be one of the crowd. . . . I've never been one of the crowd.

Yee's success in music enabled him to believe that the principle of meritocracy operated in the world, that one's talent, effort, and success mattered more than one's race. This belief gave him a sense of security and confidence in his Asian identity. He stated that a musician has the blessing of having a creative outlet and an identity in ways that most people in other professions do not have.

For Yee, the combination of his musical talent and his Chinese identity has served him well, not only in developing his own sense of self-worth but also in his career trajectory. His Chinese identity has helped him in his professional life, particularly after moving to Hawai'i. He claimed that in a community in which the majority of residents are Asian or part-Asian, his ability to fit in—even though he grew up in a predominantly white environment and is quite different from most Asians in Hawai'i—has helped him recruit students.[21]

TRIO XIA
(Courtesy of the artists)

Furthermore, he and his colleagues have been able to take advantage of Hawai'i's favorable cultural climate to Asians and to promote their music by forming a chamber group, Trio Xia. The members of Trio Xia—pianist Yee, flutist Frederick Lau, and cellist I-Bei Lin—are all ethnically Chinese, albeit from quite different origins. Yee is Canadian-born, Lau was born and raised in Hong Kong, and Lin is from Taiwan. Colleagues and close friends, the three formed the trio in 2002 to present an innovative repertoire of both Western and Asian music. The trio has performed in Hawai'i and Asia, showcasing original works by composers from Asia-Pacific in particular. Yee was initially hesitant about giving the group a Chinese name because it would not suggest any obvious connection to Western music. Yet, realizing that the trio's Chinese identities and the group's repertoire of both Asian and Western music would serve to its advantage, he came to fully embrace and proudly promote the trio's work.

Musical excellence and professional success have served as positive affirmations of Yee's ethnic identity yet played a very different but important role in the life of Taiwanese singer Jennifer Shyu. I met Shyu in the fall of 2003 at a program of the Asia Society in New York, at which composer Tan Dun gave an interview regarding his recent work, including his research and collection of indigenous music in rural China. In the audience, mostly well-groomed, older white men, I noticed a young, attractive, smart-looking Asian woman sitting in the row in front of me. During the question-and-answer session, the woman identified herself as a classically trained singer now interested in indigenous Taiwanese music, and she asked a very intelligent question about conducting research among the indigenous people in a non-exploitative way. At this fairly early stage of my research, I had rarely heard a classical musician speak about these issues, and I was intrigued by her concerns. After the program I introduced myself to her and asked for an interview, and she seemed quite interested in my project. Amidst her busy schedule touring with her jazz band that incorporates Asian music, we met at a café in the Washington Heights neighborhood in upper Manhattan.

Shyu was born in 1978 and grew up in an almost all-white neighborhood in Peoria, Illinois. She was a typical overachieving girl of the model minority: she took skating and ballet, played piano and violin at a competitive level, and earned straight A's in school. Although she was quite successful in her academic as well as extracurricular activities, she was always aware of her marginal status. She recalled that there were "like two blacks, two Asians, one Latino" in her high school at which there was a great deal of racism; she said, "I basically had to use the fact that I was doing music in the community and had other things going on as my strength to get over the terrible racism in school."

Music not only provided her a haven from racism but also became a tool for Shyu to explore the meanings of her racial identity and her ethnic heritage. She said that from very early on she was very aware of identity issues and always wanted to do something to erase the Asian stereotypes but did not know how to do so. During her high-school years she "wanted to be as white as possible." Although she was very serious about music, she chose not to go to a conservatory and entered Stanford University instead. There she started studying voice and began to develop an interest in jazz, blues, and African American culture. She said she felt very comfortable among African American students, "even more so with them than with other Asian Americans." She tried to become involved in Asian American student organizations but felt that her fellow Asian American students were "just trying to be white." She began questioning where she fit in the racial and cultural landscape of college life. After graduating, she became more involved in jazz and began exploring new musical forms. Being surrounded by people who used music to express their racial and cultural identity prompted her to explore her Chinese roots, study indigenous Taiwanese music, and incorporate Asian elements into the music she performs with her band. For Shyu, her development as a musician thus went hand in hand with her exposure to political and intellectual discourses about race relations and to African American culture and her exploration of her own Asian identity.[22]

The stories of Yee and Shyu illustrate the widely diverse meanings of Asian identity and the roles of classical music in Asian musicians' lives. Their own expressions of their Asian-ness also show the situational and relational nature of racial and ethnic identity. Their sense of Asian identity is shaped not only by their past experiences but also by the ways in which their Asian identity functions in their present lives, including their careers. Furthermore, many Asians in the United States, musicians or not, often oscillate between the desire to assimilate into white culture or to connect to their Asian heritage and claim a space as Asians in a multiethnic society. How Asians understand and express their racial and ethnic identity has much to do with the specific social, cultural, and political contexts and locations in which they are situated and is always shaped in relation to other aspects of their identity. For example, my interactions with Yee over the years suggest that his identity as Canadian is often more important to him than his identity as ethnic Chinese. Although he articulated the significance of his Chinese identity in his work and he often jokingly refers to his "typically *pake*" [Hawaiian word for Chinese, often used jokingly or in a derogatory fashion] behavior patterns (being cheap, for example), he admits that in his everyday life he is not particularly interested in things Chinese or in exploring his Chinese-ness. He has often said that he is "really culturally *haole* [Hawaiian word for white]." When his trio toured Taiwan and Japan, for the first time he was in an environment where he was surrounded by those who looked like him yet with whom he could not communicate. This experience of feeling displaced in Asia made him more aware of the particular nature of his Chinese and Asian identity. Other Asian American musicians who have performed in Asia have made similar remarks about their experience of difference and sameness with Asians in Asia.

Likewise, Asian-born musicians who relocate to the United States in their youth experience a heightened sense of racial identity after they move to a foreign country and struggle with the language and deal with feelings of displacement and alienation in a new culture.

I met pianist Makiko Hirata in the spring of 2004 at another Japanese pianist's recital at Juilliard. When I described my project to Hirata, she eagerly said to me, "These questions about Asian identity and Western music are something that I think about a lot myself, and I'm very interested in talking to you." She invited me to a chamber music concert she and her colleagues gave at a small church in Washington Heights several days later, and afterward we had an informal conversation over lunch. We conducted a more formal interview in Lincoln Center between her practice sessions at Juilliard. Our interests and sensibilities greatly overlapped, and subsequently we became close friends. She also later became my piano teacher for the remainder of my stay in New York.

Hirata was born in 1975 and spent her childhood in Hong Kong and Japan; her family moved to the United States when she was thirteen. She was then accepted by Juilliard Pre-College, and piano became especially central to her identity. Unfamiliar with American culture and unable to speak much English, she spent her teenage years on the margins of highschool life in a wealthy, suburban, almost exclusively white New Jersey town. "I really lived my high school years like I was hiding or something," she recalled, "but when the yearbook came out, I found that I had been chosen as 'the Best Musician.' The other 'Best Musician' was also an Asian boy who played jazz." Thus, music was one of the limited ways she had in setting her foot in American life and being recognized—of gaining an identity.

In addition to providing her with an identity and a sense of self-worth in a setting in which she shared few cultural references with her peers, music became a principal means by which she thought about language and communication. As a young girl, Hirata had been interested in a career in writing or acting; however, coming to the United States and not being able to speak English made her more aware of the limitations of language as a means of communication, "not just in terms of [her] fluency in English or any other language but the effectiveness of language as a tool of communication in general." She then began to think more seriously about music as her career. When her father was transferred back to Japan three years later, she decided to remain in the United States; she lived with family friends and completed her education at Juilliard Pre-College, the Manhattan School of Music, and New York University. As a performer and teacher, Hirata thinks constantly and deeply about effective methods of communicating emotions and musical ideas. She continually struggles with the balance between being true to her emotions and ideas and designing ways to deliver them effectively. She believes that her experience of being Asian—and an outsider—in America has shaped her music-making in crucial ways.[23]

As Hirata's story suggests, for Asian youth who experience exclusion and marginalization in their everyday lives, music serves as a form of language through which they can express themselves when other aspects of their communication skills are severely limited. For them, the power of music as a universal language is very real.

In addition, the conservatory setting offers a safe and free space where they can be who they are and do what they like without having to worry about fitting into a culture that sees them as foreign. Many musicians who attended Juilliard Pre-College as teenagers stressed how important the Saturdays spent at Juilliard were to their lives. In private lessons, orchestra and chorus rehearsals, and theory and ear training classes, the students are immersed in classical music all day. Some Asian students are recent immigrants to the United States and do not speak English well, but as long as they play their instruments well in performances and competitions, they are recognized and respected by their teachers and fellow students. They socialize with their peers for whom classical music is central to their lives. The conservatory functions as a democratic space for artistic pursuit, where music is the most important thing that matters and students are given merit-based recognition, regardless of their race or nationality. The conservatory gives Asian musicians an identity and self-worth that are often missing in other aspects of their lives. Other environments in which many young classical musicians study music (e.g., summer music schools, such as Aspen, Interlochen, or Tanglewood) also serve to build a sense of identity and solidarity for many Asian and Asian American musicians.

However, music does not alleviate totally the feelings of marginalization experienced by many Asian musicians. In fact, the very pursuit of classical music often marginalizes students in American schools where classical music is definitely outside mainstream youth culture. In environments where the "popular kids" typically excel in sports, play in rock bands, or are savvy in popular culture trends, classical musicians accumulate no cultural capital by spending hours each day practicing and admiring eighteenth- and nineteenth-century men with funny hair. Some of my informants told me that their high-school classmates knew nothing of their musical lives unless they won a local competition and were featured in the school or local newspaper. Some consciously chose not to talk about their involvement in classical music, thinking that their friends would not understand and that it would be considered "uncool."

Furthermore, the notion of classical music as a universal language that transcends race, nationality, or language is not always consistent with the actual experiences of Asian musicians. Although classical music does make it easy to cross boundaries, it is also the very arena in which these musicians experience the meaning of their Asian identity in America's racialized society.

Many Asian musicians told me that their lack of English-language skills not only kept them from communicating with their classmates and teachers but also made them feel like second-class citizens in conservatory life. Japanese singer Selina Miyazaki, for instance, felt a strong sense of being a minority while studying at the Mannes School of Music because of her limited language skills. The only person who understood her broken English and helped her was an African American student who became her best friend.[24] Other Asian students also mentioned that, when students formed chamber groups, very often white American students ended up in separate groups from foreign students—especially Asians; many feel that this separation was a result of subtle exclusion on the part of American students who find it cumbersome to deal with foreign students with limited English-language skills.

Many musicians also pointed out that it is necessary to master American-style social skills to succeed in the professional world of classical music. Violist Junah Chung said that, particularly in the New York freelance scene, Asians who had the American-style savvy for socializing—being able to joke and banter, for example—were more likely to succeed than more serious and reserved types with the same level of playing skills.[25] Pianist Myra Huang also stated that many Asians have difficulty handling the business aspect of the musical profession. "The fact is," she said, "to do well in business, you have to be aggressive, you have to be confident, you have to be good at communication . . . you know . . . those things inherently, I think, are hard for Asians." According to Huang, networking and self-promotion are very difficult for Asians because of the deeply engrained emphasis on modesty in Asian culture.[26] Both Chung and Huang claimed that, even though they were born and raised in the United States, they had to make a special effort to assert themselves in the business of music because their culturally shaped inclination was to be more modest and reserved. Drawing a connection between their struggles as musicians and their Asian identity in this way, Asian musicians come to understand and interpret the cultural differences between America and Asia.

Asian musicians also develop an awareness about their place in American society through their understanding of how mainstream American society perceives them. During my conversation with Makiko Hirata, she fondly remembered her years at Juilliard Pre-College as the time spent among a warm community of peers with a shared passion for music, yet she also vividly recalled the moments when she became aware of certain racial dynamics at work. She said, "When students who play orchestral instruments were doing orchestra rehearsals, all other students—piano majors, composition majors, and voice majors—had to take chorus. And I remember very well that the chorus members were almost all Asian. At least 90 percent were Korean and Japanese girls. But then, when they printed the catalog for Pre-College and they showed some pictures of the chorus, the camera had focused on Caucasian students and African American students, and all the faces of Asian kids were blurred in the background!"[27] She thus understood that, even though Asian students were well recognized and respected within the world of Juilliard Pre-College, when it came to public relations, the institution wanted to present an image that fit mainstream notions of racial diversity and that the numerical overrepresentation of Asians had a negative meaning in that context. She also remembered that African American students with less musical proficiency were admitted to conservatories while more accomplished Asian students were denied admission. Although she understood the principles of affirmative action and supported the idea of giving opportunities to underprivileged and underrepresented students, what is significant here is that it was through music that she came to a more complex awareness about racial diversity in America.

Once these musicians leave the conservatory and begin performing in diverse settings around the world, they come into direct contact with perceptions of the public—the audience, the jury, the critics, and residents of the cities in which they perform—that often continue to be framed in racial terms. Many musicians commented that it is much more common to experience racist perceptions in Europe than in the United States. Violinist Jennifer Koh said, "I think [being a minority] can be difficult when you're in Europe. There, there's a kind of a sense that they have an ownership of [Western] music. . . . Actually, people have told me straight to my face, 'I can't believe you're playing Mozart. You're Asian. I don't understand Chinese music.' And of course, not all Asians are Chinese. And they say, 'I don't understand *Chinese* music. How can you understand Mozart? It's not in your blood. And you also grew up in America.'"[28] Such comments relate racial, ethnic, and cultural identity (although Koh is not Chinese) to musical understanding. Even though musicians find their musical identity to be more meaningful than their racial identity, it is their racial identity that shapes others' perception of their musicianship.

Violist Junah Chung had vivid memories of how his white peers perceived him:

Yes, I think [my Asian identity] is definitely a factor [in my work as a musician]. . . . I have sometimes noticed that, *very* much in Europe, . . . but also here [in the United States], that people will often . . . if they see an Asian, they . . . will look at him and think, "Oh, there's that Chinese guy," or "that Korean guy." I find it different if somebody is European or [Caucasian] American. I find it a little different. I can't say it's all the time, but sometimes. And it used to upset me, that there's a kind of slight prejudice sometimes. . . . For example, when I was in Holland, I was playing with this chamber orchestra, this Dutch violinist, he's a very nice guy . . . he turned to me and said, "So, um, in your house, do you speak Chinese?" And I said, "Well, first of all, I'm Korean." . . . There was nothing malicious or anything intended by that, but I think it kind of illustrates how especially in Europe they have a very conservative [idea about race and music] . . . a lot of times Europeans think, "How can Asians relate to Western music? It's not in their culture." And they're surprised that Asians have taken to classical music so much. . . . In Iceland, in the orchestra [he played for the Iceland Symphony for three years], there were some people who appreciated having me and what I brought, but there was also a strong nationalistic resentment by several people also. They definitely wanted Icelanders. It's not only in Iceland. It's very strong in Iceland, but for example, even in New York, once my wife, who's blonde, was auditioning at the Met [Metropolitan Opera orchestra], and she was warming up in the locker room, and a string player, a woman in the Met, came and said, "Oh, thank God, a blonde violinist! This orchestra is starting to look like the Shanghai Symphony."[29]

Chung clearly felt ambivalent about these experiences. Even though he was upset by these exchanges, he qualified his statements by saying that such things didn't happen "all the time, but sometimes"; he did not characterize the remarks he received as overtly racist but as "a kind of slight prejudice"; and he clarified that his Dutch colleague who made the insulting comment was a "very nice guy" and that "there was nothing malicious or anything intended" by his remarks. His reticence in characterizing his experiences as manifestations of racism reflects his belief in music's power to overcome difference and his very articulate and confident assertion that "artists and musicians are [his] people."

Often, Asian musicians state that they are rarely conscious of their Asian identity when performing music but are made aware of it in the social aspects of their lives as musicians. The people with whom these musicians come to contact—particularly those who are not avid followers of classical music—often see Asian musicians as Asians first, independent of the content or quality of their work. When I asked Hiroko Yajima whether she was ever bothered by the audiences' perception of her as Japanese, she recalled, "The only time it bothered me was when I was spending time in Michigan as an artist-in-residence and performed with a lot of orchestras in the state. After each concert, there is a reception where you chat with other musicians and the audience. I remember being shocked at the kinds of questions people were asking me about Japan [at these receptions]. That was when I realized how ignorant Americans were about Japan—they thought we were still wearing kimonos and such."[30] Likewise, violinist Muneko Otani said,

I don't really think about [my Japanese identity] when it comes to music, but I am made aware of it in social situations, especially when I am touring in smaller cities. One time, I was performing in Oklahoma, and the person who picked me up at the airport started asking me all these questions about Pearl Harbor. . . . Then I real-

ized that this person sees me first and foremost as a Japanese . . .
He demanded my opinions about it, and I just didn't have any. . . .
More recently, I have been asked questions about how the Japanese
think about George W. Bush. . . . I feel like I have the burden of
having to represent the entire country of Japan, you know. In these
moments, either before or after the concert, I realize that people see
me not just as a musician but as an individual, as a person of Japanese background.[31]

Similarly, Hong Kong-born flutist Joel Tse lamented the many times when
he and his colleagues at the Toledo Symphony perform in local schools as
part of the orchestra's outreach program and students ask nothing about the
music but instead look at him and ask, "Are you related to Jackie Chan?"[32]

Not all such encounters are unpleasant, however. In fact, on many occasions music indeed bridges racial, ethnic, and national boundaries. In 2003,
soprano Kimiko Hata gave a recital in Baton Rouge, Louisiana, which is
known to the Japanese primarily as the city where a Japanese high-school
exchange student, Yoshihiro Hattori, was shot to death on Halloween night
in 1992. The recital was held in the church attended by Hattori's host family, and Hata chose to include several Japanese art songs in the program.
Remembering the experience, she said she felt the significance of performing
as a Japanese singer in that particular setting: the concert provided an occasion for the city's residents to reflect on their particular connection to Japan
through the medium of music.[33]

Such connections mediated by music take place in other racial contexts
as well. In February 2004, during Black History Month, soprano Selina
Miyazaki sang during a service at a Baptist church in Harlem, New York.
Miyazaki, her white accompanist, a few Japanese reporters covering her
work, and I were the only non-African Americans in the entire church. To
the audience who knew nothing about her or why she was there, Miyazaki
introduced herself simply as a "Japanese singer." Although many in the
church may not have been receptive to her presence at first, the mood noticeably changed as she started singing her first song, "Amazing Grace." As her
clear, beautiful voice filled the church, several people shouted and raised
their hands in the air; some were in tears. Miyazaki then sang "The Bells
of Nagasaki," a song written as a prayer for peace after the dropping of the
atomic bomb; before singing it, she explained, in her somewhat accented

English, the significance of the song for the people of her native Nagasaki. The audience was very attentive and clearly drawn to her singing.

These musicians' experiences and stories show the multiple functions of classical music in shaping their identity and awareness as Asians. In many ways, music serves to bridge the boundaries of race and culture that limit Asians' sense of belonging in other spheres of American society. In other ways, music becomes the setting that draws those very boundaries, either through the social aspects of the musical profession or the perception of Asian musicians by non-Asian audiences and peer musicians. Yet, in other ways, it is through music that Asian musicians come to understand the complex meanings of their "Asian" identity and their place in Western society, sometimes questioning dominant notions about the relationship among race, culture, and identity.

Negotiating Ethnic/National Identity

Classical music provides a way for Asian musicians not only to understand their racial identity in the United States but also to redefine it vis-à-vis their ethnic community in the United States or their Asian homeland. Asian musicians are often drawn into the community of their compatriots either in the United States or Asia, especially after they achieve success and fame. For example, the large number of Japanese fans who follow Seiji Ozawa's tours around the world indicates the significance of a successful musician's ethnic and national identity to the home audiences.

Asian musicians in the United States based in cities with a sizable community of ethnic/national peers are often asked to perform at events hosted by private and public organizations of their ethnic/national community. Some of these events are held at quite prestigious venues in front of educated audiences who listen eagerly to the performance.

For instance, in June 2005, internationally acclaimed conductor Kent Nagano led a performance of *Manzanar: An American Story* at UCLA; this work told the story of the internment of Japanese Americans during World War II and addressed issues of human rights and civil liberties. It was a complex, collaborative project that involved three composers, including Japanese-born Naomi Sekiya; playwright/director Philip Kan Gotanda; narrators/readers, including U.S. Senator Daniel Inouye and actors John Cho and

Martin Sheen; figure skater Kristi Yamaguchi; the American Youth Symphony; the Santa Monica College Chamber Choir; the Manzanar Youth Choir; and several foundations and community organizations.

In our interview on the morning after the concert, Nagano articulated his ideas about the significance of the performance for both the Japanese American community and the public at large. According to Nagano, all those involved in the project were aware that as the Nisei (second-generation Japanese Americans, who constituted the majority of those interned during World War II) generation passed away, the direct connection with the internment experience would gradually disappear and it was particularly important to do this project when many Nisei were still alive. Senator Inouye's participation made the performance particularly special because of his position as a senior member of the U.S. Senate and a war hero who served in the 442nd Regiment (the highly decorated Japanese American regiment during World War II). Recalling the weeks leading up to the concert and the evening of the performance itself, Nagano cherished the rare feeling of intimate solidarity he sensed in the hall. Not only was the Japanese American community deeply involved but all the major media outlets in Southern California gave extensive coverage to the event, generating an enormous amount of interest in the larger community. Indeed, the ethnically and generationally diverse audience seemed quite actively involved in the performance. Nagano commented that he rarely felt such a sense of solidarity since the early 1960s.

According to Nagano, because of the project's limited budget, its composers were driven more by the creative process than by monetary rewards. *Manzanar* was a highly complex piece of music that retained the integrity of each composer's work while depicting the multifaceted Japanese American experience, portraying the Issei's (first-generation immigrants) encounter with popular American music and the Nisei's involvement in jazz and swing. David Benoit's composition that used many elements of pop music was thus interwoven with Naomi Sekiya's and Jean-Pascal Beintus's compositions. The complex music and story, Nagano asserted, conveyed the message that the internment was not a simple narrative of good and bad: "Of course, it's a given that [the internment] was a tremendous social injustice, but the storyline involves complex individual experiences that cannot be reduced to a simple narrative."

When I asked Nagano whether it was important to include a Japanese or

Japanese American composer in the production, he recalled that he received much unsolicited advice to choose a Japanese American composer. Yet in the end the composers were chosen based on the quality of their work rather than their ethnicity. In talking about Naomi Sekiya, however, Nagano discussed the significance of her background for the specific project. Sekiya was born and raised in Japan and moved to the United States at age eighteen to pursue higher education. Nagano commented that Sekiya, who was in the process of becoming a naturalized U.S. citizen, was "a modern-day Issei": just like Nagano's grandparents who came to America in the 1880s and 1890s, Sekiya flourished a century later because of the opportunities available in the United States. "*This* is the American story," Nagano said in explaining the significance of choosing Sekiya, who is *not* a Japanese American with a family history of being interned, to be part of *Manzanar*. Through this assertion, he simultaneously presents a definition of Japanese American identity that is different from the standard historical account of Japanese immigration and also reaffirms the mainstream narrative about the "American dream." Thus, the definition, production, and performance of ethnic identity—and American identity—emerge out of complex and multiple processes that defy simple historical narratives and categorizations.[34]

These complex processes of identity formation were also reflected in a concert given by the Ahn Trio in Honolulu in 2002 as part of the centennial celebration of Korean immigration to the United States. These three young, hip, attractive Korean American sisters, often hailed as bringing "soul to classical," attracted an unusual crowd—many teenagers, young men with crew cuts, and Koreans of all ages—to the Neal Blaisdell Concert Hall, which is typically filled with the older white patrons of the Honolulu Symphony. The sisters began the program with arrangements of songs by The Doors and by David Bowie and performed several pieces written for them by contemporary composers. At the end of the program, violinist Angella Ahn announced, "We would like to dedicate this piece to all the Koreans in the audience." As the trio played a traditional Korean love song, many Koreans in the audience sniffled and wiped their tears.[35] In these events, the talent, success, and visibility of Asian and Asian American musicians serve as a symbol of ethnic and national pride for the ethnic, immigrant, and/or expatriate community.

Most ethnic events in which Asian musicians perform, however, are much smaller in scale, and some are not geared toward classical music.

However, personal connections made through participating in such events can lead to future performance engagements, and performances at ethnic/nation-based events are an important aspect of the work of many Asian musicians. For instance, in May 2004, Japanese soprano Kimiko Hata gave a salon concert at the Japanese ambassador's residence in New York as part of a series of events commemorating the 150th anniversary of Commodore Matthew Perry's arrival in Japan. According to the Web site of the Consulate General of Japan in New York, "Among the seventy guests who attended and enjoyed her wonderful performance were musicians, producers, agents, managers, VIPs from the New York City Opera, and Japanese businessmen."[36] She included a few traditional Japanese songs, such as a song by Kōsaku Yamada, and ended the program with a piece from *Madama Butterfly*. Neither the consulate nor Hata found irony in a Japanese soprano singing the part of Cio-Cio-San in an event commemorating the anniversary of Perry's arrival in Japan. Rather, the performance of *Madama Butterfly* was seen as a symbol both of the history of cordial U.S.-Japan relations and of the success of a Japanese singer developing her career in the United States. Indeed, this performance proved to be an important professional move for Hata, as it enabled her to meet an influential agent who has since helped her advance her career.[37]

In cities with large numbers of Asian nationals such as New York, Asian musicians are often asked by their compatriots to perform at events that are not musically prestigious but are important venues for networking. For example, Hata has sung at a reception hosted in New York by the Kagawa *kenjinkai*, an association of members from a particular prefecture in Japan. Likewise, in December 2003, soprano Selina Miyazaki performed at the annual concert of the New York Men's Choir, an amateur choir of male Japanese nationals—corporate businessmen, entrepreneurs, scholars, and students. In these events, the musicians' ethnic and national identity is central to the spotlight shone on them. They typically perform a combination of Western classical music and Japanese tunes that evoke the sense of home. For the encore, the choir sang a Japanese song, "Furusato [Home]," and led the audience to sing along, following the lyrics handed out with the program. As in many ethnic communities in which music of the homeland serves to express and heighten diasporic nostalgia, the song had a particularly poignant meaning for many in the audience who have spent a long period of time in a foreign country.[38]

Asian and Asian American musicians who have family and social ties to Asia and have achieved visibility in their work are often invited to perform in their home country where they receive warm welcomes. Because Asian audiences tend to admire greatly their compatriots who are advancing their careers abroad, it is not uncommon that a musician whose career in the United States is not particularly impressive gains great visibility and fame in Asia. Those who have indeed attained international visibility are particularly sought after by Asian audiences. Thus, internationally acclaimed musicians—such as violinists Midori, Sarah Chang, Cho-Liang Lin, and Kyoko Takezawa; pianists Mitsuko Uchida, Lang Lang, and Jon Nakamatsu; and cellists Yo-Yo Ma and Han-Na Chang—perform regularly in the country of their birth or of their ancestry. Many of them also teach on a regular basis in conservatories and music festivals in their home countries. Because of such demands by Asian audiences, some musicians choose to base themselves in Asia after having built a career in the United States or Europe. For instance, after decades of training and performance in Europe and the United States, tenor Warren Mok is now based in Hong Kong, serving as the executive director of Opera Hong Kong, asserting that he felt it was his "duty" to create Western opera in Hong Kong, which has had a long history of Chinese opera but no Western opera company.[39]

These musicians' relationships to their Asian homelands vary quite widely. Some spent all of their formative years in Asia, whereas others were born and raised in the United States; still others have hybrid upbringings spanning oceans and continents. However, the Asian audiences' reception of them as fellow Asians often obscures such differences. It assumes that a musician's *ethnic* identity is synonymous with his or her *national* and cultural identity, which sometimes puts those who do not necessarily identify as Asian nationals in an awkward position.

Pianist Helen Huang's experience illustrates such an uneasy tension between ethnicity and nationality. When I interviewed Huang in her senior year at Juilliard and asked her to describe her life, she immediately said that she was a product of "mixed cultures." She was born in 1982 in Japan to Chinese parents while her father was pursuing a PhD at the University of Tokyo. The family moved to the United States when she was two and has lived there since. In talking about her cultural identity, she claimed that she felt "completely American." She was a child prodigy who drew a great deal of media attention. She began her piano studies at age five, and just after her eighth birthday, she made her debut with the Philadelphia Orchestra after winning its student concerto competition. She also won the New York Philharmonic's Young Performers Auditions and performed with the orchestra in 1992. In 1995, she became one of the youngest recipients of the prestigious Avery Fisher Career Grant. Even before she reached age twenty, she was performing all over the United States, Europe, and Asia.

Huang generates an especially enthusiastic reception from audiences in Taiwan, the homeland of her parents. Yet the assumption of ethnic solidarity underlying that enthusiasm is not in sync with Huang's own sense of identity. In response to my question as to how important her Chinese identity is to her life, she said,

> It's something I feel slightly uncomfortable about. Because when I go to back to Taiwan, they make [me] out to be as sort of like "the Daughter of Taiwan," you know, and it's difficult because I actually don't feel any strong ties to Taiwan. I mean, it's definitely true that I was raised in a very Asian manner . . . but aside from that, I really don't. . . . I don't feel strongly Asian. . . . I've never lived in Taiwan at all. I was born in Japan and moved here [to the United States], and I speak Mandarin fluently, but I just spent as a toddler like a week or something in Taiwan. That's why it's very odd to me that they *claim* me [as theirs], you know. . . . And I always volunteer that information [that I was born in Japan and lived in New York], not because I really mind [being identified as Taiwanese], but I think it's just a false perception of who I am, you know, I'm not a Daughter of Taiwan [chuckles] . . .

Huang also recalled performing at Alice Tully Hall in New York in a concert sponsored by the Taipei Cultural Center in 2003:

> It was a chamber music concert of all the Taiwanese musicians. And that was a really interesting thing for me to be a part of. Because you have the musicians who have pretty much just come from Taiwan, and you have people like [violinist] Cho-Liang Lin, who I think is like me, he was raised in Australia. Then you have people like me, who is much more American because I've always lived here. So it was a strange mix to be part of. I also felt a little bit strange in that

environment. I don't know why. . . . I think it's whenever I'm sort of boxed in the Taiwanese category that I feel uncomfortable with it.[40]

Huang thus expressed unease with the nationalistic definition of ethnic identity that disregarded widely diverse forms of Chinese-ness in a diasporic context.[41] Yet, such experiences of being defined as a national subject of one's ancestral homeland, even when one may not identify at all with that nation/culture, are quite common, especially among Asian musicians who have attained international acclaim.

Conclusion

Asian musicians' racial, ethnic, and/or national identities are defined by several different parties: the community of musicians, many of whom are Asian; mainstream American society in which they live both as individuals and as musicians; non-Asians in the music world; American audiences perceiving their work; ethnic/national communities in the United States; and audiences in the Asian "homeland." The definitions are not always consistent, and the interests of these different parties are sometimes in conflict with one another. Amidst these sometimes uneasy tensions, Asian musicians shape their own understanding of what it means for them to be Asian.

For Asian and Asian American musicians, music is closely interwoven with other elements of their identity, making it impossible to separate race or ethnicity from their musical selves. Their experiences and awareness of their Asian identity have led them to believe in, and to consciously embrace, the transcendent power of classical music. Conversely, classical music is the very medium through which these musicians experience, understand, and negotiate their racial identities. Some musicians construct a sense of Asian identity that is based on and reinforces rather essentialist notions of Asian-ness. Others engage in a complex reflection on what constitutes Asian-ness, American-ness, and Western-ness.

Yet racial/ethnic identity is not the only axis of identity that intersects with their musical selves. In some cases, gender and sexuality play equally, if not more, important roles in shaping their lives as musicians and as individuals. That is the subject of the next chapter.

3

Playing Gender

Media accounts of the 2005 Van Cliburn International Piano Competition paid as much attention to the prominence of Asian musicians—especially women—and their glamorous presentation on stage as their playing. Numerous newspaper and magazine articles also offered detailed descriptions of the female musicians' physical beauty, dress, and penchant for shopping. For instance, an article in the *Fort Worth Star-Telegram* described the Chinese pianists at the competition in this way:

> The upper echelon of this musical mecca [China] is largely populated by women—confident, passionate women who tackle a technically daunting Chopin etude with bravado and then take a graceful bow, being sure to show off their Gucci glamour. Quite simply, their time is now, and they want the world to know it . . .
>
> While they pour their hearts into Chopin, many of these beautiful young pianists also pour themselves into Chanel gowns. They love their Manolos as much as Mozart. When they're not playing Beethoven's Fifth Piano Concerto, they're hitting the shops on Fifth Avenue, embracing their inner diva.
>
> "I want to wear something that makes me feel powerful, confident and really beautiful," says Shi. "I'm sort of petite, so it's easy for

me to disappear on a big stage. So I try to wear things that give me a little bit of a sparkle."

Adds Xu: "I really think about what I wear . . . for the Cliburn screening audition, I just didn't want to wear black, because I wanted something to cheer me up, restore my confidence. So I picked a happy, peachy color. I put that dress on and thought, 'Oh my God, I'm so ready to go.'"

Classical music purists have traditionally dismissed fashion and physical beauty as superficial afterthoughts, but this generation of Chinese pianists recognizes that beauty can be an all-important marketing tool.

"I believe the entire package counts," says Shi, "as much as people might try to deny it." [Texas Christian University's Tamas] Ungar [executive director of the Cliburn institute] puts it more bluntly: "Let's face it, they're gorgeous. This is no longer about the demure Chinese girl who doesn't look you in the eye. They not only look you in the eye, they are telling you: 'I am a musician equal to anyone at any time.'"

One of this year's Chinese Cliburn competitors, Sa Chen, can even be found smiling fetching on the Internet site, beautyinmusic. com. Moreover, agents from the States and England are stumbling over themselves to board planes to Beijing, Shanghai and the provinces in search of the next classical music starlet who combines musicianship and undeniable sex appeal.[1]

A reporter for the *Dallas Morning News* also commented on the prominence of Asian women in the competition and their appearance:

The dazzling didn't stop—or start—with brilliant runs and octaves and thundered chords. You couldn't help notice the snazzy, slinky gowns a lot of the women were wearing, and the big smiles and confident strides as they walked out onstage. In a noticeable change from the 2001 Cliburn, these were emphatically pianists groomed for the video age. . . . Ms. Chen wore an intensely green dress trimmed in purple, with Chinese-looking embroidery. Ms. Yang had a glittery reddish gown that lit up the stage.[2]

Asian musicians' gender, racial, and musical identities are inextricably woven together in these depictions. These connections are central aspects of the identity of Asian musicians, both within the musical profession and in society at large.

As musicologist Ruth A. Solie has demonstrated, the social roles of classical music and its practitioners are closely connected to cultural norms about gender, especially for girls and women. In the nineteenth century—when music-making in the home, especially piano playing, became thoroughly associated with young women—playing the piano became an important element of socializing young girls into appropriate forms of womanhood in both Europe and the United States. Young girls learned to assume roles in a rigidly organized family life at the same time as they acquired their musical skills from their mothers. The discipline of music; practice regimes; the image of a mother, wife, and daughter symbolically assigned to the instrument; and courtship rituals surrounding the parlor piano all worked together to define women's place and responsibility as the home.[3]

Similarly, in Asia, classical music has come to be seen as the domain of women. For instance, in Japan, since the Tokyo School of Music was founded in the early Meiji period (1868–1912), its student body has been primarily women from former samurai families or from families of equivalent standing. Along with other accomplishments in traditional Japanese arts such as the tea ceremony and flower arrangement, training in Western music quickly became a marker of bourgeois womanhood in Meiji Japan. In the postwar period, when pianos and other musical instruments became attainable by the middle class, this association between classical music and the socialization of women strengthened. As was the case in the West, this musical education was intended not to train professional performers but rather to produce properly domesticated women and educate piano-playing teachers to give private lessons to children.[4] Teaching was a particularly suitable occupation, as it was part-time, done in one's home, and involved teaching children. It therefore allowed the women to continue their musical pursuit without transgressing gender norms.

The notion that music training is intrinsic to respectable womanhood continues to have a strong hold on East Asian countries. Parents encourage both boys and girls to take music lessons throughout childhood and adolescence as a way to cultivate discipline and achieve a well-rounded education. However, in late adolescence their paths diverge when parents generally steer college-bound boys away from music and toward more stable and lucrative professional careers. In contrast, parents of girls tend to regard studying music at a conservatory or university as a desirable form of social capital that will raise their value in the marriage market. Of course, there is no question that most conservatory students are very serious about their music studies. However, in general, neither society at large nor the conservatory trains female students to see music as a means of making a living, and few institutions provide concrete career guidance. Only a small percentage of graduates become career musicians; the majority marry into upper-middle class families, a trend that leads some critics to characterize conservatories as a kind of modern-day finishing school for upper-middle-class women.

These gendered notions about music education are reflected in the composition of student bodies at major music conservatories. Since World War II, female students have outnumbered male students at the Tokyo National University for Fine Arts and Music (formerly the Tokyo School of Music), the most competitive and prestigious institution for music education in Japan. The gender imbalance has grown with succeeding decades: in 1952, the school had 266 male students and 279 female students; in 1970, the numbers were 346 and 516, respectively; and in 1988, women outnumbered men by 686 to 332.[5] Gender disparity in music education is also evident in Korea. According to ethnomusicologist Okon Hwang, although men dominate Korea's higher education ranks, female students comprised well over 70 percent of student bodies in the nation's music schools, and 89 percent of performers who gave three or more concerts between 1987 and 1997 were female.[6]

The connection between gender and music-making is also apparent in the choice of instruments. To this day, both in Asia and in the United States, female musicians are overrepresented in those instruments that are played in the home—most notably piano and violin—as well as voice. In contrast, those who play other instruments—for instance, bass, brass, or percussion—are still overwhelmingly male.

Such gendering of musical practices has a profound impact on the lives of musicians, both male and female. On the one hand, in their artistic pursuit, musicians must navigate, and often fight against, the prescribed gender norms and the sexual economy that shape the profession and society. On the other hand, for many the pursuit of music itself becomes a way to define and live their own ideals of gender and sexuality, sometimes in deviation from socially prescribed models. Solie's argument that piano playing not only socialized young women into fulfilling familial and social demands but also allowed them to resist or co-opt those prescribed identities to their own ends applies to Asian—male and female—musicians as well. This chapter demonstrates both the impact of social norms of gender and sexuality on the lives of Asian musicians and the ways in which the musicians themselves define the meanings of gender and sexuality in their musical lives.

Transgressing Bourgeois Gender Norms: Male Musicians

Because musical careers often lack financial stability and classical music is often considered an amateur or at best a semi-professional pursuit of women, many men seeking careers in classical music have had to fight social norms about gender and face opposition and pressure from their families and peers. Asian and Asian American men tend to face particularly strong opposition. Middle- and upper-middle-class families in East Asia expect their male children—especially the eldest son—to be successful and to carry on the family name, tradition, and wealth. They define success usually in terms of a professional career in such fields as medicine and law or employment in a prestigious corporation or a government office. Many regard the pursuit of the arts as unmanly and socially unrespectable, and unless one comes from a family of professional musicians, there is usually little understanding of what a musical career entails. Such gendered and classed notions of the music profession are shared widely not only in East Asia but also in Asian American communities as well.

Korean pianist Tony Cho was born and raised in Korea until age twelve and then spent his adolescent years in Paraguay and Southern California. In talking about how he became a musician, he characterized his parents as "very conservative" who "thought a man should not do music, especially piano, no." He recalled that his father never liked the fact that he was playing piano and never came to any of his recitals, even when he achieved success as a young student in Paraguay. When attending college in Los Angeles, he majored in biochemistry as his father wanted, until he transferred to another university and won a full scholarship to study music.[7] Similarly, tenor Warren Mok studied accounting for one semester because his Chinese parents wanted him to "study something practical," but it did not take him long to find out that he absolutely hated it.[8] Flutist and ethnomusicologist Frederick Lau also brought up the reaction of his father and grandfather in talking about how he became a musician. Even after he failed the exam to enter college as an engineering major and instead passed the very competitive exam to become a music major at a government university, his father encouraged him to switch his major to economics after one year; his grandfather also disapproved of his studying music.[9]

Some male informants commented that parental support for their music-making was unusual, as Asian parents typically push their sons to study law, medicine, or engineering. Chinese American violinist Conway Kuo, in talking about his decision to pursue music professionally, noted, "My parents were very supportive. And that was kind of unusual because . . . especially in my town [in suburban New Jersey], if you were Asian and played violin or piano, you usually did it just for fun, and [music] was not something that most parents pushed their kids to do professionally."[10]

Double bassist Satoshi Okamoto comes from a respectable middle-class family in Tokyo and went to one of the city's most academically competitive high schools, which sends many of its graduates to the University of Tokyo and other prestigious universities. His father, a graduate of the University of Tokyo who works for the municipal government, expected his son to attend his alma mater. When I asked Okamoto whether gender issues influenced his decision to pursue music, he said that he was not particularly conscious of social norms about gender and certainly did not choose music *despite* his gender. Although he agreed that the general public assigns clearly gendered meanings to musical pursuits, he did not feel that those who choose to pursue music professionally are particularly concerned about such issues. However, he recalled that during his teens when he started studying the double bass and decided to pursue music seriously, he also made three resolutions: "never going to the University of Tokyo, never getting married, and not having a long and happy life." When asked to elaborate on the significance of these resolutions in relation to his career choice, he admitted that there was indeed a connection between his decision to pursue music and his wish not to follow a well-trodden, conventional life of a middle-class man: "Yeah, now that I think of it that way, I guess there was a part of me that thought it was boring to do what everyone else was doing, like going to the University of Tokyo. I thought it was cool to break out of the norm, and it was cool to go to a music conservatory when everyone else was studying to get into the University of Tokyo. It was a greater challenge." In other words, his choice to pursue music was a form of rebellion against the normative ideals of middle-class life and expectations placed on him as a Japanese man.[11] These stories suggest that, for many Asian male musicians, their pursuit of classical music is itself a transgression of mainstream gender norms, whether or not they are conscious of it.

Negotiating Gender and the Sexual Economy of Music: Female Musicians

Female musicians face different challenges as they deal with the gendered expectations of both the musical profession and society at large. For many Asian female musicians, the pursuit of classical music is a way of following expected gender norms. In the middle-class milieus of both East Asia and the United States, being a diligent music student is a congruent part of being a good girl and a virtuous young woman. Yet, once they become more serious about music and decide to pursue a career in the field, the combination of their gender and race comes to acquire a much different meaning. To be successful as professional musicians, Asian female musicians often find it necessary to go against the gender expectations placed on them. Although all female musicians, regardless of race, have to negotiate between the prescribed norms of womanhood and the ideals of femininity on the one hand and the demands of artistic expression and a professional career on the other, Asian musicians must also confront gender norms specific to Asian culture. In addition, because of the gendered and sexualized meanings ascribed to Asian women in mainstream American culture, female Asian musicians have to maneuver their image and identity in ways that work to their advantage without compromising their artistic and personal integrity.

Just as many Asian musicians do not see race or racism as a particularly important factor in their professional lives, some of my female informants told me that they did not see the classical music profession as particularly sexist. Especially orchestral musicians, who are auditioned behind a screen, do not see gender (or race) as relevant either in getting hired or in their everyday work life. In addition, just as many Asian and Asian American musicians are not particularly involved in racial or ethnic issues, many female

Asian musicians do not have a particularly political language to discuss the issues of gender. In my interviews, few of my informants explicitly identified themselves as feminists.

To be sure, this lack of an explicitly claimed feminist identity may be more a reflection of the sociohistorical context than of their individual political orientation. Many of my female informants were in their twenties or early thirties when I interviewed them. As part of the "postfeminist" generation, they came of age when many of the battles over gender equity supposedly had been won by their feminist predecessors. Many thus took the pursuit of career *and* family for granted, and many also associated feminism with angry, man-hating, bra-burning, asexual women. Furthermore, although many young women today are introduced to basic tenets of feminist principles and political language when they enter universities, those who spent their early adulthood in a conservatory setting often lacked such exposure.

However, the absence of a political language to discuss feminism by no means suggests a lack of awareness about issues of gender or of the relevance of gender to their lives as musicians. Even without my asking specifically about the topic during their interviews, many female musicians brought up the male-dominated nature of the musical profession and the difficulties of a musical career for women. Many also discussed the issue of gender when talking about their career paths. In fact, the way that female Asian musicians frame their life paths in their stories reveals the centrality of gender as well as race in shaping their lives as musicians.

Pianist Helen Huang, who was in her senior year at Juilliard at the time of our interview, said that once she started traveling alone at age eighteen, she realized how lonely the life of a traveling musician is and began thinking about the difficulty of balancing career and a fulfilling family life: "As a woman, how do you deal with that? It's much easier for a man . . . *much* easier."[12] Violinist Jennifer Koh commented that, whereas she is rarely conscious of her identity as Asian in her work as a musician, "I think what can be harder in the music world is actually being a woman. . . . I think it's changing, though. But I think it used to be very difficult for a woman, an older woman, after they've been [performing] for a long time as a younger woman, and I think making that transition is *very* difficult for a woman. You know, you can have ugly men on stage and nobody will say boo about that, but for women, it's everything."[13]

Even before musicians begin their professional careers, gender shapes their daily experiences in music schools. Asian female musicians are well aware of the gendered images and stereotypes of Asian students as well as the expectations placed on them. When my informants, especially students and recent graduates of conservatories, discussed racial stereotypes of Asian musicians, they very frequently talked specifically about female Asian stereotypes. They reported a prevalent stereotype of Asian, particularly Korean, female students who go to Juilliard not to pursue music seriously but because they were sent there by their parents in the hopes that the conservatory training would help find a suitable husband back home. Regardless of their validity, such perceptions nonetheless affect Asian students who are dedicating themselves to music.

Pianist Myra Huang remembered that, while she was studying at Juilliard and the Manhattan School of Music, it was pretty clear which students were more serious than others: "Because we have a lot of performance classes, [where students play in front of others] and you notice who's always willing to perform and is always ready . . . and then there's this other person who's always sitting in the corner and giggling and talking to the friends . . . which [sic] are sometimes Asian females. . . . There were definitely visibly Asian female students who didn't seem all that serious about the career but they were just in school for whatever reason."[14] She claimed that, whereas she never experienced explicit forms of racism in the professional world, she did feel that stereotypes of Asian female students existed and that an Asian female musician had to work extra hard to stand out.

Pianist Miori Sugiyama echoed Huang's comments:

At a place like Juilliard, we Asian girls represent the majority of the piano department. . . . And because there is this stereotype that society is overflowing with female Asian pianists, in a way I feel like you have a disadvantage upfront when you're being introduced to managers. You know, you're an Asian, female pianist, and you're automatically . . . you sort of have to work extra hard in a way in order to be distinct from one another, which I feel like we already do, but it's a lot of work for us, and it's very, very frustrating. I think this culture is very much image-oriented, and they want the next representative pianist to be someone who can really represent the country. That obviously a lot of times wouldn't be an Asian person, an Asian female person. [It would likely be] more a guy with brown or blond hair, blue eyes . . . a typical American figure.[15]

The issue of gender is not just about images and stereotypes, however. Female Asian musicians have to navigate the sexual economy that shapes the profession, the most common manifestation of which is a sexual relationship between older white male teachers and younger Asian female students. The relationships between white men and Asian women, ubiquitous through the history of U.S.-Asian relations, are quite common in the world of classical music as well. Indeed, many female students in the first wave of Asian music students who came to study in the United States in the 1960s married their white colleagues or teachers. To be sure, many Asian male musicians have married or been in relationships with women of white or other non-Asian backgrounds, and in a field where there is a relatively high concentration of gays and lesbians, same-sex relationships involving Asians and whites are also fairly common. Yet my conversations with musicians—Asian as well as white, male as well as female—clearly indicated that the gender and sexual relations of Asian musicians are conceived most typically as between older white men and younger Asian women. This is not surprising considering that white men still comprise a majority of faculty at music conservatories. Many musicians can easily name several white male teachers who have had relationships with or have married their Asian students, often much younger than themselves. During my fieldwork in New York, on a number of occasions I saw a well-known white male pianist and critic, notorious for having one young Asian student after another as his girlfriend, accompanied by a young Asian woman (not always the same one) who was clearly his charge.

Of course, Asian women are not always victimized in such relationships. Some female Asian students voluntarily enter relationships with their teachers. Nonetheless, this gender and sexual dynamic is a minefield that female Asian musicians often have to learn to navigate. The extremely intimate and intensely personal, emotional, as well as physical nature of private music lessons—in which students turn their whole selves over to their teachers' judgment and guidance in many ways beyond musical knowledge and techniques—puts students in a particularly vulnerable position. Although overt forms of sexual advances or harassment are less common in recent years, several of my female informants told me of instances where they or their friends were the objects of such pressure from their teachers.

This sexual dynamic is also present in female musicians' relationships with other men who have a great influence on their professional life, such as conductors, directors, managers, and sponsors. Violinist Anne Akiko Meyers characterized classical music as "still definitely a man's business." She said that she found it astonishing that the first female conductor of a major American symphony was only appointed in 2005 [Marin Alsop was appointed as Music Director of the Baltimore Symphony beginning in the 2007–08 season]. When asked to share her own experience of the male-dominated profession, she responded as follows:

> Well, I could be working with a conductor who is really coming onto me. And I think, if I was a guy from Russia, would he be coming onto him? It's just because I'm a girl, and I'm unattached, and I'm here working professionally, that he has the feeling that he can [make sexual advances] . . . it's just mind-boggling to me. That, to me, is a disgusting behavior. I'm not interested, it's just not going to happen, and I'm not there for that. I'm not there to sleep with the conductor. I'm there to work and to make music. So that aspect of the business becomes really painful sometimes . . . that's happened many, many times. And a lot of the conductors are in a very power-ful place because they're deciding which artists they're going to work with, and so you have to walk the very fine line.[16]

As Meyers explained, particularly for musicians pursuing careers as solo-ists or as opera singers, the support of the male conductor often becomes a make-or-break factor. Many stories and rumors circulate among musicians about famous female musicians having sexual relations with powerful con-ductors or managers who helped them launch their careers.

Of course, such relationships are not always between female musicians and male conductors/directors/managers/sponsors, and certainly not all female musicians who are involved in such relationships are Asian. Nor do such relationships of mentoring and support always involve sex. During my research, I met several women who had sponsors who provided generous financial support and/or facilitated booking opportunities, either on a com-pletely no-strings-attached basis or in exchange for secretarial or other non-sexual services. Some of those sponsors were Asian men or white women. Thus, the sponsorship of wealthy and powerful patrons can by no means be explained solely in terms of gender, sexuality, and race. However, it is important to acknowledge the broader racial and gender context in which Asian musicians work, where a great majority of those who hold decision-making power in the world of classical music are older white men. Female Asian musicians, regardless of whether they themselves engage in sexual relationships with those men, are well aware of such dynamics and chart their professional and personal lives carefully.

Asian female musicians today also contend with social norms about gender roles and ideals of femininity that are often not compatible with the pursuit of a musical career. Pianist Soyeon Lee was one of the few musicians who explicitly referred to herself as a "feminist" during our interview. Lee is a very attractive, radiant, and friendly woman who at the time of our interview was a star pianist pursuing an Artist Diploma at Juilliard. Her interests are rather unusual among classical musicians: when I asked her about the musicians she admires the most, without a moment of hesitation, she answered, "The Beatles." It is quite telling

SOYEON LEE
(Photograph © Peter Schaaf)

that in response to my question, "In what ways do you think your identity as Korean or Asian is a factor in your life as a musician?"—a question about the relevance of racial identity but not specifically about gender identity—she gave me a very perceptive and in-depth answer about sexism, gender stereotypes, and ideals of femininity that affect the lives of female Asian musicians. For Lee, the issue of race is very much tied to the issue of gender:

> It's hard for an Asian person, but especially for a woman, to make it in the classical [music] world. I feel this more and more these days. Because our culture teaches us to be polite, too polite in a way that it becomes submissive almost. And what we perceive as rude behavior is actually sometimes what's necessary to get work and to make it really in this arena, you know.

Lee went on to say that she used to believe that women were capable of making similar achievements as men and that women's individual efforts enabled them to break barriers and earn recognition. Yet she reflected on how such a belief in meritocracy had blinded her to various forms of institutional sexism in the world of music, as well as the practical and psychological difficulties of musical careers for women. She discussed how she tries to overcome the disadvantage of being physically smaller than male pianists by practicing various forms of martial arts and yoga.

Lee was most perceptive in her thoughts about the racialized and gendered expectations projected onto Asian female musicians:

> I think Americans or the world in general has a perception of Asian women as submissive. And that really bothers me a lot. . . . There are so many Asian women that are doing piano. And we come out with our little ponytails and fluffy dresses, especially the Pre-College kids here, and I'm not sure that people take us seriously, really. Because so much of the value of what's expected of Asian women is to get married to a rich man and be a good mother and stay at home. Yes, in recent years that's rapidly changing, but it's not changed so much. . . . My parents in Seoul are like, "You know, [your piano] is really important, but aren't there any lawyers or doctors around [for you to marry]?" And I feel like because of that [kind of gender ideals shared among many Asians], even the faculty here [Juilliard] would

automatically think, maybe, "Well, this girl is so talented and great, but she's probably gonna one day get married and not pursue this career." And a lot of people *are* that way. So in that sense, already, the managers and society don't take us seriously. . . . Some teachers, especially the old-fashioned teachers, really do focus more on the guys [students]. . . . It's really hard to be a woman, a feminine person, *and* be really strong. People don't really want to accept that or something. I think Asian women have to work really hard to get out of this given situation that we're going to eventually get married and have a home. I think people like [Mitsuko] Uchida and, who else is there, [violinist] Chung Kyung-Wha have really pulled out of that. But it's so rare, it's two out of how many? You know, when I first came here [Juilliard] in my freshman class, it was sixteen girls and one boy. That was our class. We were a very strange class, it's not always like this, it's more or less even. But there are always more girls at Juilliard that come. And then, when they leave, the people that end up doing the doctoral are all the guys. Somehow, all those girls that were doing all the jury requirements, they somehow disappear into . . . I don't know where they go, you just don't hear of them any more. And it's that one guy that sticks around. It's a mystery, I haven't figured it out, except that you know, maybe it's that society already has a pre-conception that we won't do it anyway and so they don't even bother to make an opportunity for it. I don't know.[17]

Just like Lee, many female musicians struggle for a long time with the tension between gender norms and musical pursuits. Looking back at the psychological turmoil she went through at various stages of her life and how her own playing has evolved over the years, pianist Makiko Hirata told me that she felt that the problems she has experienced in her playing were not in small part due to her struggles with gender roles:

On the one hand, I've always been very serious about music and have wanted to "make it" as a musician. So for a long time I would just lock myself up in the practice room and cut myself off from the outside world, not caring what people think of me or what I look like or anything like that, but on the other hand, there's also been a part of me that wants to find a nice man, get married, and live the life of a normal woman. I think that part of me kept telling myself that it's not really feminine to put all my ego into music and be all out and aggressive with my emotions. And I think that desire to be attractive and feminine has held me back in my playing a little bit.[18]

Hirata is thus deeply aware of how she has internalized social norms about gender. Her heartfelt comments demonstrate that, even as musicians spend a great part of their lives in the solitary act of practicing in seclusion from the outside world, they are still embedded in and are deeply affected by the norms and ideals of larger society.

Pianist Sachiko Kato has also been caught in a dilemma between artistic pursuit and gender norms. Even though she did not frame her life story explicitly in terms of gender, the way she reflected on the different stages of her life was very much structured as a narrative about her gender identity. After Kato and her family relocated from Japan to Los Angeles when she was in her teens, she received a full scholarship to study piano at a local university. However, she felt that she could not fit into the Los Angeles scene where all the female students around her were "typical girls." Although she did not explain what she meant by "typical girls," the rest of her story revealed that her sense of her own deviance came from a combination of her attitude toward music, her Japanese identity, and gender. She talked about the summer when she attended the Music Academy of the West in Santa Barbara, California, as a catalytic time in her life. She was overwhelmed by what she perceived as other students' extraordinary talent, but she also felt that for the first time in her life she had found a circle of friends among whom she could fit and feel comfortable. She then moved to New York to study at Juilliard for her master's degree and moved to Boston after graduation.

Like many other musicians, Kato's real struggle began when she left school. She was burnt out from entering competitions while struggling to make a living. Having lost a sense of direction and feeling that being a pianist was a heavy burden, she moved back to New York and entered what she called a "long vacation." During these years, she worked at a Japanese bookstore in New York and socialized with Japanese friends who were not musicians. She reflected on that time:

Because I did not grow up in Japan, there was a period when I felt happy simply by speaking Japanese and being accepted as a member of the Japanese community. Until this time, I didn't have any Japanese friends. When I was at Juilliard, I felt that students from Japan were a rather different crowd, and with the exception of one violinist I'm still very close with, I didn't socialize with any Japanese students there. [As a sort of a rebound from that period, I immersed myself in the Japanese community during my "vacation" years.] I have felt that I am neither fully Japanese nor fully American, and when I was younger I dealt with that feeling by consciously pushing myself in one direction or another. But I now realize that by trying to be more of one than the other, I was denying part of my identity.

Kato spent her "long vacation" searching for her identity as a pianist, as Japanese, and as a woman. In explaining how she was able to resume her career, she made it clear that the process had to do with her changing notions of gender ideals. After these years of soul-searching, and especially after the terrorist attack of September 11, 2001, she came to rethink her priorities in life, and she also secured financial stability by working as a translator. Both helped her rediscover her identity and confidence as a pianist, but she added, "[My breakthrough] also had to with the fact that I had reached beyond the age where one is expected to be a 'normal girl.' I started feeling that I don't have to get married, and I felt freed from a lot of things." At the end of her story, she said firmly, "I haven't lived a normal life." It is noteworthy that what she referred to as a "normal life" is implicitly gendered female and that her sense of self has been achieved through freedom from conventional gender expectations of marriage and family.

In our interview Kato was bluntly dismissive of female Asian musicians for whom gender norms and stereotypes are serious and personal issues. In response to my question about the stereotypes of Asian musicians, she said,

I don't think such stereotypes exist in the professional world. In the world of students, there are images associated with the "typical Asian girl," but I no longer encounter situations where I feel that [stereotypes affect me]. Honestly, I don't feel that I am on the same level as the people who are worried about things like that. I think if you're worried about the audience's perception of you, you're lacking in the sense of urgency about music, really. . . . As for myself, I don't fit the image of a typical Asian woman anyway, so I don't think other people expect that of me, either.

In addition to consciously situating herself away from gendered and racial stereotypes in the United States, Kato was highly critical of Japanese gender ideals that, in her view, cast female musicians as sexual objects rather than artists. When I asked her at the end of our conversation if she had any additional thoughts, she responded in this way:

> You know, Japanese musicians, especially women, all look very formal, neat, and tidy. And women have certain glamour. . . . A couple of years ago, I was at Kinokuniya [a Japanese bookstore in Manhattan], and I was browsing through this Japanese book by a Japanese music critic. It was a collection of the profiles of Japanese musicians. So I was flipping through the pages, and there was a section on [prominent Japanese pianist] Hiroko Nakamura, and it was full of praise. But it talks about her looks! Like how her eyes are round and cute and stuff like that! What the hell does that have to do with her work? Then there was another one on this woman about my age, who is surely cute, and the book talked about how she looks good with her pink scarf and how she has this pure and pleasant demeanor and all. . . . Then I looked at the section on Mitsuko Uchida, and the book is totally trashing her, saying things like how she tries to appear intellectual by throwing out lofty ideas and confusing the listener or something like that. . . . I was totally put off after reading the first two profiles. . . . I think in Japan, people sort of expect performers to be . . . pretty, to be a beautiful person out of reach of ordinary people. . . . I think those expectations trickle down to piano teachers as well. Even if you don't perform, if you're a piano teacher, you're expected to look pretty.[19]

Thus, even as Kato clearly distanced herself from the ideals of femininity she questions, her comments show that the images and norms about gender do in fact play a role in musicians' lives, regardless of how much or little they embrace those norms.

Visual Marketing of Asian Musicians

The visual appeal of musicians as displayed on CD jackets, posters, and magazine photos plays an increasingly important role in today's market. Particularly

YUNDI LI
(Photograph © KASSKARA/DG)

for commercially successful musicians, many parties involved in the industry—presenters, managers, publicists, stylists, photographers, record companies, as well as the musicians themselves and their parents—have a stake and a say in shaping their image. For Asian musicians, dominant American images of their gender and sexuality play a role in shaping the marketing of their images and work.

The visual coding of gender and sexuality is certainly not applied only to women. Male musicians with popular appeal sometimes appear in obviously staged photographs akin to those in fashion magazines, and some capitalize on the soft attractiveness common among Asian male pop stars. The jacket of pianist Yundi Li's Liszt CD, for instance, shows Li standing in what appears like the long, empty corridor of an airport. The "soft" image of his wavy hair and facial features contrasts with his attire—his dark striped

KENT NAGANO
(Photograph by Susesch Bayat; courtesy of the Van Walsum Management)

suit and black shirt—and his sideways stance, his hands in his pants pockets and his head turned straight toward the camera. The blurred background and lighting accentuate the sharpness of Li's figure. Cellist Yo-Yo Ma's good looks, international popularity, friendly persona, and artistic innovations that cross genres and cultures have produced a wide array of visual images that appeal to audiences far beyond classical music fans. Conductor Kent Nagano, attractive and sexy with his distinctive long hair, has been asked to model for commercials for Gap and Lufthansa Airlines. The extensive use of these musicians' photographs in CD jackets, programs, flyers, and posters—much more so than with other musicians of comparable stature, who mostly are shown wearing tuxedos or business suits and holding their instruments—indicates their presenters' and publicists' awareness of the marketability of their attractive looks. Such images counter the historically held notion of Asian men as asexual and help gain popular attention. Still, the visual coding of male Asian musicians is much more subtle and less explicitly gendered or sexualized than for their female counterparts.

In contrast, the visual marketing of female Asian musicians often capitalizes much more explicitly on the visual images of Asian female sexuality. The images used to sell female Asian musicians say much about how the parties involved in the production and circulation of their images see their appeal to mainstream consumers. Visual images of female Asian musicians generally fall into one of three categories: the innocent and somewhat alien child prodigy; the young, sensuous, sexy Asian; and the mature, slightly exotic woman. Each appeals to particular notions of race, gender, and sexuality circulating in American culture.

The child prodigies who make their major debuts before they reach their teens generate attention precisely because of their deviation from the norm. Their extraordinary talent gives them an out-of-this-world persona, not only as musicians but also as children and human beings. Record companies, presenters, publicists, and even their parents choose visual images that help accentuate this quality. As extraordinary as their young age is, in many of these images these child prodigies are made to look even younger than they actually are. They are usually dressed as cute, little children in attire that erases any suggestions of their eventual development into adolescence and adulthood. Having achieved extraordinary artistic maturity yet appearing to be permanently fixed in innocent childhood, the children in these images embody multiple forms of alien-ness.

Photographs of violinist Midori from her childhood years, in which she wore childish dresses and had a childish expression, exemplify this image of an Asian prodigy. She was well known for adoring Snoopy, her stuffed animal, well into her teens, reinforcing the image of her stunted development and sexuality. The visual portrayals of other female musicians who made their debuts at a very young age—violinist Sarah Chang, cellist Han-Na Chang, and pianist Helen Huang, for instance—share similar qualities.

The most popular image of female Asian musicians is that of young, sexy Asian femininity. As many critics have discussed, the image of exotic, seductive, available sexuality has been a staple feature of the representations of Asian women in American culture for more than a century and is very much alive in popular culture today. Record companies and publicists do not shy away from capitalizing on this appeal of Asian femininity to mainstream consumers, especially in marketing female Asian musicians who fit the ideal physical type and are willing to "sell" their looks. Attractive female musicians tend to wear their hair long and straight, and they often appear in photographs or on stage with a charming, inviting smile or an air of detached coolness, wearing revealing or tight-fitting clothes that flatter their slender bodies. In recent years, some women musicians have taken a more explicit approach to highlighting their physical attractiveness by using the visual conventions of pop media.

Perhaps the most extreme and explicit example is the marketing of violinist Vanessa Mae, daughter of a Chinese mother and a Thai father who was raised in England by her British adoptive father. Mae has been transformed from a "wunderkind" who made her recording debut at age twelve into a superstar whose album sold a half-million copies within two weeks of release, making her the fastest-selling classical solo musician. Her aptly titled 1997 CD, *China Girl*, is a collection of music with a Chinese theme— the famous *Butterfly Lovers Violin Concerto*, the violin fantasy from Puccini's *Turandot*, and "Happy Valley—The 1997 Re-Unification Overture," which she co-wrote and premiered on the night of the handover of Hong Kong to China. This CD jacket features Mae as no other than the classic image of the "China girl." The black-and-white headshot shows her wearing what looks like an embroidered Chinese dress; with her bobbed hair, sharply drawn eyebrows, eye shadow accentuating her dark eyes, and smooth skin, she turns her head to the side, her mouth slightly open.

Vanessa Mae's other media images are much more provocative and explicitly sexual. Many of the images in the photo gallery of her Web site (titled "Red Hot Vanessa Homepage") show her in tight-fitting tank tops with a bare midriff. In one shot she is holding her electric violin and leaning sideways into a sofa, with her long, black hair blowing in the air. In another image, she is playing her electric violin while standing in the ocean, wearing a see-through white dress over a white bathing suit with water coming up to her crotch. In yet another photo, she sits provocatively in a chair with her legs open, wearing a tight top and pants, with her midriff showing and strands of her long, wavy hair coming down over her face. Many of these photos could conceivably be found in men's magazines or soft porn.[20]

Although Mae's explicitly sexual images set her apart from other musicians, many attractive young female Asian musicians use images that high-

ANNE AKIKO MEYERS
(Photograph by Anthony Parmelee; courtesy of the artist)

light their physical attractiveness. Violinist Anne Akiko Meyers was selected
to be photographed by Annie Liebovitz for the Anne Klein "Women of Substance" fashion campaign that appeared in magazines around the world.
Her publicity photographs highlight her physical beauty.[21] The three Korean
American sisters of the Ahn Trio also appeal to young consumers by appearing in MTV-style attire, and the media often pay just as much, if not more,
attention to their looks as their music.

AHN TRIO
(Courtesy of the artists)

In contrast, older musicians who have earned an international reputation do not employ images that directly foreground conventional feminine beauty, but rather appeal to the ideal of mature artistry and womanhood. Pianist Mitsuko Uchida, well known for her bohemian attire and distinctive style on stage—critics have made fun of her playing with her eyebrows raised, eyes closed, and her body swaying with the music—is often photographed in ways that highlight her seriousness. Whereas many promotional images of female musicians show them with a friendly smile, most of Uchida's photographs on CD jackets and promotional materials feature a much more serious look. She usually looks straight into the camera with a solemn expression that challenges the viewer. Her pose and body language—standing with her arms crossed in front or sitting with her chin rested on her hand—exude a sense of confidence and intelligence.

Violinist Kyung-Wha Chung also appears in her photographs with a look of mature beauty. Her makeup, hairstyle, and attire do not depart from the conventions of Westernized Asian female beauty, yet her posture—standing sideways with one arm at her waist and the other hand holding the violin, sitting back with her wrists on both sides of the armchair—and her daring gaze differ from the ways in which younger Asian female musicians are usually featured.

As musicians progress through their careers, their marketing images change. In our telephone interview, violinist Sarah Chang recalled that in the first phase of her career when she was hailed as a child prodigy, her mother used to dress her up in red and pink and put bows on her dresses and hair. Indeed, on the jacket of her first CD, titled *Debut,* she is shown wearing a red, puffy dress and a matching ribbon in her hair, holding her violin, and smiling earnestly with her mouth slightly open. She is standing

MITSUKO UCHIDA
(Photograph courtesy of Decca/Schels)

in front of three faceless men in tuxedos, and the top of her head reaches just above their waists. This positioning and framing accentuate her identity as a young child and her difference from the three adult—presumably white—men. Her next CD of the Tchaikovsky violin concerto, released a year later, likewise presents a fairy-like image, with Chang standing in a snowy forest and dressed in a long, bright red coat with black fur on the collar and the sleeves.

Chang remembered that when she became a teenager, however, no clothing was appropriate for her stage appearance. The only dresses that fit her

SARAH CHANG, *Debut*
(Photograph © 2007 Enrico Ferorelli; used by kind permission of EMI Classics)

SARAH CHANG, *Dvorak*
(Photograph by Sheila Rock; used by kind permission of EMI Classics)

body were prom dresses, but her mother told her they were too immodest for her to wear in performances. This uneasy stage of female teenage sexuality is reflected in her CD jackets from this period as well. She appears in plain-looking white or black clothes with her long hair knotted in the back, looking very much like a model minority Asian student. Once she reached young adulthood, her CD jackets and photos in various magazines highlight her sexiness through makeup, hair, pose, and lighting.

Chang said that, although she was happy that she was now at a point in her life where she had control over her visual self-image and she was very pleased with her CD jackets, her parents, particularly her father, were often quite unhappy with her revealing attire in some of these images. Speaking of visual marketing, she said,

> Now there are these very talented and attractive female musicians, and if their image can attract younger audiences to classical music, I think that's a wonderful thing. But I was looking at some new CDs at the store the other day, and I see this CD with all Bach music, and the musicians on the cover are wearing, like nothing! I think it's a good thing to appeal visually to the audience, but I think the images that undermine artistic integrity are maybe not appropriate.

After Chang expressed her thoughts to the CD company and the stylist during her cover session, they agreed to use an image of her that was sexy but still appropriate.[22]

Classical Music and Identity: Gay Musicians

It is hardly news that gay men figure prominently in the world of classical music, now as in the past. Some recent scholarship in musicology has adopted a queer studies approach to music, discussing such issues as queer musical aesthetics, queer relationships to music, the relationship between sexuality and musicality, and gender and sexual politics in musical institutions and communities.[23] There is hardly any agreement among musicologists and musicians on these issues, yet what is striking about these debates is that they almost always discuss sexuality independent of other variables of identity, such as race. Queer identity is thus implicitly defined as white. This tendency may be understandable, considering that the introduction of queer perspectives to musicology is a relatively recent phenomenon and, perhaps more important, the music and the musicians these scholars are discussing are European and white American. Yet, it is important to understand that sexual identity does not exist or function independently of other aspects of identity. The identity of gay Asian musicians is shaped by their Asian upbringing and their development as musicians as well as by their sexual orientation.

Most Asian and Asian American communities stigmatize homosexuality, forcing gay and lesbian individuals to remain invisible. Few Asian parents willingly acknowledge, let alone embrace, their children's homosexuality. Gay musicians thus often develop their identities amidst familial and social disapproval and exclusion. In Asia, as in the United States, there tend to be more gays and lesbians in the performing arts than in most other fields, yet cultural sensitivities and political awareness about homosexuality are generally much less developed than in the United States, and overtly homophobic statements and acts made in public are rarely questioned.

One gay Japanese musician now based in New York vividly remembered an incident from his student days in Japan. His heterosexual female teacher explained to the class that a particular piece of music they were working on was unusually difficult to play because the composer was gay. To him, this remark showed how the prejudice against gays and lesbians was tolerated by Japanese society at large. In contrast, once he moved to New York, he said, his sexual orientation has never been an issue either for himself or for others.

Despite the relatively large number of gay musicians, they still experience homophobia. In 2005, pianist Tony Cho was one of the few openly gay Asian musicians in Honolulu and worked as a pianist and coach for the Hawaii Opera Theatre. (Since then, he has left Hawai'i to work as an opera coach/accompanist at Juilliard.) He said that in the world of music he has never felt discriminated against because of his sexual orientation. However, he recalled that one of his teachers, an internationally acclaimed pianist, did not acknowledge his homosexuality publicly. The teacher believed that being openly gay would hurt one's musical career and advised Cho against being open about his sexual orientation. Cho said that while he was working with this teacher he did not really understand his point of view and thought that he should just come out of the closet, but he later came to wonder whether his teacher's concerns might have some validity.

Sexuality matters to Cho not only in terms of its impact on his musical career but also in his musical understanding. When I asked him whether he thought sexual orientation made a difference in one's understanding, interpretation, or performance of music, his first response was that it made no difference. However, he then went on to give many interesting—and often amusing—examples of the ways in which he thought gay men tended to play differently from straight men, straight women, and lesbian women. After qualifying his comments by saying that "of course it doesn't mean that straight men cannot be sensitive," he offered his general theory about the differences between the piano playing of gay and straight men. Sexual orientation made little difference when dealing with Classical pieces because the music follows strict rules of expression, but when it came to Romantic pieces such as Chopin's compositions, one could tell within thirty seconds whether the pianist was gay based on how he expressed the particular sensitivity and subtlety demanded by the music. Straight male pianists' playing tends to be strong yet often dry, claimed Cho, and it is very suited for masculine, strong music by such composers as Prokofiev and Stravinsky; however, it often misses the subtleties of Romantic composers. He said that gay musicians frequently exchange observations and remarks about other musicians' playing in terms of their sexual orientations.[24]

Many of Cho's observations about sexual orientation in the world of classical music are intricately tied to commonly held notions about gender. Although some of his characterizations may have little substance beyond stereotypes, his comments indicate that, at least for Cho, identifying characteristics of performance based on sexual orientation serves as a way to define and articulate both his gay identity and his own relationship to music. As discussed by recent scholars who have used queer perspectives on musicology, such a self-defined connection between one's musicality and sexuality is a crucial means of expression, disclosure, or communication for those musicians whose culture has instilled a sense of profound and fundamental difference based on sexuality.

Yet, gay and lesbian musicians hardly agree on the nature of the connection between sexuality and musicality—or, for that matter, whether there is such a connection in the first place. When I asked a gay Japanese musician whether his sexual orientation was in any way relevant to his understanding, interpretation, and performance of music, he told me very clearly that he did not believe in any such correlation. "The music I find truly wonderful is the music that transcends things like sexual orientation," he said. "It is widely known that Tchaikovsky was gay, but I think it's ridiculous to say this and that about his sexual identity in relation to his music. Each performer has his or her interpretation of Tchaikovsky, and that is what musical expression is all about." He recalled reading a review of a book about gay American composers [most likely Nadine Hubbs' *The Queer Composition of America's Sound*] and thinking, "What a stupid thing to talk about [i.e., making an issue out of the sexuality of composers]!"[25] He acknowledged that when he is playing pieces by contemporary gay composers whom he knows personally and with whom he can discuss the music, the composer's and performer's sexuality may become part of the creative process. "But then," he stressed, "it's not as if gay musicians can understand one another fully just by being gay. There are plenty of nasty gay musicians that I wouldn't want to work with. So as long as there is an understanding between the composer and the performer on a human level, things like sexuality are really irrelevant." For him, therefore, the power of music lay precisely in its sublime quality—the power to transcend, rather than define or express, sexuality and other forms of identities.

Only a few of my male informants openly identified themselves as gay; no female informant identified herself as lesbian. Consequently, I have limited insights into the meaning of sexuality for gay and lesbian Asian musicians, but what seems clear is that music functions as an expression of self—both defining one's particular identity and opening the self to and communicating with the world. Regardless of whether one agrees with the musical readings of gender and sexuality, musicologist Nadine Hubbs's argument about gay American modernist composers can be applied in general terms to gay musicians' sense of sexual and musical identity. She argues that the creativity of gay modernist composers allowed them to live beyond their stigmatized sexual identity and simultaneously live out their sexual, national, and social identity in the homophobic American culture of the 1920s through the 1970s:

Their culture's homophobia instilled in these queer musicians a sense of profound and fundamental difference. For queer children, adolescents, and adults, classical music was often a solitary outlet—a medium affording nonverbal emotional release, and an "abstract" channel for sublimation and expression of forbidden desires. Queer subjects' perceived socio-sexual difference, moreover, facilitated ready identification with images of bohemianism, solitary genius, and artistic "priesthood." For whereas queerness was a target of pathologizing and scorn, classical music was sublime and transcendent, and as such largely beyond reproach—and so, similarly, those deemed to possess talent in this rarefied art, who were thereby rendered exceptional and transcendent, if not vindicated. As Rorem observes of his own compositional impetus, "Much of it came from 'I'll Show Them,' those ignorant admired bullies who whipped me in grade school."[26]

Conclusion

Because of the gendered and sexualized meanings historically assigned to classical music, musicians—both as musicians and as men and women—grapple with these meanings in their lives as musicians. Many Asian musicians have to negotiate the gender and sexual norms of Asian cultures and families in addition to those of the Western society in which they live and work. Their gender and sexual identities are thus inseparable from their identities as Asians and as musicians. For men, the professional pursuit of classical music itself is often a transgression of middle-class gender norms. On the other hand, female musicians face the challenge of charting their way through the conflicting demands of artistic development, social ideals of femininity, sexual dynamics of the profession, and commercial interests shaped by the history of Asian female images. Those musicians who are gay or lesbian must find their own voices within a culture of homophobia. For Asian musicians, gender and sexual identities, like racial identities, are thus lived and defined through their musical lives.

Chapter 2 and this chapter explored aspects of Asian musicians' identities that are shaped by social and cultural ideas about race, gender, and sexuality. However, these issues are not always at the forefront of the musicians' everyday concerns. When I asked my informants what they thought was the most difficult thing about being a classical musician, many of them answered, "Making a living." Indeed, for many classical musicians, the economic conditions of the profession and a shared sense of their place in society and the market are more significant elements of their identity than race or gender. Chapter 4 addresses the economy of the world of classical music and the issues of class in the lives of Asian and Asian American musicians.

4

Class Notes

There are two, very different popular conceptions of the lives of classical musicians. On the one hand, they are seen as leading lives of glamour, spending their time on stage at such venues as Lincoln Center and Carnegie Hall, wearing beautiful gowns or tuxedos, and performing for rapt audiences who pay a large sum to hear the music they admire. They socialize with wealthy, educated, and sophisticated patrons of the arts. They tour around the world, speak several languages, and are particularly comfortable in Europe. They live fulfilling, rewarding lives performing the music they feel passionate about.

A contrasting image is the classical musician as the struggling artist who is unable to make a living. Hoping for a breakthrough in their solo careers or trying to land a stable orchestra or teaching job, classical musicians spend their days teaching small, restless children, playing a few clichéd pieces of chamber music in weddings, or working at an office job unrelated to music. They go home to their small apartments to practice the orchestral excerpts for the next audition until their neighbors complain about the noise. They have no health insurance, retirement plan, or guaranteed income.

These images of musicians' lives parallel the contrasting images of classical music itself, both as an art form and as an industry. In one view, classical music is considered the epitome of high culture. Unlike popular music that appeals to the masses, classical music—a "pure," abstract music that has no direct meaning outside the music itself—requires trained ears familiar with this musical form; thus, the appreciation of classical music itself is a mark of distinction and of sophisticated taste in the modern world. Patrons of classical music generally represent a small, well-educated, affluent segment of the population. Sociologists have demonstrated that musical tastes differ along class (as well as racial and ethnic) lines and that classical music, anchored at the upper end of the taste hierarchy, is widely considered to be a form of elite culture.[1] When French sociologist Pierre Bourdieu theorized about the connection of cultural taste to class in his influential book, *Distinction,* a significant portion of the data he collected had to do with tastes in music—illustrating the differences among those who prefer the *Art of Fugue, Blue Danube,* or the *Concerto for the Left Hand.* Underscoring the significance of music in class identity, he asserted that "nothing more clearly affirms one's 'class,' nothing more infallibly classifies, than tastes in music."[2] According to this logic, the appreciation for and the practice of classical music are quintessential forms of cultural capital that both signify and enhance one's place in the social hierarchy.

The other commonly held view is that classical music is a rarefied art form that has become irrelevant to most people and is enjoyed only by an aging few. A quick glance at the audience in most symphony concerts or the size and the placement of the classical music section in most record stores confirms this view. The exclusivity of the art form and its restricted audience in turn support the charges of elitism, especially in light of the difficulty of sustaining classical music in today's marketplace.

The economic prospects for classical music are indeed far from promising. In their 1966 study of the economics of the performing arts industry, economists William Baumol and William Bowen argued that the nature of the performing arts, in which the product is the live artists' labor itself, makes it impossible for performing arts institutions to benefit from productivity gains that technological advances bring to other sectors of the economy.[3] If they already made this prediction in the period when state funding for the arts was growing rapidly under the cultural policies of Cold War liberalism, the economic situation for the arts in the decades since the 1980s—when state support for the arts was cut drastically—has been much more dire.[4] The financial difficulties experienced by orchestras around the country in recent decades testify to the accuracy of Baumol and Bowen's prediction of the growing gap between production costs and revenue.

Even as the audience for classical music is aging and shrinking and government funding for arts education is disappearing, conservatories and universities continue to produce thousands of performers each year. A 2004 *New York Times* article traced the careers of those who graduated from Juilliard in 1990 and gave a sobering report that, after years of intensive training in what is often considered the world's best conservatory, nearly half of the respondents had dropped out of performing.[5] Likewise, a recent exposé by oboist-turned-journalist Blair Tindall, *Mozart in the Jungle: Sex, Drugs, and Classical Music,* vividly illustrates the grim paradox of the lives of classical musicians: many enter the field dreaming of a glamorous career and knowing little about their likely destination—a life of stringing together performance gigs and non-musical jobs just to pay the rent. Tindall also points out the skewed economy of the classical music field: famous conductors make millions for fourteen weeks of work a year and a handful of popular soloists perform for tens of thousands of dollars per night, whereas most orchestral musicians barely make middle-class wages even if they are fortunate to land a tenure-track position in a full-time orchestra.[6]

The economic lives of most classical musicians are fraught with contradictions. At once members of the cultural elite and workers selling their labor, they possess scarce skills and expertise, but they generally have limited control in the workplace. This chapter examines how these contradictions play out in the lives of Asian musicians and how their identity as musicians helps them negotiate those contradictions.

Although economic and class issues in classical music affect musicians from all backgrounds, for Asian musicians, the racial logic of the U.S. society and economy complicates matters further. First, aspects of one's background—such as race, nationality, linguistic and cultural fluency, and access to familial and social networks—constitute a form of currency in mainstream society and affect one's class location in important ways.[7] Deficits in these areas can put Asian and Asian American musicians at a disadvantage, impeding their and their families' ability to convert their cultural capital into economic, social, and other forms of capital. Second, each segment of society has particular valuations of "legitimate" culture, and the symbolic boundaries of cultural capital function differently across national and cultural lines. Cultural forms such as classical music have different meanings in Asia and the United States; thus, the cultural capital that Asians acquired in their home country is not necessarily converted into capital that has currency in American culture.[8]

To see how classical music works (or does not work) as a form of capital for Asian musicians, this chapter looks at both the class from which the musicians come and the class in which they end up, as well as the economic and emotional costs of classical music training. Musicians' own understanding of their work illuminates the contradictions between their economic position and their social and cultural identity.

Theorizing Class

According to the classic model of Marxism, one's relationship to the means of production (capital, natural resources, technology, labor, etc.) has a causal effect on one's material welfare and power. Capitalists obtain high levels of wealth and power by obtaining and controlling the allocation of profit; in contrast, the laboring class has less economic wealth and power because it neither possesses nor controls the allocation of profit. In the Marxist model, the capitalist and the working classes have opposing material interests, which brings about both class conflict and the potential capacity for collective action.

However, many economists and sociologists have argued that the classic Marxist model cannot account fully for many aspects of economic relationships and experiences, particularly in a postindustrial society in which many members of the middle class occupy contradictory class locations. Managers are simultaneously in the capitalist class and in the working class, in that they both control workers and are themselves employees who sell their labor. Professionals and experts have a high level of scarce skills and can exercise direct control over their own labor process, but also have to sell their labor power to an employer to earn wages. On the other hand, many in the working class possess certain forms of capital, such as real estate and stocks. In addition, individuals' class locations are often influenced by their social relationships; thus, for many, their kinship networks and family structures determine their economic conditions to a much greater extent than their jobs. These multiple class locations of individuals in the postindustrial economy make it impossible to see material interests exclusively or primarily in terms of one's relationship to the means of production and to view class relations as necessarily polarized and antagonistic.[9]

The usefulness of the Marxist framework for analyzing the economic position of musicians is particularly limited. In the classic Marxist model of production and labor, the very nature of the musical profession—in which the product of the musicians' labor perishes in the very instance of the performance and does not produce a commodity apart from itself—places musicians in the category of "unproductive labor." Needless to say, such a model is inadequate in analyzing how musicians—as well as other cultural producers—are situated in a capitalist economy. In addition, musicians' forms of employment and income vary so greatly that they cannot be classified easily in one economic category. Nonetheless, they generally share the contradictions that characterize the middle class in the postindustrial economy. Their occupation is considered an elite profession, yet many live on the economic margins. They possess highly specialized and scarce expertise and skills, yet rarely have much control over their own labor insofar as they are workers in organizations (such as orchestras, which have a notoriously hierarchical structure, or universities) or their livelihood depends on often unstable jobs that are vulnerable to changing market conditions. A growing portion of their labor depends on commodities in the media, such as recording and broadcasting, and musicians must fight to gain their share of the profit generated by their labor. Professionals in other creative and intellectual fields (such as writers, actors, and some academics) labor under similar conditions, but the extremely long and rigorous training and the costly investments required to enter the profession make the economic contradictions of the classical music profession especially acute.

Whereas Marx fails to explain these contradictions of classical music as a profession, Weber and Bourdieu offer useful approaches. In contrast to Marx, Weber does not see class structure as based strictly on the mode of production, nor does he see class relations as necessarily polarized and antagonistic. Rather than focusing strictly on class *position,* Weber looks more at class *situation,* in which the kind and quantity of resources owned by individuals affect their opportunities for income in market exchanges. Among these resources Weber includes not only the means of production but also non-material forms of capital—such as credentials, prestige, honor, social networks, and the like—which confer different economic opportunities and life chances. Those who share material interests form a status group, rather than a class.

Bourdieu takes the Weberian notion of status group further to explain the significance of symbolic systems in class relations and the ways in which boundaries between classes are produced and maintained. Asserting that class has both an economic and a symbolic dimension, Bourdieu sees "capital" as "the set of actually usable resources and powers." Central to Bourdieu's work is the idea of "cultural capital," a culturally specific competence in a particular social setting that is inculcated in settings such as the family and the educational system. A familiarity with the literary canon and an appreciation for classical music or modern art are examples of cultural capital. Bourdieu used empirical data to analyze the ways in which symbolic practices—mainly in the form of consumption—are central to the production and reproduction of class boundaries. Thus, according to his study, members of the working class, middle class, and upper middle class have different preferences in areas ranging from the style of furniture to genres of painting.

These Bourdieuian notions of cultural and symbolic capital offer useful tools for analyzing classical musicians' *practice* and *performance* of "class." Yet, despite the significant contributions by Bourdieu and other sociologists of culture, the concept of cultural capital remains generally undertheorized, and few empirical studies reveal its exact mechanisms.[10] Sociological studies of cultural capital tend to focus on consumers of culture—for instance, studies of how cultural taste or rates of participation in the arts differ along class lines—rather than on producers of culture.[11] Those that do look at cultural producers more often focus on managers of the arts (managers and board members of art institutions, for instance) rather than on the artists themselves.[12] Such studies are concerned more with the socioeconomic functions of the arts as market commodities than with the locations of artists as class subjects. Furthermore, few scholars have examined how race, ethnicity, and nationality function in the acquisition, investment, and deployment of cultural capital, especially in cross-cultural contexts. Through an analysis of the lives and works of Asian classical musicians, I illuminate the relationship between economic and cultural capital and the significance of their Asian identity in this relationship.

Class Origins

Many musicians are aware of the class-specific nature of the pursuit of classical music, and many of my interviewees opened their stories with an account of their socioeconomic background. Singer Jennifer Shyu began her story by saying, "First of all, economically, because I think that matters, my dad worked for a company as a mechanical engineer. He did engine research. Basically, we never had problems with money. But we were frugal, you know, kind of 'Asian spirit' [laughs]."[13] Pianist Ju-Ying Song began her interview by saying that both her grandmother and her mother were pianists in Taiwan, thereby locating her own upbringing not only economically but also culturally.[14] Other musicians also mentioned their parents' occupations as they began their life stories, indicating their awareness of the connection between their family background and their artistic pursuits.

At the same time, my informants generally did not use the language of class to describe their background and identity. Although most were aware of the privileges of their upbringing and the general class context of classical music practices, they very rarely referred to class per se. This was a noticeable contrast to the substantive and concrete ideas they expressed when discussing race and gender. This lack of class consciousness, which is shared by many members of the middle class, reflects the middle-class backgrounds of most Asian musicians.

Although there are no demographic data on the class background of Asian musicians in the United States today, it is safe to say that the vast majority come from families belonging to the "professional managerial class." Anthropologist Sherry B. Ortner describes this class as comprising "people who are neither owners nor workers, but rather professionals and managers who in a sense operate the system, via specialized knowledge and various forms of power and authority derived therefrom."[15] Most of the Asian musicians I have interviewed have parents who belong to this group, as far as their educational level and occupational category are concerned. Almost all of my informants' fathers have a college degree, and many also held graduate degrees. Many of the musicians' parents worked in fields that are actively connected to the global market, either in the form of international trade or as producers of knowledge shared globally. Hong Kong-based tenor Warren Mok's parents were both physicians. Hawai'i-born violinist

Anna Lim's father was an economist and her mother a mathematician, and the family moved to Vienna when she was in high school. Flutist Joel Tse's father was a Christian minister in Hong Kong who was sent on a mission to a Chinese church in Phoenix, Arizona. Pianist Yi-Heng Yang's father is a computer science professor originally from Taiwan. Korean-born pianist Heejin Shin's father is a professor of business management in Korea and had studied at New York University. Most other musicians' fathers also had similar professional and managerial jobs as business executives, civil officers, diplomats, professors, scientists, and ministers. The majority of the mothers were also college-educated, and some have had teaching jobs in elementary or secondary schools. Some Asian musicians have one or two parents who are or were professional musicians themselves or had conservatory training. Many U.S.-born Asian musicians were raised in middle-class suburban communities outside major cities, such as New York, Philadelphia, Chicago, or Los Angeles, or in university towns. Many Asian-born musicians grew up in urban areas, such as Tokyo, Seoul, Taipei, or nearby areas.

Thus, many of the musicians, including those born in Asia, were raised in families and environments infused with elements of Western arts and culture. For many, the idea of moving abroad to pursue their studies or career was well within reach. In other words, most Asian musicians come from middle-class families with a significant amount of educational and cultural as well as economic capital, which both enabled their exposure to classical music and allowed them to consider pursuing it seriously. At the same time, few classical musicians come from extremely wealthy families, which means that almost all musicians *need* to make a living as wage earners. Only those who believe that they have the talent and skill required to enter and stay in the profession and who make the necessary commitment and sacrifice can afford to pursue a career in music. A serious study of classical music is no leisure-class pursuit, and making a living is very central to the everyday concerns of classical musicians.

On the other hand, few Asian musicians come from working-class backgrounds. None of my interviewees who talked about their parents' occupations referred to blue-collar jobs. The few from less affluent backgrounds keenly felt their difference from their peers, even when in objective terms their family belonged to the middle class.

Pianist Myra Huang is a case in point. Her parents moved from Korea to the United States in 1976. Myra and her older brother spent their childhood in Oregon, where they studied piano and cello, respectively. When she was twelve, the family moved to New York so that the children could attend Juilliard Pre-College. In this sense, hers was a typical example of an Asian American family investing the entire family fortune in the children's musical training. Huang recalled the particular culture of Pre-College: "In Pre-College, the Asian mothers are very famous amongst the faculty. In fact, . . . because the faculty is very Caucasian, non-Asian, you know . . . they don't really understand such extreme supervision from the mothers. It's pretty clear to me that [the faculty] think that it's too much. . . . Because you see these Asian mothers hovering together on Saturdays, like in the lobby or in the cafeteria. . . . You definitely don't see as many non-Asian mothers doing that." When I asked her if her own mother spent her Saturdays that way, she explained that her parents started a dry-cleaning business on moving to New York and her mother could not leave the store to accompany her to Pre-College. She said, "So [my brother and I] were like one of the few 'orphans' who were there without our parents, and I had to wait at the end of the day for them to pick us up. . . . Most of the parents who were there were more wealthy. So they didn't work. You know, I think most of them either were just housewives or didn't have to have a full-time job."[16] She was thus aware at a young age of the socioeconomic differences between her family, which lived a modest life of small business owners, and other wealthier Asian families at Pre-College.

Such class marking in the field of classical music is apparent in East Asia as well. Flutist Frederick Lau remembered his first year as a music major in a Hong Kong university as particularly difficult, not only because he had started studying music much later than his classmates and had much catch-up work to do but also because he felt he did not fit into the social mold: "It's not just the music, it's . . . the whole makeup of that place. Everyone was from *proper* family, rich family, all these people. And I was really from the country, I'm from the island [off of Hong Kong], you know. So I walk around in my slippers when everyone is wearing nice, *proper* clothes, and I'm in ripped T-shirts and jeans, and I was with my friends, playing guitar and singing songs, and everybody looked down on that stuff."[17] He felt that his background—familial, economic, and musical—did not carry the cultural capital that was valued in the university setting, especially in the music department in which classical music was considered the only legitimate pursuit.

However, to characterize Asian musicians as coming primarily from the privileged middle class is somewhat misleading. The meaning of the "middle class" is highly fluid and complex in East Asia and in Asian American communities.

For instance, according to political scientist Richard Kraus, the urban middle class in China—comprising bourgeois capitalists, intellectuals, and Communist officialdom—is less a class than a status group that shares the symbols of culture. Throughout the turbulent history of modern China—from the Revolutionary War, the Cultural Revolution, to the reform era under Deng Xiaoping—the status of the urban middle class has varied greatly. In Kraus's words, "Alien yet patriotic, revolutionary yet elitist, this class continues to be alternately admired and resented in China today."[18] Western culture and artists who pursue it therefore have had a highly variable reception in China, and the lives of many of the Chinese musicians in America today who studied Western music during or shortly after the Cultural Revolution bear little resemblance to those of the American middle class.

Pianist Bichuan Li was born to a family of considerable wealth in China. Her grandfather owned a factory, and she grew up in a large house with a piano. Her aunt had studied at Juilliard, and music study was an integral part of her upbringing. She started taking piano lessons at age four. She recalled in the interview, "I didn't even know that not everyone had piano in their house until I was ten, when I realized that people in my class didn't know how to play the piano. I thought everybody had the piano and everybody had to practice. For me, it was just natural." Yet, in Communist China, children of workers and peasants were given priority in the education system, and although she auditioned three times for the conservatory, she was not admitted due to her privileged family background. Moreover, once the Cultural Revolution was underway, her family came under attack, the piano was taken away, and their sheet music was burned. She stopped going to school when she was thirteen and went to work in a restaurant from 4 A.M. to 10 P.M. seven days a week. During her long lunch break, she visited friends and relatives who had a piano and practiced on it. As there was no sheet music, she copied all music by hand. Although a handful of students, all from worker and peasant families, were admitted to conservatories during the Cultural Revolution, such opportunities were not available to Li. Thus, every six months or so, she would take lessons from conservatory teachers who were willing to teach; however, because they were not allowed to give private lessons, they would not take money but rather would be paid in the form of various favors. In this way, for eight years she studied the piano mostly on her own, with a very restricted repertoire, as the only music that students were allowed to play were revolutionary music and études.

When the Cultural Revolution came to an end and the conservatories reopened, she was too old to enroll, but she was able to pass an extremely competitive entrance examination for a teacher's college. There she studied music with a conservatory faculty member who came to teach at the college. Then, in her last year in college, she applied to travel to the United States, choosing to study at the University of Hawai'i because she had relatives on the island. She arrived with $40 in her pocket. Her parents sent her just enough money for one semester, and her relatives allowed her to live with them for four months, after which she had to find a way to support herself. With much determination, she studied English to pass the examination required for admission to the graduate program and then earned graduate assistantships that paid her tuition. She took on some teaching and accompaniment gigs to supplement her income.

Since graduating, she has made a living through a combination of teaching jobs and performances, but she stressed the difficulty of making a living as a performer. As her life story shows, it is impossible to explain a musician with her background according to the U.S. model of class relations. Both the economic status and cultural capital of the middle class had adverse meanings in China during the Cultural Revolution. After moving to the United States, she had to navigate the capitalist economy that does not easily reward classical musicians.[19]

In postwar Japan, dramatic economic growth, urban sprawl, smaller family size, and the escalation of educational credentialing led to a national "middle-classification," of which the pursuit of Western music was an important part. Yet, the middle class in Japan has fared quite differently from the U.S. middle class.[20] Despite a dramatic growth in real consumption per capita in Japan, it has lagged far behind that of the United States, being only slightly more than 60 percent of the U.S. figure, even during the bubble economy of the 1980s. Furthermore, Japan's household savings rate has been double, triple, or sometimes more that of the United States.[21] Because their disposable income is so much lower than that of U.S. middle-class families, spending by Japanese families on such pursuits as children's music lessons consumes a much larger proportion of their incomes, indicating the importance of the accumulation of cultural capital to their class aspirations.

After its liberation from Japan's colonization, subsequent land reform, and the devastation of the Korean War, South Korea went through major social and economic changes. The economic reforms in the 1960s presented increased opportunities for social mobility, and the following decades saw growth of a new middle class, which drew its membership from both former landed aristocracy (*yangban*) and commoner families. In contrast to both Japan and the West, which experienced growth in commerce and manufacturing before industrialization, in postwar Korea, growth in what is classified in other societies as the "old middle class" has been accompanied by an increase in the number of manual laborers and expansion of the so-called new middle class comprised of urban professionals and salaried, white-collar workers. Few members of the new middle class depend solely on their occupations to sustain a middle-class lifestyle, and they draw a significant portion of their income from property ownership or family businesses. The combination of three factors—the continued significance of Confucian ideas of social stratification, the status aspirations of the new middle class, and the desire of members of the old middle class to distinguish themselves from the nouveau riche through the accumulation of cultural capital rather than conspicuous consumption—has produced a competitive pursuit of status through education, occupation, lifestyle, and marriage. The enthusiasm for classical music training is one manifestation of status-seeking among South Korea's urban middle class.[22]

Although many of the second-, third-, and fourth-generation Asian Americans and first- and 1.5-generation Asian immigrants who arrived in the United States after 1965 technically belong to the American middle class, their life experiences have also been shaped by the specific experiences of their ethnic group in the United States. For example, wartime internment robbed Japanese Americans of their hard-earned assets on the West Coast, and they had to rebuild their livelihoods from scratch in the postwar decades. Although Japanese Americans' educational and economic attainment led the media to characterize the group as the "model minority," the portrayal glossed over the complexities of American race relations that the Japanese Americans and other Asian Americans still had to navigate. The Immigration Act of 1965 dramatically increased the number of Asian immigrants from Korea, China, the Philippines, and India. Unlike the earlier wave of Asian immigrants who came to the United States to engage in agricultural and other manual labor, many of these new immigrants were highly educated, urban professionals who came to the United States under the category of occupational preference. Yet, as I discuss later in this chapter, the life trajectories of many of these professionals have been hampered by the racialized economic structure, often resulting in downward social mobility.[23]

The Cost of Class(ical)

Classical music training is largely limited to members of the middle and upper middle classes not only because interest in classical music is closely connected to cultural and educational capital but also because serious training in music requires a large amount of economic capital. The cost of this training puts it usually beyond the reach of those without at least a middle-class income and lifestyle.

First, one has to purchase an instrument, and the better and more expensive the instrument, the better the sound. Many musicians who had no access to high-quality instruments until they came to the United States—particularly those from China—commented that they experienced a major shock when playing them for the first time. Many musicians and their parents sacrifice to purchase such instruments. Some musicians are loaned the instrument through patrons or sponsoring organizations, but such arrangements are rare and usually available only to those who win major competitions. Generally, the most expensive instruments are the string instruments; one that meets professional standards can easily cost five or six figures. Grand pianos also cost five figures. Other instruments such as brass and woodwinds usually cost less, yet musicians often own several instruments, and the cost of routine maintenance amounts to thousands of dollars annually.

Private lessons and tuition are another major and long-term expense borne by the family. Private lessons by reputable teachers who prepare students for competitions and conservatory auditions can cost anywhere from around $50 to more than $100 per hour, and most students take such lessons weekly. After passing the audition, the musicians have to find ways to fund their conservatory training. In 2006–07, tuition at the Juilliard School was $25,610, and at the Manhattan School of Music it was $27,400. Most conservatories charge comparable tuition. Many students receive scholarships, which make it possible for them to attend. However, even with a scholarship that covers tuition and some living expenses, few can live comfortably on financial aid alone, and many students, particularly international students from China, work to pay the bills. These jobs cut into their practice time and cause a great deal of stress and anxiety about future prospects.

Chinese violinist Wen Qian, now leading a successful career as an assistant concertmaster for the Metropolitan Opera Orchestra, told me about her first year at the Boyer School of Music and Dance at Temple University. Her parents sold everything possible and borrowed all the money they could to buy her ticket to the United States, and she arrived with a few hundred dollars in her pocket. Although she received a full scholarship, she still had to work in a restaurant for $25 a night to pay the bills. In her second month in the United States, she spilled hot soup at the restaurant and burned her hand badly, which kept her both from playing the violin and working. At the time she was making $200 a month and paying out $130 of that for rent. A major turning point in her life in the United States came in her second year, when she and her friend came up with the idea to approach a foundations center to obtain a list of hundreds of potential sponsors. She wrote letters to all of them, describing her situation and asking for any form of support. One patron of Carnegie Hall, a close friend of Isaac Stern, answered the letter and offered to provide her $6,000 per year. This patronage allowed her to move to New York where she studied with the prominent violinist Felix Galimir at the Mannes School of Music.[24] Few musicians exercise such ingenuity or have such good fortune in gaining financial support; for most, juggling academic demands and practicing while dealing with financial need is a major source of stress.

Travel expenses for lessons, competitions, and auditions also comprise a considerable cost for musicians and their families. Some students living outside metropolitan areas with a pool of high-quality teachers regularly travel hundreds or even thousands of miles to take lessons. As a child, violinist David Kim flew to New York from South Carolina every other weekend to attend Juilliard Pre-College.[25] During my fieldwork in Matsumoto, Japan, I met an eight-year-old girl and her mother from Oklahoma who had flown in for two weeks to study with a reputable violin teacher at the headquarters of the Suzuki Method. During school vacations, it is not uncommon for music students from Japan and Korea to travel to the United States or Europe for a few weeks to take intensive lessons with certain teachers. Such short-term study abroad costs at least several thousand dollars.

Many musicians pay to perform and to record. Some put up their own money to hold concerts in venues such as the Weill Recital Hall at Carnegie Hall in hopes of being reviewed and attracting the attention of sponsors, managers, or powerful musicians. Most musicians other than keyboard players also need to pay an accompanist both for rehearsals and performances. When producing their own recordings—which many musicians pursuing a solo career do—they have to pay for the recording venue, engineer, production, distribution, publicity, and so forth. Other costs, such as entrance fees for competitions or summer music festivals and clothing to wear for performances, add up to a substantial amount.

The families of musicians in training must make not only a major monetary investment but also a significant time and emotional investment. At least until the students reach their mid-teens, their parents' routine responsibilities include transporting their children to lessons, observing their lessons and supervising their daily practice, consulting with their teacher about their progress and goals, and attending their performances and competitions. Most parents of serious music students gladly take on such roles—sometimes against the wishes of their children—even at the expense of their own professional or personal lives. Still, it is undeniable that such forms of parental investment require at least a middle-class income and lifestyle.

This major investment in music training often takes a significant emotional toll both on the musicians themselves and their families. The stereotypes of overbearing Asian parents who push their children with Spartan discipline and demand excellence through constant criticism are not entirely unfounded, as the close monitoring of children's academic and extracurricular achievements is a socially sanctioned component of parenting among much of the East Asian middle class. For many young musicians, such parental pressures effectively kill any pleasure associated with music itself, leading them to abandon music altogether with much bitterness. Even among those who have chosen to pursue music professionally and have embraced music as their passion, there are many who feel scarred by the way in which their lives were defined by music early in childhood. A number of my informants told me stories, either about themselves or their friends, of deep emotional tension with parents as a result of the demands placed on them for musical excellence.

A story shared by a violist from Taiwan exemplifies such a tension. She studied piano and viola in an experimental school for talented students in Taiwan and moved to New York to live with her relatives at age sixteen to study at Juilliard Pre-College. A few years later, her parents joined her in the United States, but her father soon passed away from cancer and she had to support herself and her family through teaching and freelancing. In addition to performing, she ran a non-profit organization that provides quality music education to underprivileged children in the Dominican Republic. She thus clearly found her own way of pursuing her passion, using music as a medium for promoting communication and peace. Yet as she told me about her life, she candidly shared the emotional pain that was very much a part of her path to becoming a musician. She used the word "brainwashed" to talk about her life course: she was led to believe by her parents and her teachers that music was what she was supposed to do for the rest of her life. She remembered her school in Taiwan as a very close-knit community of students who were put in constant competition with each other; the school provided no support system and the teachers had no understanding of child psychology. She recalled that her father rarely came to her concerts, and her mother, in pushing her to achieve excellence, never complimented her. She came to the conclusion that her parents were pushing her to fulfill their own ambitions and that because they lacked an understanding of an artistic career, they were unable to provide the emotional support she needed as a child. Around age twelve she consciously cut her parents out of her life and decided not to rely on them emotionally. When her mother told her recently that she could have pursued other activities besides music, she was shocked that her mother dared make such a statement, as she felt that she was never given any other option.

This feeling of never having had any options in life but music is fairly common among classical musicians, and many musicians go through extremely painful periods of soul-searching. For some, this period occurs during their years in conservatories when they suddenly lose their special identity as musicians because they are surrounded by so many top-level musicians. Others face practical and emotional challenges as they struggle to make a living in the professional world and find themselves lacking marketable knowledge or skills outside of music.

Given the huge monetary and emotional cost of classical music training, why do so many Asian parents push their children to study music?

Although motivations vary, of course, the desire of many Asian parents to have their children study music is at least driven partly by notions of symbolic distinction and, in the case of Asian immigrants in the United States, the aspiration for assimilation and upward mobility. In Asia, Western classical music carries additional value because of its Western-ness. As discussed in Chapter 1, in East Asian countries, the familiarity with and training in Western music are associated with middle-class status and Western-style modernity. When I asked my informants why they thought Asian parents feel so strongly about classical music in particular, their answers pointed to the issue of class and social mobility. Pianist Jihea Hong commented, "Koreans value education. And I think people still believe that music will make kids smarter. . . . And . . . social status, I'm sure that's part of why people [push their children to study music]."[26] Some described their parents' aspirations in terms of Western cultural hegemony: "Western culture is idolized in Asia. It's like this blind following of classical music, and blind acceptance, like mimicking," argued pianist Yi-Heng Yang.[27]

Many musicians pointed out the significance of music for immigrants in the United States and drew a connection between Jewish immigrants of the preceding generation and Asians and Asian Americans today. Because Jews were excluded from many occupations in the early twentieth century, music became one of the few avenues open for them to advance in American society and assimilate into the mainstream culture.[28] Likewise, for Asian immigrants with limited language skills and social capital, music serves as a tool for assimilation into and acceptance by American society.[29] Classical music is particularly useful in this respect because it is a form of Western high culture and Asians' accomplishment in that field presumably proves their embrace and mastery of Western culture.[30]

These interconnected forces of Western cultural hegemony and class relations lead many Asians to believe that mastery of Western classical music is a ticket to assimilation and upward social mobility in mainstream Western society and to success in the global arena. Many Asian parents project this dream onto their children. Indeed, students who have had rigorous music training acquire discipline and focus that often lead to academic and professional achievement in fields other than music. In fact, many parents send their children to Julliard Pre-College not because they want their children to pursue music professionally but because they think that attendance there looks good on their college application. It is true that students with serious music training who choose not to pursue music professionally do tend to enter prestigious universities. Violinist Anna Lim, who has been teaching violin at Princeton University for several years, said that non-music majors who take violin lessons at Princeton play at an incredibly high level because many of them studied at Juilliard Pre-College or have had comparable training. She said that students taking music lessons as non-majors at Ivy League schools are often better prepared than those at an average music conservatory. Not surprisingly, these non-music majors with rigorous music training generally end up in high-income and high-status professions. In large cities such as New York, there are amateur orchestras consisting entirely of physicians and lawyers, indicating the number of people in those professions who have musical training. In addition, as discussed in Chapter 3, in Japan and Korea, women with degrees from prestigious conservatories are considered to have high value in the marriage market and tend to marry men from respectable, upper-middle-class families. In this sense, as symbolic capital circulating in society at large, classical music does function as an effective tool of class reproduction or upward mobility within Asian or American society. Bourdieu's argument that various forms of capital—economic, cultural, and social—are mutually convertible and together yield personal power and class position holds true for the most part. As long as one does not pursue it professionally, classical music *does* function as a form of cultural capital that is then converted into economic and social capital.

But to what extent does classical music really function as a form of capital for those who pursue it professionally? Despite some extraordinary success stories of Asian musicians who have attained international acclaim, most Asian families' investment in the child's music training does not generate a rewarding return, at least in economic terms. In fact, many Asian families end up trading in their economic capital to purchase the cultural capital of classical music. Although this investment is made in the hopes that cultural capital will translate into other forms of capital, such conversion happens only rarely and with great difficulty for Asian musicians and their families. The stories of these Asian musicians—especially the "immigrant geniuses" whose families immigrated to the United States specifically so they could study music, often at a very young age (see Chapter 2)—reveal not only the market conditions of classical music in America but also the relationship among symbolic, economic, and social capital and the terms of its conversion across national borders.

Although the life of a classical musician is difficult for anybody, Asian immigrants face additional challenges because America's racialized society and economy alters the value of the social capital their family acquired in their home country. Precisely because a musical career does not secure significant and stable economic capital, the economic position of musicians is greatly mediated by factors other than their work—including race, nationality, and social and familial ties. As a result, many families of immigrant geniuses in fact experience downward social mobility. Unlike families that emigrate to pursue professional opportunities for the adults, families that relocate internationally for their children's music training often cannot sustain the economic, social, and cultural standards they held in their home country because the breadwinner's professional or linguistic skills cannot be directly converted into currency valued in the American market. Many end up owning small businesses, which grant them a certain degree of autonomy but limited social and economic power, especially compared to the level they enjoyed in their home country.

Stories told by my informants, even those who have been successful in obtaining performance opportunities and visibility, illustrate the difficulty of the transnational conversion of social capital. Violinist Chee-Yun [Kim] won her first competition in Korea at age eight, and at age thirteen she moved to New York to live with her sister who was already studying at Juilliard. Two years later, her parents joined them in the United States. Her father was an import/export businessman in Korea. After coming to the United States, he opened a liquor store but had a difficult time and was soon hugely in debt. One day, when Chee-Yun was a teenager, her father called a family meeting at which he told the children that he was broke and that they had to develop their careers on their own and support themselves. As devastating as this news was to Chee-Yun who had depended on her parents financially and emotionally, it strengthened her musical resolve, and she entered several competitions. She won the Young Concert Artists Competition in 1989 and was granted a three-year management contract, which launched her on the path of a performing career. She is now a successful artist who tours all over the world, collaborates with several contemporary composers, and has many recordings.[31] However, many musicians are not as successful as Chee-Yun and end up leaving the classical music field.

These stories illustrate the limited cross-national convertibility of cultural capital. Although Bourdieu's analysis is useful in understanding the making and reproduction of class within a given social structure, the examination of the currency of "capital," particularly a cultural one, in a transnational context requires a modified model. Sociologist Michèle Lamont's comparative study of the French and American upper middle class shows that the valuation of symbolic boundaries of "legitimate culture," as well as the permeability of those boundaries, varies by nation (and, by implication, by social segments of a nation).[32] National differences in the mechanisms of cultural capital make it particularly difficult for transnational migrants to carry it across national borders and to convert it to other forms of capital in their new home.

The difference between the social functions of classical music in Asia and in the United States is a case in point. Several musicians born or raised in the United States who have performed in Asia commented that they were pleasantly surprised to find that classical music audiences in Asia are generally much younger than those in the United States and that prominent classical musicians enjoy popularity similar to that of a pop star. In contrast to Asia where Western classical music is associated with prestige and status to those trained in it, the relative marginality of classical music in mainstream American culture and economy assigns a much different status to those who pursue it.

Anthropologist Aihwa Ong has argued that "under . . . flexible accumulation, it is primarily economic capital that is being converted into all other forms of capital, not the other way around."[33] Discussing the constraints placed on the accumulation of capital by race and nationality, Ong shows that immigrants have difficulty converting the cultural capital acquired in the home country into social capital in their adopted society because of the perceived mismatch between the distinction of their symbolic capital and their racial identity. "The point is not that money cannot buy everything," Ong argues, "but that accumulation of symbolic capital can only go so far in converting prestige and honor into social capital that will increase access to institutionalized relationships of mutual acquaintance and recognition in particular cultural economies."[34] Ong's untangling of symbolic capital from social capital is especially useful in understanding the convertibility of capital across national and cultural borders. To convert the symbolic capital of classical music training into economic and social power in American society, Asian musicians and their families require many types of resources in addition to the musical training itself.

The Class Destination: The Economic Lives of Classical Musicians

To fully understand the meanings of the investment in classical music made by Asian musicians and their families, one needs to look at how classical musicians fare once they become professionals. The varied lifestyles of classical musicians demonstrate the diverse and often precarious nature of their livelihood, which makes their status difficult to classify.

When those outside the music world think of Asian classical musicians, they typically think of solo performers who tour around the world—such as Yo-Yo Ma, Midori, Sarah Chang, and Lang Lang—because they are the most visible and recognizable. Indeed, most musicians—especially pianists and many violinists—begin their professional training aspiring to have a solo career. However, only a very tiny fraction of professional musicians, Asian or otherwise, make a living as soloists. And even for those who manage to have a solo career, the reality of their everyday lives is often dramatically different from the glamorous image associated with a concertizing career.

Many of the musicians who make it primarily as solo performers mostly achieve the status either by being discovered by a prominent mentor and then given the opportunity for a major debut performance or by winning a prestigious competition at an early stage in their careers. Winning competitions and giving major debut performances provide visibility that leads to numerous performance opportunities. In addition, sometimes prize winners are put on the roster of a management agency that provides booking and publicity services.

Some soloists make their debuts at a very young age. When she was eleven, violinist Midori made her debut with the New York Philharmonic conducted by Zubin Mehta, who had heard about her talent from her influential mentor Dorothy DeLay. Likewise, Sarah Chang auditioned for Zubin Mehta and Riccardo Muti at age eight, which led to her New York Philharmonic debut and subsequent career. Cellist Han-Na Chang's career began with her winning the Rostropovich Competition at age eleven.

However, most soloists' debut performances occur somewhat later—mostly in their teens and their twenties. Violinist Kyoko Takezawa had won national competitions in Japan and already had performance experience when she came to the United States, but it was winning the International

Violin Competition in Indianapolis while she was a Juilliard student that launched her concertizing career. Pianist Jon Nakamatsu had an unusual background for a classical musician in that he never studied at a conservatory and all of his musical training came from private lessons. After earning a bachelor's degree in German and a master's degree in education from Stanford University, he taught high-school German while studying piano on his own. In 1997, he won first place in the Van Cliburn International Piano Competition, which completely changed his life overnight.

Successful soloists indeed make a considerable amount of money. Yo-Yo Ma, probably the most visible and successful Asian musician today, is estimated to earn more than $50,000 per concerto performance with an orchestra. Concerto fees for other international stars—Sarah Chang and Midori, for example—are estimated to be around $25,000 to $50,000. Musicians who have attained this level of prominence also receive considerable income from recordings.

Yet, the vast majority of soloists—even those who have wide visibility and extensive bookings—make considerably less. In a society where the market for classical music is rapidly shrinking and aging, only a handful of solo musicians make a living from performances alone. Even for those who earn several thousand dollars per recital or concerto performance with an orchestra, when one considers the amount of time and effort necessary to maintain and improve their level of playing and to expand their repertoire, the cost of instruments, the fees paid to management (which typically are 15 to 20 percent of the net revenue), and the physical and emotional toll of constant traveling, a solo performance career can hardly be characterized as lucrative. Sustaining a successful solo career, even after a major triumph in competitions and debut concerts, depends to a significant degree on intangible factors, such as luck, personality, and audience and media appeal, that have little to do with musicality itself. Many musicians who attain success early in their career become exhausted from too many performances and insufficient time for practice, rest, and a personal life, yet they have to keep performing to make a living and to maintain their visibility. Some are pressured by market demands to play a repertoire that appeals to the mainstream audience and so become entertainers who merely please the audience or performers who only follow conventions. In addition, performers often experience injuries from constant practicing that keep them from practicing or performing for a considerable period of time. Not a few musicians experience depression and other forms of mental illness because of the intensity and uncertainties of their work.

Many young musicians who play orchestral instruments pursue their musical training with the dream of becoming a member of a major orchestra that will grant them the opportunity to perform a broad repertoire with talented musicians and to attain economic stability. Although there are more opportunities for an orchestra career than for a solo career, it is still extremely competitive to gain a position in a full-time orchestra. Positions open only sporadically. During the 2003 calendar year, there were a total of 159 openings for musicians in all the orchestras that belong to the International Conference of Symphony and Opera Musicians (ICSOM; comprised of fifty-two American orchestras that pay a full-time living wage).[35] For instruments that have a small number of positions in each orchestra—for instance, harp, bass trombone, tuba, and timpani—an opening may come only once in many years. Consequently, auditions are highly competitive. An opening for a section violinist in a mid-level orchestra such as the Buffalo Philharmonic or the Phoenix Symphony typically draws more than 100 applicants. Musicians have to pay their own way to travel to auditions, even those across the country or overseas. Auditions often occur over the course of several rounds, and although the musician must prepare a wide range of music—concerti as well as orchestral excerpts from different periods—their fate is determined in only a few minutes of "anonymous" playing behind a curtain. Although the auditions are generally conducted in a fair and systematic fashion, sometimes such factors as one's schools, teachers, and personal connections play a role as well. Then, even a musician fortunate enough to land a position in an orchestra is hired on a probationary basis for the first year or two, at the end of which the music director can decide to deny tenure without providing specific reasons.[36]

Working conditions in orchestras vary widely. Large orchestras have 52-week contracts with a full performing season, which give musicians the opportunity to play a broad repertoire with a range of conductors and soloists.[37] The salaries of orchestra musicians are determined by collective bargaining by the local union. The Big Five orchestras in the United States—the Boston Symphony, the Chicago Symphony, the Cleveland Orchestra, the New York Philharmonic, and the Philadelphia Orchestra—also have endowments ranging from $100 million to $280 million, which allowed them to offer a minimum salary for the 2004–05 season of more than $100,000.

Other major orchestras, such as the Los Angeles Philharmonic Orchestra, the San Francisco Symphony, and the Metropolitan Opera Orchestra, have comparable or higher base salaries. First-chair players can sometimes triple their base salary, and most section players also earn more than the minimum because of overtime, seniority, recordings, and media appearances.

Yet, the vast majority of orchestras in the country offer nowhere near such excellent working conditions. During the 2003–04 season, for musicians in the ICSOM, the average minimum salary was $57,370, with the lowest being $23,000.[38] To support themselves and their families, musicians receiving salaries on the low end of the scale often take on dozens of students (if they play instruments that draw many students) or a second job in addition to playing in rehearsals and concerts every week. Because they have shorter seasons and more infrequent concerts than big orchestras, the repertoire they get to play is also more limited. The orchestra's ability to bring in top-level guest conductors and soloists is also dependent on their finances. As most orchestras have a shrinking and aging audience base and modest endowments and outside funding, a handful of wealthy individual and corporate donors wield huge influence. Contract negotiations are often tense, strikes are not rare, and frequently orchestra musicians are pressured to accept drastic pay cuts in their already modest salary under threat of bankruptcy. In addition, the public's perception that classical music is not a bread-and-butter issue for a community makes the musicians' salary struggles even more difficult. Technological advances and changing audience expectations for musical performances also threaten the profession. When asked what he thought was the biggest challenge about being a classical musician, Conway Kuo, a violinist for the New York City Ballet orchestra, reflected on the time when the orchestra went on strike and the management weathered the situation by playing a tape in lieu of a live orchestra: "Basically [the management] showed [the orchestra] that it is possible to have a performance without us."[39]

Under these circumstances, unlike many others in intellectual and cultural professions who usually prefer not to think of themselves as the laboring class and are reluctant to unionize, orchestra musicians are generally well informed and actively involved in union matters and have an acute sense of their profession being under siege. Symphony musicians are among the most highly unionized of all industries in the United States today.

In addition to landing an orchestra job, another way for classical musicians to gain economic stability is to become a member of the faculty at a university or conservatory. A faculty position grants musicians a combination of economic security, the freedom and flexibility to pursue their performance career, and the ability to impart their knowledge and skills to the next generation. Many musicians seek a teaching position in a university or conservatory by earning a Doctorate of Musical Arts (DMA). After landing a tenure-track position in a university, music faculty have many responsibilities, including giving private lessons; conducting master classes; teaching classes, such as music theory, keyboard literature, or ear training; coaching chamber groups or orchestra; and directing thesis/dissertation research. Faculty are also expected to give recitals on a regular basis. Particularly in smaller cities with a limited number of performing musicians, faculty perform in various venues in the community, serve as judges and faculty at regional competitions and workshops, and also often give private lessons to interested students outside the university.

Most classical musicians who do not have a position in an orchestra or a university/conservatory work as freelance musicians. Their activities range widely from giving solo concerts, playing as an accompanist, substituting in orchestras, and playing in chamber ensembles and in musical theater to playing various gigs such as weddings, making recordings for films or commercials, and teaching private students. Although some musicians welcome the freedom and flexibility of a freelance career, freelancing has the serious downside of the lack of security and benefits. Most freelancers also spend a considerable amount of time traveling from one gig to another. Many musicians think of freelancing as their temporary situation until they land an orchestra job or make a breakthrough as a soloist; however, because they are playing in many gigs to make ends meet, they often have little time to practice, and it becomes increasingly difficult to effectively prepare for auditions or give polished performances. It is also difficult to maintain one's artistic integrity and autonomy when one must perform whatever music is required, sometimes without even a single rehearsal, to audiences that are not always fully appreciative of the music or their performance. In addition, because of the limited number of available gigs, making a living as a freelancer is next to impossible in many places outside of large metropolitan areas.

Moreover, unlike orchestra and university positions where the hiring process is systematized and mechanisms are in place that prevent discrimination, the freelance market has few such institutionalized safeguards. To sustain a living as a freelance musician, one needs to have many personal connections in the local and regional music scene as well as the personality, social skills, and political savvy that facilitate networking and working with others. Therefore, recent immigrants or those without linguistic and cultural fluency find it difficult to navigate the freelance scene. A Chinese violinist who has been working as a freelance musician in New York since graduating from Juilliard in 1990 commented, "In the freelance world, getting jobs has nothing to do with the level of playing; it has everything to do with schmoozing." Some Asian musicians do market their Asian identity to their advantage, and metropolitan cities with large numbers of Asian musicians, such as New York and San Francisco, have networks that support Asian musicians. For instance, when a well-known Korean American agent in New York books musicians for gigs such as film recordings, she first calls on Asian musicians in her professional network. Yet it requires personal connections to enter such a network. In addition, employers can make negative judgments based on racial prejudice without being held accountable, and more often than not, Asian musicians experience negative associations with their Asian identity in the freelance scene. Interestingly, most of my informants who said they felt there is racism in the field of classical music were working as freelance musicians.

Given the far from lucrative nature of their work and their unstable relationship to the market, it is difficult to pinpoint the class position of classical musicians, even within the fluid field of the middle class in late capitalist society.[40] A musician's economic position is contingent on several factors, including the form of employment, the size and stability of the employer, the availability of performing opportunities in a particular region, and access to professional and social networks. Often their economic position is mediated by social relationships, such as kinship networks and family structures that provide varying degrees of economic support and stability. Classical musicians are also situated in a contradictory economic position as being professionals and laborers simultaneously. This contradictory position shapes the ways in which they understand and articulate their place in the larger economy and society.

Performing Class: Maneuvering the "Field" of Cultural Production

Most classical musicians occupy an economic position that is highly ambiguous and unstable; yet, the material dimensions of their work and lifestyle do not exclusively determine the meaning of their "class." For many musicians, pride in their cultural standards and values compensates for a lack of economic capital and social power. For them, "class" is more meaningful as a form of social, cultural, and occupational *identity* with a shared value system than as an economic *position*. Such an identity is *practiced* and *performed* through articulations and enactments of the values governing the field of classical music, which are often juxtaposed against those shaping other fields, especially that of dominant society.

Bourdieu's notion of "field" is useful in understanding the world of classical music. In Bourdieu's model, society is structured by a combination of related but also mutually autonomous "fields," such as an economic field, political field, religious field, educational field, or cultural field. A field is a social arena that has its own arrangement of various forms of capital according to its own logic, rules, and value system; in each field, individuals maneuver to pursue resources that have currency in it. Although economic capital plays a central role in all fields, each field also has laws of operation that are not governed by economics. Hence, the field of cultural production, particularly the "restricted" field of intellectuals and artists for which the goal is not necessarily to reach the mass market, has its own hierarchy of different forms of capital; economic capital occupies a relatively low place in this hierarchy.

The often oppositional way in which my informants talked about their own economic and class position illustrates the nature of the field of classical music. On the one hand, by emphasizing their and their families' educational background, lifestyle, and appreciation of the arts, the musicians position themselves implicitly and explicitly in the middle class. On the other hand, the musicians are also quite aware of the relatively marginalized position of the classical music field in mainstream American society, and they articulate their values in opposition to what they see as the materialistic pursuit of wealth, mass commercialization of the arts, and conformity to mainstream culture and popular taste. By thus situating themselves in juxtaposition both to those outside their economic status and to those who do not share the same cultural values, the musicians map out their own value economy that shapes the field of classical music. It is this positioning in the field of cultural production rather than their location in the economic market that constitutes the shared social identity—if not class position or class consciousness—of classical musicians.[41]

Violinist Mari Kimura's articulation of her own position and values exemplifies the concept of the field of classical music. Kimura began our interview by commenting that "[i]n the United States, class determines who can afford to study classical music." She contrasted this with Japanese society in which, according to her, "the majority of the population belongs to the middle class or above," and therefore more people have access to classical music training. She then began telling her own story by describing her parents' background. Her maternal grandmother was a college-educated social worker in Kochi Prefecture in Japan, and Kimura's mother grew up listening to her mother counseling battered women while she was practicing the piano in the next room. Although Kimura's mother wanted to study music, she felt inspired by her mother's work and became a legal scholar instead. Kimura's father was a pioneer in the study of solar energy. Her parents met when they were on the same ship from Japan to America; he was on his way to study at MIT and she at Mount Holyoke College. Kimura thus grew up in a family with experiences and connections to life in the United States.

Having been raised in Tokyo, Kimura left Japan in 1985 to study violin at Boston University and then at Juilliard. After meeting a professor of artificial intelligence, she became interested in electronic music and gradually became involved in architectural acoustics and computer music. She now composes and performs music using both acoustic and electronic violin. In explaining her interest in this genre of music, which is quite unconventional for a classically trained musician, she said,

> Perhaps it had something to do with the fact that I was raised in a family where my father was pursuing solar energy. I grew up watching my father pursuing something that nobody in Japan took seriously at the time, and I saw him eventually make a big success. Maybe it was my father's influence that led me to think that it's boring to be just playing the violin and pursuing a solo career like everyone else. I

wanted to do something different. Plus, the name of Juilliard serves as a status symbol, so just the fact that I got into Juilliard gave me enough sense of accomplishment, and I felt like I was now free to do whatever I want [without having to think about whether something was prestigious or not].[42]

Kimura's narrative is interesting in several ways. It begins with an explicit commentary about the connection between class and classical music, thereby revealing her awareness of the class-specific nature of classical music practice. The foregrounding of her family background also suggests her awareness that it was her place in Japanese society that allowed her to pursue musical training and American education. She also makes it clear that the prestige of Juilliard mattered to her, even though she eventually came to value the pursuit of her own interests over those defined by mainstream standards. At the same time, she assigns important non-economic values to her family background. She credits her mother and grandmother for their dedication to serving less privileged women, and she admires her father for pursuing his ideals and passion even though he received neither respect nor recognition for a long time. Thus, for Kimura, non-material values and qualities, such as service to society, pursuit of ideals and passion, and a willingness to go against the mainstream, are elements of her social identity that are at least as important as her economic background.

Likewise, a Japanese pianist commented on the socioeconomic disparity of American society as she observed that her students' and their parents' attitudes toward lessons and practice fell along ethnic and class lines:

Students from families on welfare are the biggest problem [when it comes to teaching the piano]. They are coming to school because it is free, and the students as well as their parents are used to the life-style of not working. It's unclear to me which comes first, their lack of competence or their laziness. . . . But all this derives from much larger historical issues, starting with slavery. So, of course I think it's a good thing to provide opportunities for music education to all children, but I think there are things that society needs to deal with first, like decreasing the vast economic gap between the rich and the poor.

In these remarks, she clearly sees her students whose families receive government welfare as being her "class other." At the same time, it is through her experience of teaching the piano to these children that she came to contemplate the legacies of slavery and the issues of economic disparity. Immediately after making this comment, she compared the American social structure to the Japanese one: "On the other hand, in Japan, for instance, where society is more leveled, everything is more uniform and few truly outstanding things come out of it." Here, although she implicitly acknowledges the merits of a less stratified society, she associates the relative lack of economic disparity in Japan with a culture of conformity that can stifle artistic expression and genius. By making a U.S.-Japan comparison in terms of music, she thus articulates a complexly intertwined notion of class that incorporates economic structure, behavior, lifestyle, history, and culture.

Yet, not all Asian musicians place their own middle-class identity in opposition to the working-class and the poor. Rather, many musicians engage less privileged people and communities through classical music. A sizable number of my informants are actively involved in working with underprivileged communities through their music. High-profile organizations such as Midori and Friends—a non-profit organization founded in 1992 by violinist Midori to provide children in underserved public schools in New York City with comprehensive music education programs at no cost—have received much media attention, but other less well-known Asian musicians also engage underprivileged communities through music. For example, violinist Jennifer Koh began her Music Messenger Program, through which she brings presentations, seminars, and master classes to children and young adults. Through his involvement in the Chinese Christian Herald Crusades in New York's Chinatown, Sidney Yin, a young, Hong Kong-born pianist, teaches children who cannot otherwise afford music instruction.[43] For these musicians, such activities are their way of addressing social issues, such as poverty, education, and the lack of state funding for the arts. They use their music to engage and give to those who do not have the privileges they themselves had.

Classical musicians also define their work, lifestyle, and value system in juxtaposition to those above them on the economic scale by distancing themselves from the materialist accumulation of wealth and America's commercially driven culture. This self-distinction is an extremely important dimension of their identity, especially in American society where the field of what Bourdieu calls "restricted cultural production" is relatively marginalized.

Ayako Watanabe is a Japanese harpist who came to the United States to study music in 1965. Since graduating from Indiana University, she and her husband Haruka Watanabe, a violinist for the St. Louis Symphony, have lived in St. Louis and played for the symphony as well as in freelance chamber gigs. When asked why she thought Asians have become so successful in classical music, she explained it in terms of "the high sophistication of the Japanese people cultivated through the country's long history" and the "artistry that has been developed through centuries"; she observed that "the Japanese mentality of constantly aspiring to create something that is more refined is never an accident." She then commented that "in comparison, American culture is still shallow, and the monetary concerns are primary, and there is a whole different mentality [about culture]." She lamented that, in the United States, classical music tends to be seen as a form of recreation for intellectuals and that many orchestras around the country are on the verge of extinction while sports events have no difficulty collecting millions of dollars in revenue.[44] Her cross-cultural commentary is thus framed as a critique of the profit-driven, anti-intellectual culture of mainstream America. Her identity as a classical musician—and as Japanese—derives in considerable part from her sense of pride in belonging to a group that prioritizes the rigor and integrity of an artistic pursuit over profit.

Younger musicians share this anti-materialist, anti-commercialist sentiment. Double bassist Kurt Muroki, born in Maui in 1972 and who has been playing with various orchestras and chamber groups in New York since graduating from Juilliard, was quite explicit about his views about art and money:

One thing I really feel strongly about is that money and music do not mix. You either have money, or you have music. Once they get together, there are problems. The best performances I've heard are the performances where there was no money involved, where you're doing it for the love of the music. That's the only way you really do well in music . . . you have to do it for the love of it. I know many people who are in the orchestras that are very disillusioned. They're earning the money, but they're not happy. I think it has to do with the fact that the emphasis is on the money. That's a big deal for me.

I'd rather be playing chamber music and not earning a penny and living on the street than making a million bucks. It's much more rewarding.[45]

Certainly not everyone can maintain such purist ideals of art when they have to worry about paying the bills. Nonetheless, the notion of art for art's sake is an ideal that most classical musicians dearly embrace, regardless of the extent to which they can actually live up to it in their real lives.[46]

Anti-commercialism, anti-materialism, and resistance to conforming to popular taste shape their attitudes in other ways as well. For instance, many of my informants were partly puzzled by, and partly derisive of, Asian parents who, in their view, pushed their children to study music and enter competitions not because of their love of music but because they thought it would enhance their educational and career prospects. Both male and female musicians also often spoke contemptuously of "successful" classical musicians who, according to them, have gained popularity either by selling their ethnicity (by appearing in ethnic garb at recitals or by playing ethnic music, for instance), by telling stories of their difficult upbringing (in their war-torn country or during the Cultural Revolution), and by flaunting their sexuality (in the case of attractive, young, female musicians, as discussed in the preceding chapter). They argued that such pandering to commercialized exoticism is a déclassé pursuit of popularity at the expense of artistic integrity and authenticity. Musicians also often lamented what they consider the "prostitution" of their labor that is required to earn a living or to satisfy their audience and donors—having to play under a conductor for whom they have no respect, having to play music that is far below their level of skill and artistry, or having to play in venues where music is nothing more than background entertainment. Through such disapproval (of practices they cannot themselves entirely avoid), they express a sense of pride in embracing a value system other than one determined by commercial success.

Musicians thus espouse a particular value system that operates in what Bourdieu discusses as the "economy of the artistic field." Bourdieu stresses that "[t]here is a specific economy of the literary and artistic field, based on a particular form of belief. . . . The work of art is an object which exists as such only by virtue of the (collective) belief which knows and acknowledges it as a work of art."[47] Such beliefs "always involve recognition of the ultimate values of 'disinterestedness' through the denunciation of the mercenary compromises or calculating maneuvers of the adversary, so that disavowal of the 'economy' is placed at the very heart of the field, as the principle governing its functioning and transformation."[48]

Most classical musicians, and not just Asians, embrace such a value system. However, for Asian musicians, this sense of identity serves an additional function by strengthening the notion that the "class" of classical musicians—occupying an economically marginalized position in the larger society and comprising a field with a shared value system—is more important than their racial identity as Asians, as discussed in Chapter 2. It also serves to diminish the meanings of the actual socioeconomic differences among Asian musicians, as the chosen values are often more important in their everyday lives than objective material conditions that are beyond their control. In other words, the boundaries drawn by their non-economic values highlight their sense of difference from those outside those boundaries and strengthen the bond of those within.

Classical musicians embrace and practice values and meanings that operate autonomously from market relationships, even as they as social agents live in those relationships. As Bourdieu noted, "In contrast to the field of large-scale cultural production, which submits to the laws of competition for the conquest of the largest possible market, the field of restricted production [such as classical music] tends to develop its own criteria for the evaluation of its products, thus achieving the truly cultural recognition accorded by the peer group whose members are both privileged clients and competitors."[49] Musicians' embrace of non-economic values is their class *practice* and class *performance* that justify their ambiguous and contradictory class *location*.

In his book, *Who Needs Classical Music?*, musicologist Julian Johnson makes this point eloquently. He claims that music-as-art is not fundamentally a sign for a cultural position, a style, or a social status, but rather "a thing whose enactment makes possible the realization of a noncontingent sense of value." He thus identifies the inadequacy of using the language of cultural capital—and treating it as objects of market exchange—to fully address the meanings of classical music:

> Fundamental to our notion of humanity is the sense that who and what we are exceeds such misappropriation [of people as commodities]. We vehemently oppose such a reduction of what we consider to be inalienable and irreducible: the absolute value of the human

spirit. . . . The high value accorded to art, classical music included, derives from its opposition to the social devaluation of the particular and individual. In a social world in which individuals become increasingly interchangeable and dispensable, art dwells on the particular and finds in it something of absolute value. In this way it redeems not just things but also people, whom society increasingly turns into things.[50]

Arguing for the "absolute value of the human spirit," this idealist position rejects the Marxist model of production as a means of understanding art. Until recently, this understanding of art as an essential expression of the human spirit and individual genius independent of the realm of political economy has shaped much of musicological scholarship. Although this type of idealist subjectivism cannot sufficiently analyze the social contexts for the production and circulation of art, such an understanding is at the core of musicians' own sense of cultural identity and of their place in a society that often does not reward such a view. As Bourdieu points out, "Intellectuals and artists are so situated in social space that they have a particular interest in disinterestedness and in all the values that are universal and universally recognized as highest (the more so the closer they are to the dominated pole of the field of cultural production)."[51] In other words, classical musicians' socioeconomic marginalization and their investment in what Bourdieu calls "inner-worldly asceticism" and their sense of "mission" go hand in hand in shaping both the field and their own identity.

Conclusion

It is extremely difficult to analyze classical musicians as class subjects in economic relationships. Their class location defies clear classification, as their authority and autonomy at work, income, and wealth are incongruent with most other occupational groups with a comparable level of education and expertise. In addition, their forms of employment, income, and lifestyle vary so widely that it is almost meaningless to discuss them under a single socioeconomic category. In addition to their origin and upbringing in the professional managerial class, the only other element that ties the majority of them together is actually the very absence of the language and perspective to talk about their own class position. Like most middle-class Americans, classical musicians generally lack explicit class consciousness.

Classical musicians nevertheless express their sense of class identity in several ways. They position themselves explicitly and implicitly in opposition both to those above and below them in the socioeconomic structure by articulating the emphasis they and their families have placed on discipline, education, and the accumulation of cultural capital and by distancing themselves from the materialist pursuit of wealth and commercially driven culture. In many ways, it is this oppositional stance to the economic valuations of art, work, and status that marks the classical musicians' identity as a group in the field of restricted cultural production.

These values and stances have particular meanings for Asian musicians whose class position and identity are shaped and mediated by their race and nationality. In many cases, especially for immigrants, the fulfillment of their families' dream of cultural assimilation and upward mobility through the pursuit of classical music is hampered by the economic and cultural differences between Asian and American society. The cultural capital of classical music is thus rarely converted smoothly into other forms of capital that carry currency in American society. Yet, the non-economic logic of social identity for classical musicians, in which their worth is judged by their adherence to artistic goals rather than by economic factors, forms the basis for their sense of a collective identity. How, then, do Asian musicians fare on the "purely artistic" scale of evaluation that they embrace so dearly? Chapter 5 addresses the issues of identity and musical authenticity in classical music.

VOICES

Pianist Margaret Leng Tan was born in Singapore in 1953. She came to the United States at age sixteen when she won a scholarship to study at Juilliard, and she later became the first woman to earn a doctorate in music from that institution. After meeting avant-garde composer John Cage in 1981, she developed a strong interest in world music and contemporary music. She became Cage's close friend and collaborator for the last eleven years of his life and was hailed as "the most convincing interpreter of John Cage's keyboard music." Her association with Cage also led to her fascination with the toy piano and prepared piano (a piano in which foreign objects have been placed on or between the strings to create special sound effects), and she has performed and recorded many works for the instruments. In addition to Cage, she has been inspired by other avant-garde composers who have been influenced by non-Western music, such as Henry Cowell, George Crumb, Lou Harrison, Harry Partch, and Philip Glass. She has also worked with contemporary Asian composers, such as Tan Dun,

MARGARET LENG TAN
(Photograph by Yvonne Tan)

Somei Satoh, and Ge Ganru, who have composed works specifically for her. She has created a unique niche as an interpreter of Western and Asian music. As someone who has her foot in both Asian and Western worlds, she sees herself as a "logical inheritor of the history of musical exploration."

In December 2003, I went to listen to a concert of the contemporary music ensemble, Alarm Will Sound, held at the World Financial Center atrium in downtown Manhattan, where Tan played the world premier of composer Aaron Jay Kernis's Concerto for Toy Piano and Chamber Orchestra. The combination of the sounds of toy piano and regular piano was unexpectedly natural and interesting. As she does in many performances and media appearances, Tan, who has bobbed hair reminiscent of Anna May Wong, was dressed in "Asian exotic" wardrobe in bright red and purple. A week later, I went to meet her at her brownstone in Park Slope, Brooklyn, for an interview. She is an avid animal lover, and as soon as I rang the doorbell I could hear her large dogs rushing to the door to greet me. Tan took me to her piano room on the second floor, which has two grand pianos, and also showed me her toy piano collection on the third floor. She showed me a new toy piano she had just received from a manufacturer in China. We then walked to a neighborhood diner and conducted the interview there. Both the owner and all the customers who walked in knew her by name (and vice versa), and our conversation was interrupted several times by friendly customers stopping by to greet her.

MY: I know you were born in Singapore.

MLT: The fact that I'm from Singapore puts me in a rather unique position, as opposed to someone from Korea, Japan, Hong Kong, or Taiwan, because Singapore is a multiracial society. . . . Singapore is really multiracial because the majority are Chinese, then there are the Malays, the indigenous people, then there are South Indians who came as immigrants at the turn of the century. And we live pretty much in harmony with each other; there's no racial strife, racial tension. It's a wonderful mix of cultural diversity. I think it's because I'm from Singapore that I have this unique position. To give you a concrete example, when I first met John Cage in 1981, I played some of his pieces for the prepared piano, and I heard that he was really struck by the way I prepared the piano. . . . You know, as some people say, Cage's music reminded me of *gamelan* [ensemble of Indonesian instruments]. And it's because I'm from that part of the world that I have this kind of ethnic music sensibility embedded in me just from my background, which wouldn't be true if I had been raised in Hong Kong or Taiwan, where I would have been exposed to Chinese culture and nothing else. Because Singapore was a British colony, the Western influence is very strong . . . and there is also the Chinese, the Malay, and all the mix. So it's in a very unique position. And I think that's why I have this curiosity about world music. Ethnic music and world music was something that I was really interested in long before it became the hot thing in the 1980s . . .

I can play Chopin and all that as good as anyone else. But the thing is, I can also do a lot of other things that a lot of other classical pianists can't do. I mean, all these things I developed, like techniques inside the piano and everything. . . . I use [my classical training] as a springboard [for playing new music]. I mean, if you're going to play with your elbows and your fists, you have to do it with certain finesse. And that comes out of your training as a classical pianist. That kind of discipline and control also applies to all these extended piano techniques when I work inside the piano. It's a whole other dimension, but at the same time, you can't just start doing that without having some classical background.

I think what's really interesting for you to know is how I got into all this. Because I am trained as a classical pianist, got my doctorate at Juilliard. . . . And it's because I was getting very restless as a classical pianist. Just before I met John Cage, everything was ripe for me. You can meet somebody and it doesn't mean anything to you unless you're ready to receive what they have to offer. And around 1980, I was getting really restless and was starting to explore world music. I was getting interested in listening to ethnic music on recordings. Then I thought of putting together this program to take on tour in Asia. I decided to put together a program of music by Western composers influenced by Asian aesthetics. Because I thought this was a tour in the Far East, it would be interesting for Asian audiences to see the impact of the East on significant composers in the West. So I chose Debussy as my point of departure, because he was fascinated by the *gamelan*. . . . So I put in the concert *Image* Book II, because that is a really multi-layered writing, not to mention the titles like "Pagoda" and other Asian imagery. So I used that as a springboard, and then I included music by Messiaen, which was influenced by Indian rhythms . . . and Cage, and Charles Griffes. Do you know Charles Griffes? [MY shakes her head.] You should explore that, because he was an Orientalist if there ever was one. American turn-of-the-century Impressionism, at a time when there was such a fascination with Eastern exotica, he's right out of that tradition. I included a Griffes Sonata to end my program. . . . I performed this program all over Southeast Asia, and I even did it in New York at the Asia Society. So that's how I got started in this direction. That was in 1982, and I met Cage in 1981.

How did I meet Cage? See, I had a friend who was from Malaysia, a dancer. She was a traditional dancer, and she was also interested in contemporary dance and she was here studying different styles. . . . And we put together this song and dance which she choreographed, so I thought, "Hm, Cage should see this." So I called him up, I didn't know he was so famous; if I'd known I would never have done it [laughs]. . . . And then he did come to see us, and he was very taken by what we did, so much so that he wrote down our names. That was the beginning of a long friendship. . . . Of course, Cage's whole philosophy is so entrenched in Asian aesthetics, whether it's his own brand of Zen Buddhism or I Ching [Chinese "Book of Changes"] or Indian philosophy. . . . You cannot understand his music without understanding his aesthetics. You cannot separate them out. So for me, that was a way to bring me back to my own Asian roots. My life really had a turning point when I met Cage in 1981. Because I didn't really abandon my classical music past, but I relinquished [it] gradually. I just found this [new music] much more challenging and interesting. The possibilities seemed to be infinite. And then composers started to write [pieces] for me. So it was a natural turn of events. After exploring the influences of Asian aesthetics on Western composers, you just flip the coin over and look at what Asian composers have done with their own heritage as well as their knowledge of Western music and see how they put it together. And in the mid-1980s, all these talented Chinese composers came to Columbia. Tan Dun, Ge Ganru, they all came in the '80s. At the time I was also interested in Western composers like Philip Glass, John Adams, Steve Reich, and all the minimalists who were influenced by Asian aesthetics. . . . So it became a very fascinating and exciting time in the mid-'80s to discover not only the Western composers but Asian composers. . . . Then I got an ACC [Asian Cultural Council] grant to go to Japan to meet Japanese composers and spend some time there. So all this fed into the curiosity that I have to take my piano, my repertoire, into a new territory . . .

MY: Before you got interested in this new music, your training was strictly classical?

MLT: Strictly classical. I didn't know any better. [laughs] And I feel I've made a very special niche for myself in this repertory. I feel that my responsibility as an interpreter of new piano music by Asian and American composers is very important. I have a responsibility to this particular niche that I've committed myself to. See, the West has taken a great deal from the East. Cage, who has had such an influence on artists in all disciplines in the twentieth century. And just imagine how his vision is reaching out to a whole other generation of musicians, dancers, writers, painters, through his aesthetics. It's really mind-boggling if you think about it. . . . And even before that, there were all these other musicians, Lou Harrison, Henry Cowell, Harry Partch, you know, who were all into other musics. They weren't just interested in Western music . . . all these people were way into other cultures long before it became a vogue, from the '40s . . . so I feel I'm just a next step in the logical progression through the generations . . .

MY: Do you feel that because you're Asian, you have . . .

MLT: A vantage point. And not only because I'm Asian, but I'm who I am, I have a foot in either door, because of my whole Western background and my Asian roots, you know, my Asian colonial background. In a way I feel very privileged to be in both worlds. My name kind of sums it up, right? Margaret Leng Tan.

*C*ho-Liang (Jimmy) Lin is one of the most sought-after violinists in the world today. Born in 1960 in a university town in Taiwan, he began taking violin lessons at age five. When the resources available in Taiwan became too limited for his talents and goals, his parents sent him to Australia to study at the Sydney Conservatorium. In 1975, he moved to New York to study with Dorothy DeLay at Juilliard. In 1981, through the influence of Isaac Stern, he went on an extensive tour of mainland China and other parts of East Asia. He has since achieved an international reputation both as a soloist and chamber musician, performing regularly with his close friend and colleague, Yo-Yo Ma. In 1997 he founded the Taipei International Music Festival, the largest classical music festival in the history of Taiwan. In recent years, he has collaborated with contemporary composers such as Bright Sheng, Aaron Jay Kernis, and Tan Dun. He is also on the faculty of the Juilliard School.

He is an extremely collegial, generous person who is highly respected and dearly loved by all those who know him personally. I interviewed him in January

CHO-LIANG LIN
(Photograph by David Weiss)

2004 at his studio at Juilliard amidst his busy performing and teaching schedule. He was very generous with his time and in sharing his thoughts, and he took great interest in my project.

CL: My musical upbringing was rather abnormal, exceptional, in that there's no musician in my family ever, and musical education was considered a luxury in Taiwan in the early 1960s. Taiwan was still a poor country. Musical education was not only considered a luxury but also there was no career possibility. Why bother taking music lessons? An engineer, lawyer, or doctor or some sort of a scientist, those were the lofty jobs to have. So it was very unusual for my parents to not only encourage me to learn the violin but also at age twelve to send me overseas. Compared to my surroundings those days, that was very unusual. And to make it even more interesting, I did not grow up in Taipei. If anything, Taipei's musical environment was beginning to take shape, but I grew up in the town of Hsin-Chu, which is now the Silicon Valley of Taiwan, but it was not so then in the 1960s, so it was basically a very quiet university town. So what I did was even more unusual in that I could grow up basically in an intellectual environment with not much musical life. . . . My father was an avid record collector. He brought home many records and put them on, so I grew up with classical music in the house, and also radio broadcast. So violin was something I encountered by chance, through my neighbor who was taking lessons. . . . I think it was because it was the university environment with many intellectuals around—engineers, college professors—my father was a physicist, a researcher, and my mother was a high school teacher—so I was able to follow. . . . I went to watch my neighbor practice every day, and I was five, so my parents gave me a violin. . . . Then my father went to Japan on a business trip and brought back a quarter-size violin. See, in Taiwan in those days, it was very hard to find even a quarter-size violin. That's how backwards things were in Taiwan . . .

[One reason for leaving Taiwan] was that my violin playing had progressed to a level that even my teacher thought that I needed to go to a better musical environment. And secondly, I would be stuck in Taiwan for a long time if I stayed because of the military service. I think after age fourteen all male Taiwanese citizens would have to stay in service until two years after college so I would be twenty-four by the time I finished. . . . So I went to Australia as a first step. I had an uncle living there, and second, I won a scholarship to the Sydney Conservatory with a high school attached to it, so it seemed like a very good fit. That's when I learned English, Western culture, a bit of history, and so when I eventually came to New York at age fifteen, I was far more ready for New York than I would have been otherwise . . .

MY: In what ways do you think your identity as an Asian plays a factor in your work as a musician?

CL: I've gone through different phases, generations of identity. When I was first a student here at Juilliard, I tried everything I could to be as American as possible. In fact, for a period of three or four years, I didn't speak any Chinese. And I've seen that in some of the students here. It's interesting to see that they go through the same stages. They want to assimilate, you know, just like I was trying to. Now, you can come to Juilliard and be in a Korean student clique and not get out, there are all these Koreans forming a group, but in those days, I tried not to [hang out with other Asians]. . . . There were many Asians around, many Japanese and many Koreans, and most of them studied piano or violin. That's another interesting thing about Asians, they don't want to play the trumpet, they hardly play the clarinet, but they have to play a solo instrument, piano or violin, or maybe sometimes cello, but bassoon, out of the question, you know. Double bass, ah!

But back to the identity thing, in my early twenties, I also tried to be as non-Chinese as I could. But then, something changed in my thinking. I began to pay attention to Chinese history again. I began to follow what China was doing. I went to China. I began to take great pride in what Taiwan was achieving economically and politically. And I noticed that there were some wonderful Chinese musicians out there in the world starting to do things. And so my identity started to change and I began to think that it's a great thing to be Chinese. So I began to go back to Taiwan more, and I was very keen to make sure that I speak Chinese well again. I was actually very embarrassed about how badly I spoke Chinese. And this fascination with both Chinese culture and Taiwanese culture and Asian culture at large grew. Now, I'm pretty much at ease in that part of the world. In the old days, I didn't really like being in Taiwan. I thought Taiwan was horribly congested and I always got sick when I was there. But now I'm much more at ease. In fact, I have started a music festival in Taipei. And I'm trying to do things to bring good people back to Taiwan and China. China is less tangible, it's harder for me to contribute directly . . . but I want to go back to China more because that's where my roots are historically and I find it very interesting.

MY: Do you think that a Chinese person has a different interpretation of Western music?

CL: This is just based on my own observation. . . . Well, I used to think that musicians from China in the 1980s came out in a technically brilliant way, but recently I have noticed that some of them have developed beautiful interpretation. So I thought, "Geez, if that's the case, that has to do with their environment." So interpretively, or, in the way you put it, if we look at the standard piece differently, yes, of course I looked at a piece differently when I was fifteen than I do now. You go through different experience and come to a new interpretation based on your own experience. So I don't think there's a generic Chinese way of doing Bach or Japanese way of playing Brahms, you know. I have noticed fantastic players from different parts of the world. . . . If you look at Mitsuko Uchida's interpretation, I'm sure it's radically different from the way Kyoko Takezawa plays Beethoven. So I think it goes back to personality, how open you are to new interpretive possibilities and also your environment . . .

Back when I was still in Australia, when I was beginning to learn about style, I was always drawn to performers I thought were stylistically interesting or stylistically bright. When I came to New York, one of my great learning opportunities was occasional encounters with people like Itzhak Perlman and Isaac Stern, and from working with them as well as listening to them perform, I learned a lot about what makes Isaac Stern's interpretation of Mozart different from Heifetz's Mozart. So I must say, it's interesting that I came up with my own way of playing Mozart from different observation of players. My own instinct is very much shaped by what I heard. . . . In fact, it's very interesting that English conductor Raymond Leppard who recorded the complete Mozart concerto cycle with me said, "Your Mozart is different. When you hear Stern and Zukerman play Mozart, it's too Jewish. [laughs] You have this certain purity about your Mozart." I don't know how I came upon that, he never really told me how he heard the difference, but I hear the difference when I hear my own recording of Mozart compared to Isaac Stern's Mozart. [MY: Do you think Stern's playing is Jewish?] I can't really tell. I mean, there's a certain vigor and romance in a Jewish violinist's playing, especially in older players like Heifetz, Stern, and Oistrakh, there's some robust quality to it. There's definitely like a Russian school, and there was for a long time a French school. But I can't say there's a Chinese school of violin playing. It never got famous. And all the good Chinese players all went overseas [laughs]. So it's more that I'm a product of Juilliard, but some people say that I don't sound like a typical Juilliard product. My style is different from what people think of Galamian and DeLay students with big sound and a lot of aggressive qualities. That's not my style. So I'd like to think that my style is unique, and it's a combination of my own thinking, my upbringing, my various teachers, my observations.

Chinese composers are becoming prominent now. And I'd like to find out . . . I'm just beginning to experiment with this . . . whether a Chinese violinist or Chinese pianist would necessarily play a Chinese composer differently. I'm not sure, I'm not 100 percent sure. For instance, I really wish, a few years ago when Gil Shaham was going to record the *Butterfly Lovers Concerto,* which is like number one greatest hit for violin concerto ever written in Chinese repertoire. It would have been very interesting to hear this Israel-born violinist interpret a Chinese concerto, especially a traditional Chinese concerto, and of course, I'm learning the piece myself, and I'm planning to record it. So one day, maybe ten years from now, when both our recordings are out, people can say, here's one Chinese and here's one Jewish [musician] playing a Chinese concerto, that would be very interesting, it would be a point of comparison.

MY: Do you personally feel that when you play a Chinese composer's piece you have a better understanding of it than another musician?

CL: That's a very good point. I tend to think that I understand it a little bit more, but I don't dare to make that claim in a strong way, because I find myself very ignorant about Chinese music. I've learned a lot in recent years, but I'm no expert on ethnic Chinese music, and therefore how I'm qualified to interpret Chinese music, I'm not sure. But I know how to interpret what's written on a page, and I've also learned how to learn from composers. . . . Like, for example, when I first played *Out of Peking Opera* by Tan Dun, when he first showed me the music, I had no clue. And this is the early 1990s. He gave me a whole bunch of recordings of Peking opera for me to listen to. And it still didn't register. I listened to Peking opera, but this is a violin concerto, I didn't understand the connection. And when I met Tan Dun finally, he began to explain to me, and then I made the connection. Then I realized that you don't have to be literal, you don't have to write a piece that sounds like a violin transcription of a Peking opera but rather it's an impression of a Peking opera, like Debussy. . . . it's more in the mind . . . there's a certain philosophical and poetic connection in Asian music. I'm thinking of Takemitsu, and Tan Dun, there's a recurring theme, like in Debussy, each of these preludes has a recurring theme very much like a Chinese opera. . . . Whether that makes that piece better or not, I'm not sure [laughs].

M akoto Nakura is a marimbist born in 1964 in Kobe, Japan. Trained at the Musashino Acadmia Musicae in Tokyo, he studied in London for a year. In 1994, he became the first marimbist to win the Young Concert Artists Competition in New York, which launched his concertizing career. He moved to New York in 1997 to take advantage of the rich cultural resources and encounters with creative artists in the city. He has performed in forty states in the United States, tours and teaches regularly in Japan, and also performs in other parts of the world. He collaborates with many contemporary composers, and the majority of the pieces he performs in recitals are compositions he commissioned. Working with an instrument that does not have a vast repertoire written for it,

MAKOTO NAKURA, marimbist
(Photograph by Yukihito Masuura; courtesy of Makoto Nakura)

he is making an important contribution to creating new music, expanding the repertoire for the instrument, and exposing the audience to marimba music.

I met Nakura when I attended his solo recital at Merkin Concert Hall in New York in October 2003. Not knowing anything about Nakura or the marimba, I had bought a ticket for the recital after seeing it in Merkin Hall's season program, thinking that it would be interesting to listen to a Japanese musician who plays an unusual instrument. The performance immediately drew me into the world of marimba. In addition to his technical brilliance, what was most striking about his performance was his gentle and organic sound that con-

veys the texture of the instrument as well as the music. On the percussion instru-
ment, which does not produce sustained sound and on which one cannot control
the tone after hitting a note, Nakura produces an amazing range of sonority.
When he played an arrangement of "Amazing Grace" for an encore, the older
woman sitting next to me (because it was a weekday matinée, the majority of the
people in the audience were from the senior citizens' home nearby) and I looked
at each other and smiled. It was the kind of concert that created such moments
of shared appreciation for beauty and depth.

As it turned out, he and I happened to have a friend in common—a Japa-
nese flutist—who was helping out at the recital selling his CDs in the lobby. A
few days later, all of us had a delicious and jovial dinner at his apartment on
the Upper West Side. (Nakura is an excellent cook.) The interview took place in
the same apartment several days later. Nakura and I subsequently became good
friends. He generously introduced me to many musicians; he invited me to con-
certs and dinners; and he let me be a helping hand at one of his recording sessions
where I got to witness the painstakingly meticulous process of recording, not to
mention the hassle of transporting and assembling a marimba.

As is probably clear from the interview excerpts below, as an artist and as an
individual, Nakura is someone who holds high standards for himself, for music,
and for others. He thinks deeply about what it means for him, as a Japanese
musician, to be a marimbist based in New York. Yet he does not resort to a facile
marketing of his Japanese identity or create music that shallowly uses "Asian"
sound. The music that he creates in collaboration with the composers is, although
extremely beautiful, not the kind of music that easily entertains the audience. It
demands the audience to face music seriously.

MY: What surprised you the most when you arrived in England?

MN: Everything was very different from Japan. I had never been outside
of Japan until then. So the value system was different; the ways people see
things and think about things are different. So the most fruitful thing I gained
from going to England was that I realized that there can be different ways of
looking at things. That was very productive both for me as an individual and
for my music. In Japan, one tends to be constrained by a single value system,
since it's a homogeneous society and people tend to think in similar ways,
and the education system is oriented that way. But once I left Japan, I learned
that there can be different value systems and that I can express myself in my
own way. That was the most fruitful thing I learned . . .

MY: How did you choose London as your destination?

MN: Having been in Japan all of my twenty-two-year life, I felt suffocated by the environment. I had never been abroad, and I am studying Western music, so I thought I should go to Europe. And London is a place with a lot of different musical traditions. I didn't want to be limited to a single tradition of music, like the German tradition or the Italian tradition, so I wanted to be in a place that has multiple traditions.

MY: Having learned that there can be different value systems, how did that manifest in your music specifically?

MN: Listening to other students' performance, I was surprised to see how freely they express themselves. I felt that Japanese students probably wouldn't express themselves quite so explicitly. Also, everyone [in London] is very opinionated. In Japan, people don't express their opinions too much. There is an atmosphere that you shouldn't be so candid. But the students in England were very knowledgeable as well as articulate. Also, in everyday life, London is a place where people from all over the world come together, and having been exposed to different cultures, I understood that I can say what I think and feel without hiding it. It made me feel very liberated . . .

MY: How does New York compare with Tokyo and London in terms of your musical life?

MN: Compared to Tokyo, New York is so much more multicultural, and people think about things in so many different ways, so it is very stimulating. The diversity is incomparable. That has been tremendously important for me as an individual and as a musician. That's why I decided to relocate to New York. . . . Putting myself amidst this diversity forces me to ask myself what kind of a musician and a human being I am. That's very important for an artist. There are things and people here that I would never have encountered in Japan, like composers, performers . . .

MY: Specifically speaking, what are the things you would not have thought about if you had stayed in Japan?

MN: It relates to what I said about diversity. It also relates to asking myself who I am. My chosen instrument, marimba, is far less constrained by the classical tradition compared to, say, the piano or violin. It was first born in Africa, developed in South America, and modernized in North America, but it uses the basic tuning of the European music. So the instrument itself has roots in many places around the world. Adding to it the fact that I,

Makoto Nakura, a Japanese musician, am playing the instrument, I think my playing is truly multicultural, a real mix of different cultures. And I think that is how the audience [in the United States] sees my playing. . . . I think what I'm doing—a Japanese marimba player collaborating with American and other composers in New York—is something that is possible precisely because of this age in the twentieth and twentieth-first centuries. So I think I should create projects that reflect this reality. So for instance, I did a program where all the pieces were commissioned to contemporary composers in America; all the pieces were premiered at this recital. I'm thinking of doing a program that reflects the global history of the marimba, showing not only the classical tradition but the different ways in which the world's peoples engaged the culture of wood. If I had stayed in Japan, I would never have thought about such things, and even if I had, I wouldn't have had any contact with American composers . . .

MY: In your life as a musician, in what ways do you think about your Japanese identity, if at all?

MN: Unlike piano or violin for which the main repertoire is European, in my case, marimba is not something deeply rooted in Europe. Plus, many of the music I play are the repertoire I produced myself. Many pieces I play were written for me, and I also arrange music myself. In the case of piano, if you are playing Schubert, you might wonder if you need to be German in order to really understand it, and the audience too might think that a German musician's performance of Schubert is the most authentic. In that kind of climate, you might have to think about what it means to be a Japanese musician playing Schubert. But in my case, the situation is completely different, and the issue is really about who I am as an individual and what kind of music I make rather than about my race or nationality. Of course, as I grew up and was educated in Japan, I think there are things about my aesthetics and ways of thinking that are deeply Japanese. I believe that musical performance reflects the performer's self, and I think if the playing does not reflect the person's life, it's meaningless. So in that sense, I am sure that the place and the culture I grew up in is reflected in my music. How exactly it's reflected is not something I can see for myself, but I'm sure it is reflected. It's not something that I'm conscious of; it's futile to try to play something "like a Japanese." It's an unconscious process that's involved in the choices I make among different options of playing. I'm sure it's part of my influence, but it's less a matter of being Japanese than a question of who I am as an individual. . . . I have come to feel resentment toward having my playing characterized as "a Japanese performance." I want people to hear "Makoto Nakura's performance," not "a Japanese performance." . . . And I am rarely characterized as a Japanese or an Asian anyway. There is little basis for comparison in the case of my instrument. If I were playing Beethoven, there may be orthodox ways of playing Beethoven, but I play music written for me by young composers, and the composers and I create the music together. So in a way I am the orthodox in that music, so I don't feel a sense of inferiority; all I think about is expressing my own ideas.

MY: When you commission works to composers, do you think the fact that you are Japanese is an important element as they write music for you?

MN: I think it depends on the composer. When I commission pieces, I have them understand some things about me as a musician and an individual, as well as about what the marimba can do as an instrument. So I think when they write music, they write not just for the marimba in general but specifically for Makoto Nakura. In that sense, some composers may think about the fact that I'm Japanese, but others probably don't. And if the composer's music is the type of music that actively tries to incorporate Japanese elements, that person may think about it; if it's something more neutral, my being Japanese won't matter. . . . I would never ask a composer to write something that's "Japanese." I think it's very shallow to say things like that. Composers wouldn't know what's Japanese. Even I who grew up in Japan don't really understand it. I really hate compositions that make superficial borrowings from *kabuki* and what not. I would never suggest such a thing . . .

MY: Beyond the marimba, for instruments like violin and piano, do you think that cultural identity is relevant to playing?

MN: Classical music was born in a small part of Western Europe and eventually spread so widely across the world. I like to believe that that fact alone is a reflection of the nature of classical music, which is inherently universal and has the capacity to absorb diverse cultures. So the idea that German music should be played by Germans or that the German style is the orthodox style of playing is very far from how I like to think about classical music. Classical music ought to have universality that goes beyond such thinking. Classical music today is different from classical music of two centuries ago, because it has absorbed diverse cultures. But a hundred, two hundred, three hundred years from now, what we think of as a distinctly contemporary form of classical music may not seem too different from the music of Beethoven. So we are all part of that history.

Classical music has long been stimulated by the infusion of different ethnic groups. So I believe that the new groups [like Asians] will be a force in producing something new in classical music. Mozart, for example, wrote the Turkish March because he was inspired by Turkish music, and there are many examples like that in the music that we know today. Mozart wrote Italian opera as well as German-style opera. Bizet wrote Carmen inspired by the Spanish gypsy. That's how classical music has evolved and developed. So I believe that the day will come when [Asian musicians] will be a powerful force in creating a new form of classical music. Two centuries ago, communication and transportation was limited compared to today, and Mozart didn't have a chance to learn about Asian cultures, and Japanese didn't have a chance to listen to Mozart sonatas. But now, living in these contemporary times, we cannot be fussing about questions like what is authentic or orthodox. There is much more important work that we musicians have to do.

K*enji Bunch is one of the most promising up-and-coming composers. Born in 1973 and raised in Portland, Oregon, with a Japanese mother and American father, he began piano lessons at age five and violin shortly thereafter. At age thirteen, he switched to the viola, which he felt suited his personality better. He entered Juilliard as a viola major, but during his music theory class he was extremely excited about small composition assignments and wrote pieces that were much bigger and more complex than those by other students, who thought of the assignments as a chore. He then started taking composition lessons on the side and later entered Juilliard's master's program as a double major in viola and composition.*

Both his background as a performer and his network of performing friends helped his composition career flourish. Of particular importance is his friendship with the Ahn Trio. While at Juilliard, he arranged a few pieces for the trio and wrote a solo violin piece for violinist Angella's graduation recital. Then he began to write trio pieces for the sisters, and the collaboration has continued since then. Thanks to the trio's success, the pieces the trio plays have been performed in more occasions and venues than all of his other compositions combined.

KENJI BUNCH
(Courtesy of the artist)

Bunch is a musician who is not bound by the conventions of Western classical music. He says that he grew up living a "pretty average suburban life," and music was not part of his life at public high school. On entering Juilliard, he was shocked to meet all the prodigies, who had been playing music at an extremely high level for many years, and he realized how "normal" his childhood had been. His music reflects his background and interests, which are not limited to the conventions of Western music. He draws from the musical languages of pop, rock, and jazz; he regularly performs fiddle in a bluegrass band (he occasionally yodels as well). When I asked what musicians he admires the most, among the names such as Shostakovich, Ravel, Leonard Bernstein, John Adams, and John Corigliano, he unhesitatingly listed Johnny Cash. I interviewed him at a Starbucks on the Upper West Side, Manhattan.

KB: [The collaboration with the Ahn Trio has been great.] A lot of people that came out of Juilliard are quite conservative musically and not that comfortable playing new music. They [the Ahn Trio] sort of made the point of playing the music of today . . .

In general, I found myself while at Juilliard, I was drawn to hang out with a lot of brass players. They were somehow more similar to me in terms of our backgrounds. The brass players were generally more mainstream white American guys who went to regular high school. So many of other string players, violinists especially, or pianists, went to Pre-College here, and moved here just to go to Pre-College. . . . One of my suite-mates [in the dorm] was a violinist from Korea. . . . He and I were good friends . . . we both enjoyed improvising and enjoyed trying to play non-classical music on our instruments. . . . He was a sad yet unfortunately typical story of someone who had grown up at the Pre-College and Aspen [summer music festival]—you know they all go to Aspen [laughs]. His mother was very, very attached to his music and his Juilliard career. She would call every morning at our suite at 8, 8:30 in the morning to make sure he was up and going to class. Of course it was very annoying to the rest of us [laughs], but it was also hard to see the effect it had on him. It was such a strain. In the next few years he started having problems with drugs. He had a nervous breakdown. And again, this was not that uncommon for people to lose it [at Juilliard]. . . . He ended up spending some time in the psychiatric care and he ended up on medication for bipolar disorder. . . . It was sad to see how the whole thing played out. There was a Japanese violist who killed herself. She was a year younger than me, she had an apartment in the 60s [of Manhattan] and jumped out of her window.

The weird thing about it is that I couldn't personally relate to that kind of pressure. I never knew it. I could see it going on, I could see it with these people with their parents and maybe the pressure from their teachers, but I never felt it. It was always fun for me to be there, I loved Juilliard and I had such a great time. It's been hard for me to sort of wean myself from that place. I guess it's a lot like childhood, there are some things you end up resenting because they keep you from growing or something. But there were times that I felt very angry and resentful at Juilliard. Ultimately I think it was a little misplaced. But the school does a great job at a very specific thing—they train you in the traditions of Western classical music. But beyond that, you sort of have to provide the rest for yourself. I got to a point musically where I wanted to explore more creative, non-traditional, avant-garde issues, and I felt like I had suddenly become this freak at Juilliard, like I was rebelling against something. And I didn't want to feel that way. I felt what I was doing was continuing this tradition. And I still think that. But it's just hard for people who are so rooted in something; sometimes it's hard not to be threatened by newer things.

These days I do a lot of non-classical playing. I'm in a bluegrass band, and I have another group that's a string quartet, drum and bass, and we play our original music. It's a blending of classical and non-classical traditions that we come from. . . . I've noticed that with myself and other people in the group, the Ahns, with a lot of people who sort of eventually try to step outside of the box of the conventional classical world, everyone sort of goes through the same issue of trying to reconcile this guilt about leaving the rigidity of the classical world. And I think the reason for that is that, for so many of us, classical music is so tied in with parents and discipline. Especially the Asians. It's such a part of the childhood experience of being a good boy or a good girl, practicing, playing this thing well, to impress your parents. And it becomes a sort of familial, generational thing. . . . And the teachers are sort of an extension of parents in a way. I know I felt a little of that, I think I have a very mild version of that experience. And for some people for whom music was discipline, it's very hard for them to break away from that . . .

So that's the conflicting feeling over the years, and there have been times when I felt myself writing things sort of to rebel or act up against this tradition or something. But I wouldn't be happy doing that, and I came to terms with it. A lot of my music incorporates elements of popular music, and it's not really that tied into classical traditions. But I do make it as much as I can to be respectful of the traditions, and I don't see my music really as innovative as much as an extension of very old traditions of incorporating popular music into classical music. I don't see it as very different from what Mozart and Haydn did, or Bartók or Gershwin. Thinking of it that way, I feel like I'm able to reconcile both worlds.

Another thing about classical learning and the classical tradition is that it's so anachronistic. To grow up in this country and be trained in this tradition that comes from a hundred years ago in Germany or something. And every once in a while, I've found there are people of the generation above mine who had that same awkwardness about the anachronistic training and they sort of affect this European kind of mannerism. There are a lot of American classical musicians in their forties and fifties who affect this faux European manners [laughs]. . . . It doesn't really make sense to do that; I want to be a part of my time and place. That's another thing we all have to reconcile at some point, how to be relevant to the rest of ourselves and do the thing we love. That's another thing that drove me to music, because that's the way I can play the music of today and still play this instrument that has a long tradition. But I don't want to turn my back on classical music, I still love it. If I do a lot of different things, I feel comfortable moving in and out of that scene.

I think in terms of cultural issues as an Asian American, I guess I would be classified as a biracial. And I think that combination of cultural experience has given me an extra sensitivity or appreciation for this kind of incongruous thing that I see in music. I end up wanting to celebrate that rather than hide it. I'm intrigued by any kind of unlikely juxtapositions. That's why I love New York. What better example of the co-existence of so many incongruous elements. . . . My whole life is sort of like that . . .

MY: There's a common perception that Asian musicians are technically proficient but artistically inexpressive. Do you think that's just a stereotype, or is there any grain of truth to that characterization?

KB: It's an unfortunate stereotype because it's very easy to say that. . . . The thing is, though, it doesn't really matter how musical you are if the technique isn't there. . . . There are times I felt frustrated because of that generalization about Asian musicians who are just very cold and technical. On the other hand, it's still genuine, and at least they're not imposing some artificial emotive things superimposed onto their playing. I think in some ways that's worse. That relates to what I was saying about creating this faux Viennese persona of the people who feel connected to classical music in some special way. That's also very false to do that. I'd rather see someone who very honestly is sharing what his or her work is. And if it means that they somehow don't associate the music with their emotions, I'd rather see that honestly than to see someone saying, "I have to move around a lot, I have to emote right now." . . . So it's an interesting issue, and ultimately I think that if a performer is happy and rewarded personally by playing and sharing the music, that comes across. If the person feels uncomfortable or disenfranchised by doing that, then that also comes across. That happens regardless of culture. Talking about the incongruity of growing up in present-day America and learning this traditional European art form, that incongruity is ten thousand times more so for an Asian musician who grew up in Asia and learning this very foreign thing and trying to have it become an organic part of their person; it's a challenge. I have an appreciation for how difficult that might be.

5

A Voice of One's Own

Japanese violinist Hiroko Yajima remembered well her first tour in the United States in 1965 as a member of a student orchestra. The orchestra, comprised mostly of college and some high-school students at the Toho School of Music in Tokyo, had meticulously rehearsed Arnold Schoenberg's *Transfigured Night* for the performance at the New York World's Fair. For decades following this performance, Felix Galimir, a world-famous violinist from Vienna who later became one of her mentors, repeatedly told the story about how astonished he was by the performance of this group of "cute, young Japanese students in identical black and white outfits." He could not believe that "a student orchestra from Japan could possibly play Schoenberg at such a level." Galimir was not only impressed by their impeccable technique but was also particularly surprised by the way in which the Japanese students, presumably so "foreign" to the cultural and musical ideas of the Second Viennese School, had truly grasped the "essence" of this extremely difficult piece with its changing rhythm and sonority and played it so convincingly. A few years later, when Yajima was a student at Juilliard, she and two other Japanese students performed the Schubert Piano Trio in B-flat Major at a recital sponsored by the Schubert Society. The young trio members, having been trained by Galimir, were quite confident about their mastery of the piece and had a wonderful time performing, as it had never even occurred to them that anything other than their playing would matter to the audience. The audience—especially the Viennese—did praise their playing, repeatedly telling them that they "did not think that Japanese could play Schubert like this." Both of these anecdotes illustrate audiences' inclination to assume that musical understanding and expression have a natural connection to the musician's geographical, historical, cultural—and by implication, racial and ethnic—background. Despite asserting that she is not very sensitive about such matters and did not feel offended by these incidents, Yajima did remember these instances in which the apparent mismatch between her Japanese identity and her fine playing of European music seemed to evoke a cognitive dissonance on the part of the audience.[1]

More than thirty years later, in 1999, when pianist Makiko Hirata performed Chopin's Second Piano Concerto in Livingston, New Jersey, the local newspaper reviewed the performance as follows:

> The highlight of the concert was Chopin's Second Piano Concerto performed by soloist Makiko Hirata.
>
> Ms. Hirata was born in Japan, and it always surprises me that people born into a very different tonal system cannot only adapt to our eight-note scale but do it so well!
>
> While the orchestra was working with familiar music by one of the well-known Polish composers, Miss Hirata was working with something that would be as "foreign" to us as if we were trying to play Japanese music. She played the concerto from memory, while all the "grownups" on the stage—players and conductor—worked from printed scores.[2]

Even in praising Hirata's performance, the writer displays several assumptions fraught with contradictions. First, because Hirata was born in Japan (never mind that she has spent the majority of her life outside Japan, much of it in New Jersey), she was "born into" a different tonal system than that of Western music (never mind that she has been trained in Western music almost all her life and had studied at Juilliard, the Manhattan School of Music, and New York University and has no training in Japanese music). Second, for the members of the Livingston Symphony Orchestra, the music by a well-known Polish composer is "familiar" (never mind that most members of the orchestra are American, nor that Chopin spent much of his life in France). Third, "we"—presumably the American readers of the *West Essex Tribune*—all share the same musical sensibility, which finds Polish music familiar and Japanese music foreign (never mind that Japan not only adopted Western music well over a century ago but also is one of the most culturally as well as economically modern nations in the world). Finally, in contrast to the "grownups" in the orchestra Hirata is clearly a "child" (never mind that Hirata was twenty-five at the time), and therefore it is even more impressive that she performed from memory when the orchestra members used music (never mind that, with a few exceptions, concerti are always performed from memory).

It is easy to dismiss such comments as those of a provincial reviewer ignorant of either classical music or Asian culture. To be sure, such a response is certainly not typical among today's classical music audiences. Most audiences and critics are more knowledgeable about music itself as well as the multicultural nature of today's classical music world. Nonetheless, the idea that classical music is a province of European descendants to which Asians—as the racial and cultural outsider—are alien is not held exclusively by those ignorant of classical music. In fact, as discussed later in this chapter, many of my informants have encountered situations where their fellow classical musicians questioned—or conversely, noted as a pleasant surprise—the "authenticity" of their playing, singing, or composition of classical music, given their Asian identity or upbringing.

Is such an invocation of "authenticity" in classical music simply an outdated purist illusion about cultural traditions bound by geography and ethnicity? Or does the concept of authenticity have any validity or usefulness in understanding the nature of classical music? How would Asian musicians themselves answer these questions? If they believe that racial and cultural identity has any relevance to their music-making, how do they come to terms with the relationship between their identity and their work?

The idea of authenticity has been highly contested in both the arts and academia. As Walter Benjamin noted in his famous essay more than a half-century ago, modern technologies of mechanical reproduction have fundamentally altered the nature of artistic production and the meaning of authenticity.[3] Supporting Benjamin's point, postmodern artists' often playful engagement with the idea of "reproduction," "copy," and "simulacra" and their demystifying of the aura accorded to the "original" have challenged the dichotomous thinking underpinning the real versus the fake.

Meanwhile, in academia, scholars in such fields as history, anthropology, folklore, and literature have revealed that what are commonly regarded as ancient traditions of a people or culture are instead products of historical and political processes—many of them having to do with the shaping of modernity—thus debunking the notion that authentic traditions transcend time and context.[4] Moreover, the theoretical challenges brought by deconstruction and poststructuralism have pushed scholars toward an increased awareness of the forces that define their subjects and the processes by which "legitimate" knowledge is produced. No longer can scholars in these fields assume a fixed and pure—"authentic"—object of inquiry that exists and operates completely independent of the forces outside the bounded field, including the presence and the gaze of the inquirer.[5] Furthermore, postcolonial studies have shed light on the ways in which the histories and legacies of colonialism have made cultural hybrids out of both the colonizers and the colonized subjects. Studies of globalization have also shown the multidirectional and dynamic ways in which cultures—along with capital, labor, information, and technology—are spread and practiced across geographical borders, making the idea of authenticity almost null and void.

Yet, despite these critical debates, the ideas and ideals of authenticity remain a basis for important political and moral struggles for many people and groups. The concept of authenticity continues to have significant power in part because it invokes an organic connection between place/people and cultural artifacts/practices that is diluted under the conditions of modernity and postmodernity. Particularly for the people who feel that the integrity of their culture is threatened by the history and legacies of colonialism, global capitalism, or mass culture, authenticity has extremely high stakes. In a sense, the call for authenticity expresses a resistance to a commodified, disembodied culture and tries to realize a historically and culturally rooted, socially located self. The acts of "strategic essentialism"—a conscious invocation of particular elements of one's history, culture, and identity—are powerful tools for minority people in forging alliances toward shared political goals. Advocates of classical music as a distinctly European tradition—to which Asians are theoretically cultural outsiders—operate on similar notions of authenticity, stressing the importance of the historical and cultural rootedness of art forms such as classical music.

Far more than other art forms, classical music professes an ideal of rootedness in the music's historical and cultural origins. The orthodox understanding of classical music assumes that the role of the performers is to communicate the composer's intent, and so the performers' racial or ethnic identity should theoretically be irrelevant. In other words, whereas the composers and compositions are grounded territorially, historically, and culturally, the performers are largely disembodied. The vast majority of musicological literature focuses on composers rather than performers, revealing this emphasis on the primacy of composers in the world of classical music. Yet, the large presence of Asians in the classical music world challenges these premises because, in the United States, Asians are rarely seen as transparent conveyors of Western traditions.[6] Racially marked as cultural Others yet widely recognized as excelling in the musical form to which they are presumed to be outsiders, Asian classical musicians force us to rethink commonly held premises underpinning the classical music field, particularly the notions of authenticity.

This chapter discusses how the notion of authenticity is articulated in the field of classical music. I first address the historical, cultural, and musical context that shapes Asian and Asian American musicians' identities, which compels us to rethink the presumed connection among geography, race, culture, and musical identity. I then discuss how different areas of classical music—instrumental performance, opera performance, and composition—define criteria for authenticity. Although most of my informants are instrumentalists—as the vast majority of Asians in classical music are instrumental performers—it is important to discuss these fields within classical music separately, as there are important issues specific to each.

Within this context, I analyze Asian musicians' own understanding of the relationship between racial and cultural identity on the one hand and music-making on the other. Their ideas about the notion of authenticity vary widely from a universalist position that refutes the presumed connection between race/ethnicity and music-making to a particularist position that sees the culturally specific nature of musical expressions. From an academic standpoint, it is easy to criticize both of these views: the universalist position can be criticized as being devoid of historical and social specificity, whereas the particularist position can be charged with essentialism (i.e., treating a particular element of culture as the unique core that is shared by all members of its community while ignoring the conditions under which that element came to be seen as a valuable representation of that culture and eliding the diverse relationships that different members of the community have to that element). Yet, the range of the musicians' experiences and ideas illustrates the inadequacies of making such critiques without grounding them in the actual practice of music-making. Asian musicians' experiences, ideas, and work enable a conception of authenticity that is simultaneously faithful to the original music and to themselves—one that is at once relevant both to the tradition of classical music and to its practice today—and does not see them in dichotomous terms.

"Insiders" and "Outsiders" of Classical Music

When audiences, critics, or peer musicians question the authenticity of Asians playing or composing classical music, the underlying assumption is that Asians have a natural affinity for Asian music, not Western. Many Asian and Asian American musicians indeed note that they have been asked to play pieces of traditional music from their country (i.e., the country of their Asian ancestors, regardless of the musicians' own place of birth or upbringing) or compositions by their compatriots (i.e., those who share their ethnicity, regardless of the musicians' nationality or cultural identity) at performances. Such requests reflect the current American climate of multiculturalism that valorizes non-Western cultural forms; identity politics, which often equates one's racial and ethnic background with one's cultural identity; and perhaps, a desire on the part of the audience to be exposed to and understand other cultures. However genuine and well intentioned their motivations might be, such requests assume that racial and ethnic background is synonymous with national identification, cultural knowledge, and musical expertise. According to this premise, a Korean American violinist playing a traditional Korean song would supposedly convey a deep, instinctive connection to the spirit of the piece that is different from her playing of, say, Shostakovich. Faced with these assumptions, Asian musicians often agree to play an arrangement of some piece with recognizably ethnic tunes—such as Korean "Arirang," Japanese "Sakura," or Chinese "Mo Li Hua."

However, most Asian musicians working in classical music are far from familiar with Asian music. In fact, for many Asian musicians, Asian music is much more foreign than Western music, and their relationship to Asian music is no more authentic or innate than their relationship to classical music.

As discussed in Chapter 1, since the nineteenth century when East Asians eagerly adopted Western music, their musical training has been largely Westernized. Traditional or folk Asian music has continued to be practiced among certain segments of the population, but it is rarely a substantial part of school curricula or mainstream cultural consumption, and the urban middle class with its Westernized cultural upbringing has come to see Asian music either as low class or as a rarefied art form and a legacy of premodern times. Especially for the generations raised after World War II, Western functional harmony, Western scales, and the sonority of Western instruments have played a central role in shaping their musical sensibilities. "School songs" written for schoolchildren used Western harmony and became a central component of musical training in Japan, Korea, and China. Advanced music training in Asia was modeled after the Western conservatory system, with private lessons, classes in theory and musicology, orchestral or choral studies, and so forth.[7] To be sure, traditional Asian music has a greater importance in some East Asian countries than in others. Whereas in Japan, traditional Japanese music such as *gagaku* or *koto* music has come to be seen largely as an esoteric pursuit of the upper class, in China, Beijing opera has remained an important part of the culture; interest in and the practice of traditional music also remain fairly widespread in Korea as well. Furthermore, in recent decades there has been a resurgence of interest in traditional and/or folk music in many parts of East Asia, as seen in the popularity of Okinawan music in Japan. Nonetheless, on the whole the groups active in such music do not overlap heavily with the practitioners of Western classical music.

In Asian American communities as well, traditional Asian music has been practiced over generations and has played an important part in community life and ethnic cohesion, and the rise of ethnic nationalism in the 1970s and 1980s encouraged many Asian American youths to turn to Asian music and other forms of performance arts as an assertion of their ethnic identity.[8] However, the generations that were raised in the United States going to American schools and living under the pressure to assimilate tended to be drawn more to Western music. Although a few of my informants were raised in households in which traditional Asian music was played frequently, most Asian and Asian American musicians grew up with little exposure to or interest in Asian music.

For many Asian musicians, their lack of interest in Asian music stems from their upbringing. For example, Frederick Lau, a flutist and now also an ethnomusicologist specializing in Chinese music, recalled that when he was growing up in Hong Kong, he had no interest in Chinese music at all: "I thought it was backward, low-class music." It was his exposure to ethnomusicology during graduate school that opened his eyes to non-Western music and expanded his musical vocabulary and appreciation.[9] However, most classical musicians never have such experiences and thus continue to hold views about Asian music derived from their childhood. A number of my informants made it quite clear that they were not particularly interested in Asian music and that they believed in the superiority of Western music over Asian music. Violinist Pei-Chun Tsai remembered that, when she was in music school in Taiwan, all students were required to learn to play a Chinese instrument but that she did not enjoy it: "I just wasn't that crazy about it. . . . I think [Western classical music] is much more beautiful. There must be a reason why Western classical music is played by the whole world but not Chinese music, right? It's just a lot more beautiful and it's got a lot more culture."[10] She thus attributes the global spread of Western music and the relative isolation of Asian music not to differences in the systems of music production and dissemination or to political, economic, or social structures but to the quality of the music itself. Hong Kong-born pianist Siu Yan Luk said that she is not interested in playing traditional Chinese music or contemporary music inspired by traditional Chinese music because she does not find it musically challenging. Chinese music, according to her, tends to be harmonically simple, the melody is always the same, and it imitates antique tunes from traditional Chinese instruments.[11] Chinese violinist Duoming Ba's comment sums up these musical sensibilities of Asian musicians raised with and trained in Western music: "When I listen to Chinese opera, it sounds more foreign to me than Mozart or Brahms."[12]

Asian musicians' attitude toward Asian music is also shaped by the training they received in classical music, which does not encourage the study of non-Western and contemporary music, let alone non-classical musical genres.[13] Conservatory training typically focuses almost exclusively on the European repertoire prior to 1945. Not surprisingly, many of my informants, especially young musicians, told me that they are not especially interested in playing works by Asian composers, as they are quite happy playing Western music: "It's not that I consciously avoid works by Asian composers, but I think perhaps that there is an unconscious part of me that thinks that if I'm going to bother to learn a piece, I might as well learn something European. I think I should change this way of thinking. On the other hand, I don't necessarily seek out music by Japanese composers specifically because they are Japanese," said one Japanese pianist. Whereas this musician displayed a critical awareness of her own bias against Asian compositions, many other musicians are quite uncritical of their own prejudice.

Even the musicians who now actively explore works by Asian composers admit that their experience of playing such works is too limited to allow them to make any meaningful comparison between their understanding of the works by Asian composers and that by Western composers. Pianist Sachiko Kato, who has been producing and performing recitals comprised entirely of works by living Japanese composers, said that although she feels that composers such as Toru Takemitsu convey particular Japanese aesthetics, she has not played enough works by Japanese or other Asian composers to be able to make a comparison between their works and those of Western composers.[14]

Many musicians also note that they do not find anything specifically Asian in most contemporary Asian music, because contemporary musicians have been trained in the Western medium and influenced by many musical traditions and many Asian composers today do not use stereotypically Asian sounds such as pentatonic scales. Pianist Helen Huang commented that, although Tan Dun is seen as a quintessential contemporary Chinese composer and his music that has specifically Chinese themes (such as the music for the film, *Crouching Tiger, Hidden Dragon*) sounds Chinese, his piano music does not strike her as particularly Chinese or Asian.[15] Cellist Han-Na Chang said, "As for Asian composers who compose in the tradition of Western classical music, I wouldn't group them under Asian cultures, I would rather say 'this individual' or 'that individual.' . . . Whether I find any personal link to them depends on the musical language they write in and whether I feel that I can convey something special in that particular musical language."[16] When harpist Ayako Watanabe played contemporary works by Japanese composers, she did not find the music particularly culture-specific, nor did she feel that she understood the piece any better because of her Japanese-ness.[17] Many others said that they do not feel a particular affinity with contemporary works in general, Asian or otherwise. Many Asian musicians actually find it challenging to play contemporary music that incorporates Asian musical traditions and sonorities because they have not been trained in those musical languages. Violinist Jennifer Koh made this comment on the music of Tan Dun, the first Asian composer with whom she has worked: "For me, it's more of an experiment to be playing Tan Dun, which is inspired by Mongolian fiddle, than it is for me to play something like Brahms, because, to be quite honest with you, I've never heard a Mongolian fiddle."[18] Thus, for Asians in classical music, their relationship to Asian music, whether traditional or contemporary, is tenuous at best.

In contrast, many Asian musicians see American music as their own. Several of my informants mentioned instances where they heard non-American musicians play works by American composers—particularly those who incorporate specifically American musical forms such as jazz and swing—and asserted that "it just did not sound right." After giving a detailed, thoughtful response to the question about authenticity in European music, conductor Kent Nagano rather abruptly said, "On the other hand, when I have heard European groups playing American music, I have said, 'That's not right.' As an American, I can tell [when American music is not played right]."[19] Similarly, flutist Joel Tse recalled that, when he was working for an orchestra in Hong Kong, he felt that the way Chinese musicians played the works of American composers such as Gershwin or Copland was lacking in flavor and swing and that the Toledo Symphony for which he currently plays was far superior in this regard than the Hong Kong Philharmonic, which was otherwise a very competent orchestra. Of course, such an observation needs to be understood in a larger context: many members of the Hong Kong Philharmonic are European and American and the rehearsals are conducted in English; thus, attributing "non-American-ness" to the orchestra because of its geographical location may be misleading. Yet, the observation is still meaningful as Tse's assertion of his understanding of American music. "I was brought up in the States, so I guess I can play American music better than Chinese or European musicians."[20] Many other Asian musicians, even those who were raised mostly in Asia, made similar remarks, even as they qualified them by saying that, like most classically trained musicians, they were far from versed in jazz and other forms of American music.

The assertiveness with which these musicians declared their ability to distinguish between the "right" and "wrong" ways of playing American music is striking, especially in contrast to the nuanced way in which the same musicians responded to the question of authenticity in playing European music, which I discuss later. Notably, these musicians, whose interviews as a whole conveyed their multifaceted, fluid sense of identity as both Asian and American, almost unquestioningly claimed an American identity when they were discussing their understanding of American music. Just as some Western critics insist on European ownership of Western classical music, these musicians claimed their own authentic understanding of American music. Especially for Asian Americans whose place in American society has historically been challenged on legal, economic, and social terrains, such an assertion of cultural belonging performs a powerful work of claiming citizenship in America.

As these stories indicate, for most Asian and Asian American musicians, the musical repertoire and idioms they have the closest relationship to are European and American rather than Asian. Western music is not their cultural Other but rather at the center of their identity.

Whose Voice?
Part I: The Instrumentalists

Classical music differs from other forms of music in that its central repertoire is the music written in a bygone era, which is meticulously studied and rehearsed by the performer. In this sense, much of classical music performance is about connecting the present in which the performer and the listener reside with particular moments in the past in which the composer produced the music. Compared to other forms of music, the performance of classical music places a much higher demand and value on the accurate understanding of the musical styles and conventions of each period and the faithful realization of the composer's genius and design.[21] Thus, as ethnomusicologist Bruno Nettl writes, institutions such as music schools place highest value on the preservation of purity of the musical tradition: "[T]he value of purity is illustrated in the music school's great interest in authentic performance, on so-called authentic instruments of the composer's time, and in works rendered in accordance with composers' presumed intentions and ideals."[22]

Yet, implicit in Nettl's use of words such as "so-called" and "presumed" is the contingent nature of such notions as authenticity and purity. As most of the classical repertoire was written before sound was recorded, it is impossible to determine exactly what the music was intended to sound like. Moreover, the understanding of the ideal way to play, for instance, Baroque music, changes over time as musicological knowledge and performance practice evolve. Thus, there is no fixed, authentic way to play a particular repertoire. What remains essential to the form, and what lies beyond the scholarship and careful study, is individual interpretation and expression.

Nonetheless, the primacy of the composer and the original context in classical music shapes the issue of authenticity in ways quite different from those in other forms of performing arts. In the orthodox discourse of classical music, the locus of authenticity—the point of origin—lies first and foremost in the composer and his or her (mostly his) musical, cultural, historical context, *not* in the performer. Regardless of interpretive innovations or technical brilliance, a performance that does not adhere to the musical understanding shared in the profession is not deemed legitimate. In Nettl's words, "In general, what is most emphasized about musical works and styles, about composers and performers, even about instruments, is—broadly speaking—their origin, their place in history."[23] This centrality of origin inherently shapes the relationship between the composer and the music on the one hand and the performer on the other.

Within such a framework, concepts such as the performer's identity are quite secondary to the musicians' artistic goal. Conductor Kent Nagano articulated this point quite clearly, stressing the utmost importance of "assimilating" oneself into the culture and language of classical music: "[The ideal behind] classical music is very different from [the idea underlying comments like], 'I perform this music this way because this is how I feel.' This art form has too much tradition to respect. One needs to embrace the responsibility to assimilate, evolve, and improve. Only by doing so, one can evolve to a different level."[24] He described his endless search for an understanding of the art form: "Working within the art field, I am faced with constant humility. The more you know, the more you realize how much you don't know. Every time I go back to Beethoven symphonies, I realize how much more I need to do." Central to classical music performance, therefore, is the realization of the composer's music, rather than of the performer's emotions, ideas, or ego.

In a sense, then, in classical music performance, any performer today—regardless of race or ethnicity—is inherently an outsider to the composer/music that is the locus of authenticity. However, given the primacy of the original, it is easy to understand the issue as a matter of racial identity if one presumes a correspondence between geography, race, and culture and authenticity in territory-bound terms. It is such a premise that leads to the argument that Asians are cultural outsiders to the European tradition of classical music.

Some Asian musicians regard this argument about authenticity as offensive. It is worth noting that some of the most prominent Asian musicians I contacted declined to be interviewed. Although I can only speculate about their reasons, their representatives' explanations suggested to me that, from the way I described my project and the questions I was interested in, the musicians thought that I was trying to make an argument for the racially and culturally based nature of music-making, a view with which they did not wish to be associated. Their response indicates that for some Asian musicians, even the mere suggestion that one's racial and cultural identity might play a factor in music-making is offensive.

Some of the musicians whom I did interview made this point quite clearly by promptly dismissing the question of authenticity as irrelevant and offensive. From the outset of the interview, Korean violinist Chee-Yun clearly stated that she found the suggestion that race matters to music-making quite appalling. "If you listen to a recording, you can't tell the race of the performer," she declared. She claimed that, as far as music-making goes, she never thinks of herself as Asian. She recalled an incident when a French musician asked her if it was difficult for her to play Western music because she was Asian. "I was very offended by that," she said very adamantly. "He said that because he's French, when he plays German music, he has a hard time understanding it. And I thought, 'You know what, this guy is probably never going to have a career.'" She characterized his comment as "completely stupid" and remarked, "Especially these days, when we are able to travel across the world within a day, you can go and experience just as much what other people are experiencing, taste their food, adapt to their lifestyle. . . . To say something like [what the French musician said], in the year 2000, it's pretty silly. I think it's almost impossible to feel your nationality or race in music. It has never, ever crossed my mind."[25]

Pianist Sachiko Kato similarly commented that it is the role of a professional performer to play all types of music convincingly. When I asked her to elaborate on the issue of authenticity, she immediately said,

I don't think there is such a thing as an 'authentic' performance. I
don't think composers expect an 'authentic' performance [of their
music], either. . . . [Pianist] Peter Serkin's playing of Takemitsu is
a lot more imaginative than the playing by many Japanese pianists
I've heard, and I think it's up to the talent of the performer to capture, absorb, and express the essence of any music. If an American
performer cannot convincingly play a piece of music from another
culture, that's because that person has no talent. Especially in this
day and age, you can have access to the world, you can get music
from another culture through the internet or whatever, so understanding the music of another culture is not something beyond
imagination.[26]

There are several common threads to these musicians' views. First, no
particular culture or group of people "owns" classical music any more legit-
imately than others. Second, the flow of information in the world today
allows open access for musicians to gain understanding of other musical
cultures. Third, the sign of a competent and talented musician is the ability to capture and express musical ideas, including those that originate in
cultures other than their own. And finally, to think of musical understanding as geographically and culturally bound is not only provincial but also
racist. Underlying this reasoning are the universalist, cosmopolitan, human-
istic ideals of individual free will, independence from the bonds of nations
and other forms of affiliations, a devotion to the interests of humanity as a
whole, and a belief in and commitment to a shared global culture. They also
share the conception of globalization as a condition in which the free flow of
information and goods gives all people access to them.

This universalist position partly echoes the neoliberal rhetoric of globalization. As many scholars have demonstrated, such views tend to ignore
the vastly unequal access that people around the world have to the resources
and institutions that enable such ideals; the particularities of places and
histories that shape the experiences of universalism or cosmopolitanism
in enormously different ways; the ways in which nationalism often works
hand in hand with the goals of universalism or cosmopolitanism; and the
ways in which such rhetoric functions as a guise for reinforcing Western
and capitalist hegemony.[27] In the context of classical music, this rhetoric
is manifested in an argument that "(classical) music is universal," ignoring

the vastly different access that people from different regions—and, more important, classes—have to classical music, as well as the numerous forms of state and civic interventions in promoting, shaping, or suppressing music at various points in history.

At the same time, these universalist ideas also make important interventions by turning the often Eurocentric underpinning of such rhetoric on its head. In the dominant discourse of classical music, the values and logic of its particular musical culture have often been cloaked under the rhetoric of universalism, and non-Western musical traditions have been accepted only as far as they are seen as contributing to the development of Western music.[28] Yet, in the hands of Asian musicians, this universalist rhetoric comes to carry quite a different message. By de-territorializing classical music from Europe and thereby de-centering the logic of universal humanism, Asian musicians do not simply extol the superiority of classical music but challenge the Western hegemony that enabled its spread by claiming their own place in and ownership of classical music. Just as the claim by Asian and Asian American musicians to have an authentic understanding of American music serves to assert their place in American culture and society, these musicians declare their rightful place not only in the Western culture but also the world at large by demonstrating their ownership of classical music.

In our interview, double bassist Satoshi Okamoto deftly articulated this issue of ownership: "If you think of classical music as a form of European ethnic music, you might find it strange to see so many non-Europeans playing it. But I think classical music is beyond the level of ethnic music and has been raised to a more universal level that doesn't necessarily belong to any particular group of people. Christianity originates in the West, but so many different elements have been added to it, and it is no longer solely a 'Western' religion. Similarly, classical music doesn't necessarily belong to Europe . . . I don't think of classical music as specifically Western."[29] In this last statement, Okamoto reflects that the adoption and appropriation by Asians of classical music were not simply unidirectional from the West to the East, as shown in Chapter 1. Those who have embraced classical music have made their own meanings of it and used it to advance their own goals. In the process, at least according to some Asian musicians, classical music even lost its significance as a specifically Western cultural form.[30]

In addition to claiming the universalism of classical music, Okamoto also explained the act of music-making as he sees it:

Ultimately, playing music is a very concrete act of making sound through physical movements. I don't think there is anything particularly esoteric involved in that physical act, like something made up of some secret that you cannot attain. It's really a matter of how to hold the string and how to move the bow and how to make the sound big or small . . . anyone can do those things [as long as one acquires the proper technique]. Even the things that are often attributed to innate musical sensibilities, like rhythm, are ultimately a very concrete physical thing that can be learned.

He thus refutes the idea that there is some culturally specific essence to classical music that non-Western people cannot capture. By objectifying music as a combination of concrete elements that anyone can learn and then practice, he demystifies classical music and rids it of an authenticity defined in territorialized cultural terms.

Yet not all Asian musicians hold a universalist position. Many believe that one's racial and cultural background does shape music-making in one way or another, and they thus express a particularist position in regard to authenticity. The musicians who make this claim often use such words as "blood," "soul," "instinctive," and "innate" in describing their feeling that a musician who shares the national or ethnic culture of the composer possesses an authenticity in playing that music that is not held by musicians from another culture.

Such an argument carries an undeniably essentialist overtone. Attributing musical expressions to primordial ties such as race and ethnicity does not account for the historical and social forces that shape musical production, and it also ignores the diversity within ethnocultures. At the same time, those who see the specificities of musical sensibilities along ethnic lines also have an understanding of culture and identity that is more situated in specific contexts and that resists a universalist rhetoric that elides differences in histories and circumstances. They thus pay greater attention to the culturally specific nature of musical practices.

Violinist Angella Ahn said that, when she heard a Bulgarian musician play a piece derived from Bulgarian folk music, she felt there was an "innate feeling" and "natural rhythm" that she would never be able to capture.[31] Similarly, trombonist Kōichirō Yamamoto said,

[W]hen Europeans play music like Mahler, Mozart, or Beethoven, it's hard enough for me just to follow along. . . . I do feel that those people who have it in their blood relate to it differently. After all, I am a Japanese musician who has *studied* Western music, and there is a limitation that I have to acknowledge. When Russian musicians play Russian music, it's very clear and easy to follow, but if I had to do the same thing all on my own, I couldn't do it. When someone like James Levine [of the Metropolitan Opera] conducts Mahler and other music by Jewish composers, I am in awe of how he does it.

When asked if such cultural boundaries can be crossed, he said, "It will take a whole lifetime. You keep working hard, with open ears and open mind, and maybe at the end of your career you will reach that goal."[32] Pianist Mariko Furukawa commented that the difference in the performers' cultural background is manifested most clearly in their sense of rhythm: "What we have in our blood is inherently in us. . . . The sense of rhythm that's culturally specific becomes most clear when we play ethnic dance music, like polonaise, Hungarian dance music, things like that."[33]

The feeling of foreign-ness to the music is not always based on a primordialist understanding of race or ethnicity but also comes from the notion that a shared culture shapes the classical music tradition. Violinist Mari Kimura explained,

Specifically speaking, the difference is in minute details, but those details are what distinguishes the essence and superficiality. So, in music, for example, a Japanese playing Mahler sometimes would do things that a German musician would never do. It is a really minute thing, but still definite and specific, and it makes a difference. [The Japanese playing] is not necessary wrong, but because there is an unspoken agreement between the performer and the listener that has been made historically and culturally, if those rules [about how a piece of music should be played] aren't met, the listener feels betrayed, and the playing is characterized as inauthentic.[34]

Some musicians had more specific explanations for how a shared culture affects music-making. After commenting that she has never thought about her

Asian identity as it relates to her actual playing, collaborative pianist Hiromi Fukuda said, "But I think in studying music, especially lieder and other music that has verbal text, and particularly religious pieces are hard to understand on the level of feeling. I may feel differently if I were Christian, but I'm not."[35] They thus attribute the difference in musical understanding not to race or blood but rather to cultural elements at the basis of classical music.

Oboist Kaori Kato came to an awareness about the culturally specific nature of musical expression through her work as a music therapist. After studying at the Toho School of Music, she came to the United States to study oboe performance at the New England Conservatory and Temple University. Although she did some freelance work in various orchestras and chamber ensembles after graduation, she did not feel that the life of a freelancer suited her and so she decided to study music therapy. After obtaining her degree, she started working as a music therapist for a psychiatric hospital in the Bronx, New York. When I asked Kato whether she is ever conscious of her Japanese identity in her work as a musician, she said that, although she rarely thought about her Japanese identity when she was playing, she came to be much more conscious about it once she started working as a music therapist. She talked about how, through her work in music therapy, she came to deeply understand that people from different cultures express themselves musically in completely different ways, and she often felt the difficulty of building a relationship with her patients from different cultures. When I asked her to talk about a time when she felt that way, after thinking carefully, she said,

> For example . . . there's a song called "Swing Low, Sweet Chariot." It's a spiritual about going to heaven, about death. But in terms of the feeling of the music, from my Japanese sensibility . . . it's in F Major, so it has a cheerful tone to it, and it doesn't sound too depressing. A Japanese person, if somebody dies, would choose something darker, in a minor key, you know. So when I see a patient singing this song and crying, I find it difficult to understand and empathize with that musical sensibility. In Japanese music, even "Sakura Sakura" [a traditional song about cherry blossoms] is in a minor key, and lullabies are also in minor keys. . . . So I think in music, in terms of things like key or rhythm, there are things that are consistent throughout the world's cultures, but there are also things that are very different

along cultural or racial lines. I have come to feel that my own musical language is a little different from other people's, because of the culture I grew up in.[36]

Through learning that people from different cultures have very different ways of understanding and expressing themselves through music, Kato arrived at a more heightened awareness of her identity as Japanese, both as a musician and as an individual.

Such an understanding of the culturally specific nature of musical expression requires a reconsideration of the oft-used phrase, "Music is a universal language." The connection between music and language is better understood by focusing on the process of language acquisition.

Pianist Ju-Ying Song's experience illuminates this point. Song recalled that during a summer music festival she attended, a student from Hong Kong, who was a highly proficient and accomplished pianist, had an unusually difficult time getting the phrasing right in the Chopin Third Sonata. Then a friend of Song pointed out that the problem was that the student played like she spoke in Cantonese. Convinced by this explanation, Song recalled,

> That's [the student's] language, and the inflections of Cantonese are completely different from the inflections of French. And that's why she's phrasing the way she's phrasing, and it doesn't sound idiomatic. . . . [My friend] did an imitation of Chinese opera [and sang] the Chopin melody with the inflections of the Chinese opera. And that's exactly what [the student's playing] sounded like, in a bizarre way, and I think [the student] really understood completely that that's what it was all about. It's basically like you're trying to teach a foreign language to somebody. . . . It doesn't matter that she's hitting all the right notes. She plays very musically, and her natural musical instincts are very good. But in terms of where she chooses to put the accents and how she's phrasing, it doesn't sound idiomatic. . . . At the end of the month, I think it changed a little bit, but it still didn't sound quite right.

The concept of "idiom" is key to this idea of language as a metaphor for music. Idiomatic expressions—whether linguistic or musical—are those expressions that are in common use yet whose meaning is not logically deducible from the concrete meanings of its components; as such they are the most difficult parts of language for non-natives to acquire. It is these elements that are often characterized as culturally specific expressions. However, it is important to note that neither Song nor her friend who made the connection between the student's playing and her native language was making a *racial* or *ethnic* argument per se. Without my prompting, Song volunteered a comment saying that Asians raised in Europe (like herself) or in the United States might have a different relationship to Western music than those who grew up in Asia, thus asserting that one's racial or ethnic identity does not always correlate with one's linguistic or cultural identity.

Song's observation about language and musical expression led to a unique insight about what the language-music connection means exactly. She asserted, "I never believed that music is a universal language. It's always said [that music is universal], but I don't think it is. It's an *acquired* language just like anything else." Reflecting on her experience of hearing an Indian classical music concert, she remembered that she found Indian music generally rather monotonous and repetitive; yet the Indians in the audience were responding physically to the rhythm in ways that were very different from how she understands rhythmic patterns.

> I realized right then that there is a tremendous cultural gap. Until I understand how this music is put together and I feel the feeling that they're conveying, I won't be able to feel the music the way [the man whose head was bumping throughout the concert] was feeling. And then it made me think, if I were to play for him Chopin Berceuse, would he appreciate some of the subtleties there? You know, there are these ever so slight color changes that can be such a heart-wrenching moment, but it's so subtle, and for the average listener, it's just boring, perhaps. . . . So I think it's an acquired thing. Understanding music is like understanding a verbal language, an acquired skill. You *learn* to understand what emotions are being conveyed. You *learn* to understand the meanings behind the notes.[37]

By linking music to language and seeing both as acquired rather than innate, Song thus not only challenged the equation between language and race but also questioned the very idea of the universality of music. In other words, linking music to language has helped her see the culturally specific nature of music, rather than reifying the notion of music as universal. Although Song's culturally varied upbringing—born in Taiwan, raised in Geneva speaking French, and currently based in New York—may have much to do with her insights, her story illustrates the complexity of the notion of "music as a universal language."

For some musicians, their Asian identity affects not only how they express particular musical traditions, styles, or elements but also that very act of self-expression through music. Hawai'i-born double bassist Kurt Muroki said, "A lot of times, [when I'm in the context of] Asian culture . . . [I feel] I'm not allowed to speak, I'm not allowed to express myself. And in music, you're allowed to do that. . . . Growing up, I wasn't a good speaker, [and] I didn't express myself very well. My father was very strict and stern, old-style, and [especially in his presence] I often didn't know how to say what I wanted to say. And music allowed me to [express myself]. I have a lot of friends who feel that way that are Asian."[38] Similarly, violinist Conway Kuo said,

If I can make a generalization, I definitely feel that in Asian culture we're a little bit inhibited musically. . . . If I were a little child among Chinese grownups, I would be reserved and not make too much noise . . . you're not going to see me dancing wildly on the dance floor. And a lot of times, in music, to really express certain ideas with a wide range of emotions requires a really high level of expression, and I would say for myself that I find myself a little too inhibited. I think it's a cultural thing, because [in Asian culture] it's just not considered appropriate to show too much [of your emotions] to other people. Just the way we're brought up in our culture, the natural inclination is to go inward, and it might require some extra element to let myself loose.[39]

For these musicians, Asian norms about social interaction and emotional expression are at odds with the demands of musical performance, and it is through conscious effort that they have learned to express themselves through music. At the same time, it is through classical music that they can express themselves in ways that are not restricted by cultural norms. In other words, it is classical music that allows their authentic voices to break through and beyond the layers of socialization.

In all of these arguments about the particularism of music-making, the performers themselves are the outsiders to the authentic music written by the composer. As essentialist as such constructions of the "authentic" Western music and the "Asian identity" might be, their ideas about the particularities of cultural practice and experience present an alternative to the universalist notions of music that gloss over differences.

The universalist and particularist views of music and identity need not be incompatible, however. Most Asian musicians' viewpoints fall somewhere in between the two or, more accurately, combine them. Even musicians who clearly took the universalist position sometimes acknowledged that there were musical sensibilities and aesthetics that were particular to Asian culture. For example, although half-Japanese violinist Anne Akiko Meyers emphasized that she thinks the issue of authenticity is largely irrelevant as all professional musicians play music by composers from all over the world, she also said that her part-Japanese background and her fascination with Japanese culture help her better understand contemporary Japanese music: "I've done a lot of CDs recently with Japanese music, like [Toru] Takemitsu, [Somei] Satoh, things like that. And Takemitsu always said that the Japanese do not understand the word 'allegro.' That, philosophically, I can totally understand, because the Japanese just love that space in between the notes, it's almost more important than the note itself. And that kind of quietness and reflection is like an identity stamp. So maybe I'm more sensitive to things like that."[40]

On the other hand, those who gave elaborate explanations about the musical "essence" specific to certain cultures also said that expressing that essence is not necessarily the ultimate artistic goal for a musician. Mari Kimura, who commented on the subtleties of authenticity manifested in minute details of musical expressions, followed up by saying,

> But actually, as a musician, it is not my goal to learn the essence of Western music and to acquire its ultimate truth. My goal is to learn the Western musical form and make it my own. It is not my goal to play Viennese music like a Viennese musician. As more and more people who don't follow the conventions come to play Western music, those conventions themselves will eventually change. . . . If you really tried, you can probably learn to play German music

like a German musician, but it's up to the individual whether to make it one's goal to "become German." I think it's unclear whether the authenticity debate is a crucial one or simply a reflection of prejudice.[41]

Many musicians saw the benefits of the encounters between cultures, celebrating the hybrid nature of musical practice. Harpist Ayako Watanabe commented,

Of course, from the standpoint of authenticity, someone from the culture which produced the music may have an advantage. But I think classical music is something more universal. Today, both the musicians and their audiences travel all over the world, and the idea of authenticity itself is becoming meaningless. . . . Japanese people have a particular notion of what a *toro* [tuna sushi] ought to taste like, but an American person might put some lemon on *toro* and think that's the best thing in the world. That makes sushi a whole different thing, producing something totally new. So I feel that musical authenticity is not particularly important.[42]

Although acknowledging cultural particularities and differences, these musicians do not place ultimate value on pursuing the essence of the originating culture of classical music; rather, their artistic goal is to find their own voice that emerges through their rigorous study of Western music.

The range and combination of these musicians' ideas demonstrate the relevance and power of both the universalist ideals they embrace as artists and the experiences and insights about cultural particularities they have gained as musicians and as individuals straddling multiple cultures. As discussed in previous chapters, Asian musicians experience the various meanings of their Asian identities in their everyday lives, both in and outside the world of classical music. At the same time, they pursue classical music precisely because they believe in its power to communicate across the particularities of social categories. Asian musicians seek their musical and personal voice that is true both to the demands of the original music and to their individual self.

Whose Voice?
Part II: The Opera Singers

Issues of authenticity have quite different meanings and manifestations for musicians in fields of classical music other than instrumental performance. Opera singers face the particular issue of casting as well.

In opera, a multi-media art form that involves visual spectacle and theatrical performance as much as musical art, authenticity becomes a matter not only of faithful realization of the original music but also of visual and theatrical believability. Most roles in the standard opera repertoire are white, and in the cultural climate in which white performers playing non-white roles have been hailed for their ability to bridge the cultural gap through their artistry whereas non-white performers playing white roles were often seen as unbelievable, Asian opera singers have faced special challenges in developing careers in the opera world. Since the early twentieth century when Tamaki Miura became the first Japanese singer to have an international opera career by playing the role of Cio-Cio-San, female Asian singers have historically been cast in few roles other than as Asian characters in *Madama Butterfly, Turandot,* and a handful of other operas in which they play the stereotypical role of the exotic geisha.[43] For male Asian singers, the issue of the emasculation of Asian men in dominant Western cultures—resulting in the audience's resistance to seeing Asian men in powerful roles traditionally played by white men—is compounded by the sheer absence of substantive operatic roles for Asian men, except for the presumably "Oriental" character of Calaf in Puccini's *Turandot.* Such casting and audience perceptions—which often equate the Asian roles created by Western imagination with the real Asian singers—are based on Orientalist racial and gender stereotypes of the librettists' and composers' times, some of which persist to this day.

Moreover, the history of Orientalism in opera itself further complicates the meaning of authenticity in opera performance. In such operas as *The Mikado, Madama Butterfly,* and *Turandot,* the Asian setting, the characters, and the story are nineteenth- and early twentieth-century Western Orientalist constructions of Asia. Some operas are more realistic than others, but all reflect the fantasies about Asia shared by the Western producers and audiences. Although a handful of Asian singers built careers in the early twentieth century by singing these roles, none of these operas was written with the intent of casting Asian singers in Asian roles. In other words, a production would be no more authentic by casting an Asian singer in an Asian role. Such a paradox highlights the entangled nature of authenticity, culture, and race in opera.

Under these circumstances, Asian opera singers work hard to maintain their artistic integrity and to carve their place on stage by honing their musical and acting skills so they can play non-Asian roles convincingly while coming to terms with the reality of casting that is often racially based. "Just like many Japanese people would find it strange if they saw a white singer playing the role of Cio-Cio-San, I think one can't blame the white audiences for finding it strange to see an Asian singer playing a white role. Some people say that it's stupid to think that Japanese singers should be cast in *Butterfly* and African American singers in *Aida,* but I do think that visual considerations are a factor in opera production," said Japanese soprano Kimiko Hata. She said that she even found her own performance of Juliet somewhat strange when she watched the video recording of the *Romeo and Juliet* production in which she starred. Such visual expectations—to see Asians performers playing Asian roles and white singers playing white characters—have little to do with the musical and theatrical demands of the opera. For example, many Japanese singers are not suited for the heavy voice demanded of Cio-Cio-San. In addition, some Asian singers say that, in terms of acting, Mozart operas that are less overtly dramatic than many Italian operas tend to be easier for Asians to perform, yet Asians tend to be cast more often in Italian operas with "exotic" roles than in Mozart operas. Although some Asian singers, such as Hei-Kyung Hong and Sumi Jo, have had increasing success in opera companies around the United States and Europe, race still often plays a part in casting considerations. Hata told me that when she auditioned for an American opera company, she was asked to sing a *Butterfly* aria for future reference even though *Butterfly* was not on the program for that season.[44]

In the world in which Asian femininity is seen as exotic, the meanings attached to Asian or part-Asian appearance may be at odds with the musicians' artistic goals. Lea Woods Friedman, a Hawai'i-born soprano whose parents are of Singaporean Chinese and Russian Jewish heritage, said that she has been told by company directors and her colleagues that she should "play up her Asian [ethnicity] more. . . . I've been told in this past audition season that I should try to look 'more Asian' because supposedly the trend now is to hire Asian." The suggestion that one can play up one's Asian-ness and look more Asian (or, by implication, play down one's Asian-ness and look less Asian) reveals the arbitrary and performative nature of Asian identity in this context. Such a cultural climate that fetishizes the visual appearances of Asian women makes it awkward for Asian (or part-Asian) musicians to balance their artistic integrity with their desire to be cast. Friedman contemplated this balance: "When I go to sing in an audition, I sing because I'm me. I haven't grasped the idea of making myself into something else. . . . So really in this industry, the challenge is to stay true to what you've been born with and what package we've worked on for ourselves."[45]

As an increasing number of Asians enter the opera world not only as performers but also on the production side, they gain greater influence in shaping the productions, including casting. Henry Akina is an ethnically mixed opera director who grew up in Hawai'i, studied theater on the East Coast, and worked in a Berlin opera house for fifteen years until he returned to Hawai'i in 1996 to become the artistic director of the Hawaii Opera Theatre. On the politics of race in casting, he said that although his predecessors were very insistent about casting only Asian singers for Asian roles, he has tried to avoid that issue as much as possible. "I cast usually for voice and a kind of physical energy. And to the extent that that is governed by ethnicity or physical presentation or something, certainly that's an influence. But for instance, this year's casting for *Turandot* is a little strange, because we have a Swedish Irish Turandot, who is a princess of China, and all the Chinese are playing the Tartars. So that's all mixed up. [laughs]" He commented that in Hawai'i, where there has historically been a high degree of racial mixing among whites, Native Hawaiians, and Asians, the audience is more open to such casting.

Akina's direction of Gilbert and Sullivan's comic opera, *The Mikado,* for the Hawaii Opera Theatre in the summer of 2004 approached the notion of operatic authenticity in an innovative, contemporary manner. Opening in London in 1885, *The Mikado* was inspired by librettist William Gilbert's visit to a cultural exhibition displaying real Japanese people for the curious Western audience. Gilbert and composer Arthur Sullivan hired some of the Japanese displayed at the exhibition as consultants to authenticate the manners, movements, and costumes of the characters. The absurdity of the work—its characters have such un-Japanese-sounding names as Nanki-Poo, Pitti-Sing, Yum-Yum, and Pooh-Bah, and it is set in an equally un-Japanese-sounding village named Titipu—has led twentieth-century critics to see the work as a most outrageous piece of Orientalism. Indeed, many opera companies that produced the work eliminated what they saw as offensive elements of the opera or changed the setting altogether to translate Gilbert and Sullivan's intended social satire into a contemporary context. Instead of following such a "politically correct" direction, Akina chose to highlight the Orientalist and satiric nature of the piece by keeping the Japanese setting and the characters intact while adapting the political and social commentaries to the context of contemporary U.S., Japan, and Hawai'i. He did so by changing or inserting lines to make references to politicians and events familiar to the audience and casting such well-known figures as taiko drummer Kenny Endo and sumo wrestler Ace Yonamine. The most surprising element of the production was the appearance of the then-Consul General of Japan, who at the beginning of the second act walked onto the stage in a business suit and declared in a somber, deadpan tone, "On behalf of the Hawaii Opera Theatre and the government of Japan, I assure you that what takes place in this opera has nothing, absolutely nothing, to do with the country I represent."[46]

Akina explained his directorial choices this way: "I wanted to make this silly opera into something that is relevant to us today. . . . In trying to make it less offensive and more fun for everybody, the idea was to include lots of Japanese elements that we like and bring in characters like the sumo wrestler." He commented that, because Hawai'i has a large number of people of Japanese ancestry, these Japanese elements have relevance to the audience who would appreciate the absurdity of the theatrical staging of such elements for what it is—deliberately absurd staging—rather than to take it literally and be offended by it, as audiences in other locations might do.[47] Akina's ingenuity in playing with the idea of authenticity—instead of pursuing it uncritically or debunking it altogether—illustrates how today's artists may engage the authenticity question. The production's locale in Hawai'i, with its large ethnic Japanese population and a history of ethnic mixing, also demonstrated that environments far from the centers of Western classical music and less bound by the orthodoxy of its tradition can produce a unique, new artistic work that opens new horizons while using a historical art form.

Warren Mok, a tenor born in Hong Kong and raised in Hawai'i, now produces opera in Macao and Hong Kong as well as singing many leading roles internationally. He said that being on the production side has made him understand the art of opera in its entirety, rather than only focusing on the singing. When asked about casting, he asserted that there was no particular pressure to hire Chinese singers for Opera Hong Kong, as opera itself is an international art form and singers come from all over the world:

> I go for the quality. If they're good for the role, I'll hire them, regardless of what they look like—I mean race, that is. For me, it's important to look the part, of course. I'm talking about body size. Nowadays, visual art is very important. In the old days, they didn't care what you looked like, even if you weighed 500 pounds, that was okay as long as the voice was there. For me, voice and looks are equally important. A princess should be beautiful. That's why Calaf [the prince in *Turandot*] falls in love with her at first sight. If we had a 500-pound princess, the audience would laugh![48]

Mok's comments shed light on the disproportionate attention that has been paid to racial identity at the expense of other elements that enhance visual believability—body size, for instance—which, in his mind, are more important to artistic realism. In the world of opera, it is extremely difficult to negotiate the authenticity demanded by the art form, the authenticity expected by the audience, and the authenticity of the musicians' own inner voice.

Whose Voice?
Part III: The Composers

Authenticity has a very different meaning for composers whose role is to create their own music rather than perform the music written by others. In the classical music world the composer is granted the role of innovation and change, whereas the goal of the performer is to realize and preserve the composer's intentions. Nettl describes the position of composers in the context of the music schools: "In the music school, composers are the principal promulgators of change and see change and innovation as the main characteristics of history and the present. They can be classified in categories from reactionary to radical, but all composers regard innovation in musical style and content as the main requisite of a successful compositional career, if not a successful composition."[49] In this environment, composers are held to a different standard of authenticity than that expected of performers. Rather than capturing existing music or musical traditions, composers are expected to produce original music distinct from others in the past or the present. In other words, composers are expected to have and to communicate a voice unique from others and authentic *to themselves.*

Yet, for Asian composers whose cultural and musical identities might be at once deeply Western and Asian, the question of what their authentic voice is and how to represent it with the tools of Western music is highly complicated. Many Asian composers feel that their musical sensibilities are indeed deeply Asian; however, what they mean by their "Asian" musical sensibilities is quite different from recognizably Asian sounds that permeate the popular media. In some cases, the realities of the market—in which the mainstream American audience expects cultural and musical Other-ness from Asian music and musicians—might compel them to use Asian musical elements expected by their audiences. Yet, because many Asian composers' cultural and musical identities are deeply Western, when they do choose to use Asian musical elements that may be quite foreign to them, they may be liable to charges that they are doing so for the sake of marketing—and by implication, commodifying their Asian identity for commercial purposes. It is impossible to distinguish which elements of a composition—its Western musical language, Asian sensibility, or multi-genre influences of much of contemporary music—are the most authentic voices of the composer, as it is the very product of those mixtures that becomes his or her individual voice.

For Akemi Naito, both her Japanese cultural identity and her current base in New York City have played an instrumental role in shaping her voice and defining her identity as a composer. In the liner notes to her CD, *Strings & Time,* she makes it clear that the productive tension she finds between her Japanese upbringing and her New York surroundings is highly important to her work:

> New York City, where I have lived since 1991, enables me to examine my own being. Here, the spirit of individual style fit me like a glove, and I felt I wanted to delve myself as deeply as I could. Yet here, as a Japanese, it is necessary to nurture in myself a perspective, a struc-

ture which is different from the Western ideas of time. For me, time is malleable, and can be sublimated from a melodious moment into a time-space of infinite continuity.

In this city where various cultures intersect, one is made aware of one's roots. But simultaneously, things that are pure and moving leap easily over barriers of language and ethnicity.

I am convinced that the most beautiful moments in history are when something is communicated. That is why I continue speaking through music.[50]

In talking about her first arrival in New York, Naito said firmly, "I felt that this is where I belong." Yet, as much as she underscored the importance of having lived in New York in shaping her sense of self and her professional identity, she asserted that she is first and foremost Japanese in terms of her musical sensibilities. When I asked her to what extent she is conscious about her Japanese identity in her work as a musician, she answered immediately, "I am constantly aware of my Japanese-ness, in all kinds of circumstances. . . . I always feel that I am a 'Japanese living in New York.'" She stated that her Japanese upbringing has made her musical sensibilities very different from those of Western people:

Starting with phrasing, everything is very different between Japanese and Westerners. . . . Japanese feel sound very differently. I think [sensibility about sound] is one of the superior aesthetics of the Japanese people. For instance, Japanese people pay close attention to things like the sounds of insects and consciously listen to them, you know. . . . Every time the cicadas start making sound in summer, I listen to them carefully. I think that's a uniquely Japanese sensibility. American musicians I know here don't seem particularly interested in things like that. The sense of *wabi* and *sabi* [a feature of Japanese aesthetics and philosophy that evokes serene melancholy and spiritual longing out of a sense of impermanence] is ingrained in our bodies, just like South Americans have the dynamic rhythm of samba in their bodies. I think my sense of sound comes from that sensibility that was nurtured through my years of being raised in Japan.

Whereas many performers said that they are made more aware of their Asian identities in their social relationships rather than in music-making itself, for Naito, her Japanese identity is much more important in her musical work than in social settings. "In my aesthetics, I am thoroughly Japanese," she declared.[51]

Yet, it is important to note that Naito's music, like that of many other contemporary Asian composers, does not sound overtly Asian, at least not to lay listeners. Although she has been commissioned to write some pieces using traditional Japanese instruments such as *satsuma biwa,* most of her compositions are for Western instruments, including electronics. She does not use stereotypically Japanese tunes, unusual tuning system, or timbre. Rather, her Japanese sensibilities are expressed through more subtle aesthetics of time, sonority, and movement. The essence of her Japanese-ness—from which her authentic voice derives—lies in elements quite different from stereotypical characterizations of Japanese culture.

Moto Osada, who grew up listening to traditional Japanese music and has always liked *noh* music as well as having been a serious rock musician, also claimed that distinctly Japanese aesthetics and sensibilities are a natural and primary part of his identity. At the same time, like Naito, his musical ideas are shaped also by the decade-long experience of living in New York. For him, the New York surroundings have been meaningful not only because of his encounters with rich cultural resources and creative ideas but also because of his experience as a member of a minority group:

I feel that my music is becoming more and more aggressive. Other people have told me that my music is getting more intense and aggressive. Living as a minority in New York, I feel like I want to say something really loud so that I can be heard. . . . I identify with composers like [György] Ligeti because I feel in their music their sense of being minorities in their own societies. I think being a Jew in a small country like Hungary that is surrounded by big nations, [in Ligeti's music] there's a strong sense of nationalism as well as identity as a minority. That's different from music born in countries like France or Germany. . . . There's a fundamental difference in terms of why you create music in the first place. There is a much more strong sense of urgency.

What defines Osada's music in New York is not simply the musical and cultural resources of the city but more important, the identity he developed as a racial minority, a consciousness he would not have had if he were living in Japan. Osada's racial identity also plays a factor in marketing his career. He was not shy to admit that there are times when he thinks about using his Japanese identity and musical ideas as a strategy to create his place in the New York music scene. He is aware that when he receives a commission to write music, the commissioning party often expects some sort of Japanese flavor in the music: "They don't always say so explicitly, but listening to their response to my work, it's clear that what's interesting to them about my work is those elements [that use audibly Japanese musical ideas]. This is called 'playing the race card,' and people like Tan Dun do it quite effectively." When I asked him if he is disturbed by being labeled as a Japanese composer, he acknowledged that he might feel upset if he did not like Japanese music but because he has always been an enthusiastic fan of Japanese culture and music, he is not particularly bothered by it. While some people criticize composers like Tan Dun as commodifying his ethnic identity, Osada held that the commercial success of such musicians benefits all living composers by broadening the audience for contemporary music.

Although he is savvy about his racialized identity and the cultural politics of the market, at the same time, Osada asserted that the most important thing for the composer is "to be true to oneself, and to do something that you really want to do without worrying about things like audience preference. When you do that, you inevitably will face the question of what your true self is about."[52] He claimed that the reason he uses Japanese elements in his music is first and foremost because that is what comes most naturally to him and that strategic considerations about marketing are secondary to his goal of creating his own music. Osada therefore does not simply pander to the popular taste even as he is aware of the market expectations, and he expresses his multiple and hybrid musicality in more digested forms. Many of his pieces do have Japan-related titles and themes. For instance, *JoHaKyu* for cello and piano (1999) refers to a tripartite form commonly used in Japanese *noh* performance; *Kaguyama Dance* for viola and piano (2003) is inspired by the Japanese mythology of the Sun Goddess Amaterasu-Ohmi-kami; the title for *Mifune,* a viola solo suite (2001–02), comes from the legendary Japanese actor Toshiro Mifune.

Yet the music is far from recognizably Japanese, and the Japanese-ness of these themes is expressed on an abstract level. For example, *JoHaKyu* is sonically quite Western in its use of the cello's wide range of tone color; yet it expresses a distinct concept of the sequence of time or objects used in Japanese performing arts, in that the musical idea moves in a linear structure rather than in the A-B-A form commonly found in Western music. The primal energy and barbaric beauty of the Sun Goddess in *Kaguyama Dance* are expressed not through a programmatic reference to the story but rather through the intensity of the fast, repetitive rhythm. Much of his music is characterized by the juxtaposition and melding of different sounds, musical ideas, and structures, drawing not only from Western classical and traditional Japanese music but also from other genres, such as jazz, pop, and rock. *Atomotium* for piano (2001) draws inspiration from the polyphonic weaving of sounds heard in Bach, Chopin, and Ligeti as well as from the scales of Japanese *noh* and the orchestration of *gagaku*; it also combines the overall structure of motif development in a Western classical fashion with a juxtaposition and sequence of independent musical ideas that are more common in contemporary music. *Take the Six* for marimba and electronics (2003), incorporating sounds from Jimi Hendrix and Prince, pits the organic sound of the marimba against the electronic voice generated by CD playback.

Just as Naito and Osada attempt to produce truly authentic Japanese compositions without relying on stereotypically Japanese sounds, a generation of Chinese composers has risen to fame by composing avant-garde music that defies the popular notion of Chinese music. The success of such Chinese composers as Bright Sheng, Chen Yi, Zhou Long, and, most famously, Tan Dun has drawn much attention. These composers share a similar background: they were raised in China during the Cultural Revolution, developed their experimental compositional style in the years when China began to open its doors to the West, came to study in the United States in the early 1980s, and established their careers in the United States as composers who successfully synthesize Western and Eastern musical elements. As ethnomusicologist Frederick Lau explains, these composers consciously moved away from the stereotypical uses of Eastern sound in order to break from Orientalist traditions in music. They thus pursued "their own relationships to sound, instrumental technique, and underlying philosophy rather than making direct musical references to China."[53] Yet these Chinese composers' career paths since emigrating to the United States illustrate how social contexts and cultural politics shape musical production as much as aesthetic concerns. In Lau's words, "what they are trying to do is to assert and negotiate a cultural space and cultural identity within the globalized network of cultural commodity and the multiculturalism that is at the foundation of the avant-garde music circle."[54] They produce what one might call the "East-meets-West" genre of contemporary music, in which the composers appropriate Chinese musical elements in ways that appeal to the commodified, globalized aesthetics of predominantly Western audiences. However, such music often draws criticism from musicians and critics in both the United States and China. According to Sheila Melvin and Jindong Cai, "Sometimes it seems that the general rule among culture critics in China is that if foreigners like it, it can't be any good and it most certainly can't be authentic because a foreigner could never understand anything that is truly Chinese. Thus do some Chinese critics make the claim that composers use their music to trick foreigners, who are naturally assumed to be dumb enough to fall for this."[55]

These debates over the Chinese-ness of works by Chinese composers illustrate the complexity of the notion of authenticity. Even if a composer's musical style indeed shifted partly in response to demands of the audience and the market, it is difficult to differentiate between his or her genuine search for a Chinese sound and appropriation of audibly Chinese sounds for commercial appeal. A more useful line of analysis is to examine each of the voices that make up these composers' music, none of which is any more or less authentic than the others.

Like the other U.S.-based Chinese composers of his generation, Ge Ganru grew up during the Cultural Revolution and was among the first cohort of Chinese composers who came to study in the United States in the 1980s under the tutelage of Chou Wen-Chung of Columbia University. Describing his evolution as a composer, he recalled the moment during his study at the Shanghai Conservatory of Music when he suddenly began to feel that his training in Western compositional methods and styles did not provide him with adequate tools to create his own music:

> All I was taught was Western [music]. . . . We didn't have any opportunities to encounter anything [other than standard Western repertoire]. But I had some urge at that time. . . . I couldn't just write like

Beethoven. But I didn't know how to write other things. . . . When I started composing, because all my training was in Western music literature, I just wanted to write in Western style, like Schubert. I was using Western harmony and what not. Then after a while, I started to feel I needed to go to another stage. I'm Chinese, and why don't I use some Chinese tone. . . . Then I thought maybe I could borrow ideas like Debussy or Bartók because they use some Oriental materials. But when I tried to imitate some of them, I still felt that that's not really what I wanted.

Ge began to feel that music that uses exclusively Western musical tools was inadequate for representing his authentic voice, which he felt was rooted in his Chinese upbringing. It was only when he encountered the sonority of the works by such composers as John Cage, George Crumb, and Toru Takemitsu that he found new possibilities of breaking the boundaries of Western music and began to define his own compositional style. He started exploring ways to use Chinese materials, not by using traditional melodies but by incorporating the system of pitch, rhythm, timbre, and dynamics of Chinese music.[56] This breakthrough in his musical thinking resulted in his work for unaccompanied cello, *Yi feng* (1982), which won him the reputation as the first Chinese avant-garde composer; it also made possible the subsequent series of work he composed since emigrating to the United States in 1983. He discussed the development of his ideas:

I always found that Eastern and Western music were very contradictory . . . I was born and grew up in China; naturally I heard all this folk Chinese music, just like the language you're born with. But in the meanwhile, when I was very young, I was educated in Western music, that's the language I learned. If you just want to be a music lover, these two things are fine as they are, but if you want to be a composer, these two things that are contradictory to each other were very difficult to deal with. At heart, I feel Chinese music. But on the other hand, I really loved Western music. I loved Chopin, Mozart, I adored all that. . . . I thought all this Western music was very beautiful and Chinese music was very backward. I had that kind of feeling for a long time. . . . I spent a lot of time trying to reconcile and to solve this question.

To solve this question, he delineated the differences between Eastern and Western music in terms of pitch, rhythm, timbre, and dynamics. Yet, after explaining the ways in which he synthesizes the different musical ideas in his compositions, he concluded, "For me, whether to have Chinese or Western influence or how to use the materials, those questions are of secondary importance. The most important thing for me is how to write music that only I could write."[57]

It is this goal of "writing music that only I can write"—put differently, writing music that is authentic to their own voice—to which all composers aspire. All attempt to convey their own, unique voice through the tools of Western music tradition in which they have been trained. At the same time, for music to have social and cultural meaning—and, no less important, for composers to obtain commissions, performances, recording, and publishing contracts and thus to be able to earn a living as composers—the audience needs to find the music meaningful and distinctive. In the society and market that see Asian musicians as the cultural outsider, what often makes their music meaningful and distinctive to the audience is their ethnicity marked in their music.

The venues, audiences, and reviews of Asian composers' work reveal this point. As much as critics praise the universal appeal of the works of contemporary Asian composers, performance of their works often carries racial, ethnic, or geographical markers—for example, concert series titled "East Meets West," "Ears to the East," "Pacific Rim," "Fusion," and so forth. The audiences at the concerts featuring these works tend to be predominantly white intellectuals with an interest in contemporary music or Asia. Program notes, liner notes, and interviews repeatedly discuss the composers' Asian upbringing—in the case of Chinese composers, with a particular emphasis on the Cultural Revolution—and their professional success in the West, as well as characterizing the music as a blending of Eastern and Western traditions. In fact, it is almost impossible to find a review that does not mention the Asian composer's ethnicity.[58] All of these indicate both the difficulty for Asian composers of operating without a racial marker (it is much rarer to find reviews that specifically mention the racial or ethnic background of, say, Milton Babbitt, Pierre Boulez, or John Adams) and the usefulness of such markers for Asian composers in creating a niche in the market.

Conclusion

All Asians in classical music pursue music-making despite the constant challenges because they find classical music to be the most effective medium through which to express themselves and because they believe in the power of music to communicate to others. The degree and the ways in which Asian musicians find their racial identity and cultural upbringing relevant to their pursuit of classical music vary widely, as do the specific demands and expectations placed on their form of musicianship based on their field of music. What they do share are the components of their individual voices—their Asian cultural heritage, their everyday experience of living as Asians in the United States, their lifelong dedication to classical music, among other factors—that are equally authentic parts of who they are. Being Asian does not make them any less authentic as classical musicians, and being classical musicians does not make them any less authentic as Asians. They play and create classical music because that *is* their authentic voice.

The debates over authenticity in classical music become mired in issues of culture, race, and identity because its European origin and the particular emphasis it places on the composer and the original music render the Asian performer as the cultural outsider. In addition, the racial politics of American multiculturalism and the racialization of Asians in America often demand recognizable forms of Asian-ness from the musicians and their music, even though their truly Asian voice may consist of sounds very different from such expectations. In reality, the cultural and musical environment in East Asia and Asian American communities in the past century has rendered Asians' and Asian Americans' musical sensibilities—their "voices"—deeply Western.

Within these demands, expectations, and constraints, Asian and Asian American musicians strive to create their individual voices—voices that are faithful both to the history of the music and to the present practice, voices that simultaneously embody the particular and communicate universally, and voices that are authentic both to the art form and to themselves. Folklorist Regina Bendix points out, "*Authenticity . . . is generated . . . from the probing comparison between self and the Other, as well as between external and internal states of being.* This search [for authenticity] arises out of a profound human longing, be it religious-spiritual or existential, and declaring the object of such longing nonexistent may violate the very core around which people build meaningful lives [emphasis in the original]."[59] As Asian musicians grapple with their identities and their endeavors, there arises a conception of authenticity that is not defined in terms of self vs. the Other or external vs. internal, but rather is achieved through connecting the past and the present, the music and the performer, the musicians and the audiences. Classical music allows them to simultaneously live through and beyond their Asian identity.

Asian musicians embrace classical music, make it their own, and express themselves through it in a complex and intense process of engaging a culture, tradition, and art form. For most Asian musicians—who were raised in culturally hybrid environments and have been trained almost exclusively in Western musical traditions—this process is not necessarily dichotomous. For them, all that informs their music—their understanding of Western music acquired through many years of rigorous study, their expressive language formed by the Asian cultures in which they were raised, and their musical and cultural sensibilities shaped by their experience of being raised in, or having lived in, the United States—are equally integral parts of who they are.

Conclusion:
Musicians First

Much writing about classical music tends to be about composers and their work. The classical music section in most bookstores (if there is one) is usually filled with biographies of Bach, Brahms, Chopin, Mahler, and so forth. There are entire books about Beethoven's Ninth or Mozart's *Don Giovanni*. In contrast, far fewer books focus on performers of classical music. Except for celebratory biographies of some star performers, such as Vladimir Horowitz, Leonard Bernstein, and Maria Callas, few books give a glimpse of what the lives of classical musicians—orchestral and chamber musicians, freelance performers, and teachers—are like.

By shifting our attention from the composers and the musical text to other parties in the musical activity—the musicians who perform and the listeners who make meaning out of the music—we gain a different understanding of classical music, one that looks at the ways in which music is *experienced*. Thinking about the experience of and in classical music urges us to consider not only the aesthetic qualities of compositions but also the investments, backgrounds, and values that the musicians and audiences bring to the musical experience. These non-musical aspects include people's socioeconomic positions and cultural aspirations, ideas about what the music symbolizes in the larger culture, and various identities prescribed by others or claimed for themselves. By focusing on a particular group—Asians and

Asian Americans—we see how these non-musical aspects that make up the musicians' and listeners' lives interact with the "music itself" to create powerful meanings that are unique to this particular art form. Classical music continues to have power for Asians and Asian Americans because it can both express and transcend their social and cultural identities and experiences. Yet that power does not reside solely in the musical text; it is the musicians and their audiences who create that power and experience its meanings.

In examining Asian and Asian American musicians' relationship to classical music, I have addressed four key themes: Western modernity and class aspirations, agency, field, and identity.

The beauty of Western music no doubt has moved a large number of Asians to study it seriously and make it an important part of their own culture. However, their investment in classical music also had a great deal to do with its association with Western modernity and the aspirations of the growing middle class in East Asia and Asian America. Of course, labels such as the "West," "modernity," and "middle class" have had multiple and ambivalent meanings for Asians at various points in history, and they were not always models for Asians to simply emulate. As can be seen in the uses of Western music during nationalist movements in Japan, Korea, and China and particularly in China's Cultural Revolution, the music associated with the West was subject to dramatically diverse interpretations and treatments. Yet, the belief that the pursuit of classical music was an important part of achieving status in modern society has driven many Asians to make the sizable and long-term investments required by that pursuit. Asians' association of classical music with social aspirations is manifested in the class-specific nature of classical music practice among Asians, both in Asia and the United States.

At the same time, Asians did not passively receive and uncritically practice Western music. Theirs was a process of selective adoption, adaptation, and appropriation. Asians adopted some Western instruments, such as the piano and violin, more eagerly than other instruments, because they signified higher symbolic capital. They treated skeptically other areas of Western music, such as opera, which as a result developed more slowly in Asia. Asians adapted Western musical elements intelligently and skillfully and melded them with their own musical traditions and cultural languages to create their own music. Such adaptations resulted in a wide repertoire of compositions and arrangements, ranging from school songs at the turn of the twentieth century and instructional pieces used in the Suzuki Method to contemporary avant-garde music. In addition, Asians appropriated Western music—its instruments, compositions, and performance practices—for their own political and social goals, sometimes even to fight the West and to assert Asian nationalism. By the latter half of the twentieth century, Japan, Korea, and China were sending their own musicians, musical instruments, and musical works using the tools of Western art music to the West. The growing presence of Asians in classical music at all levels—from neighborhood music studios in Asian cities and youth orchestras in American suburbs to professional performers and composers on the international stage—is making a clear imprint on the way the world's audiences think of culture and music. Asians' remarkable achievements in classical music require reconsideration of the seemingly natural connection between the music's European origin and the music as it is practiced today. At the same time, Asian musicians define musical and cultural authenticity in their own terms, sometimes claiming the universal nature of classical music and at other times stressing the culturally specific nature of the musical language. They develop and articulate these ideas through the serious and intense process of working through the relationship between their own cultural identity and the music they make their own.

Although the social functions of classical music on both sides of the Pacific have been shaped by historical, political, and economic contexts, the world of classical music also operates as a relatively autonomous field with its own currency of capital. In this field (both in common usage and in the Bourdieuian sense of the term), non-economic values and the ideal of art-for-art's-sake often occupy higher places than economic capital. In fact, the disavowal of economic considerations and resistance to the capitalist logic that governs mass culture are very important in the world of classical music and form the basis for both the individual and collective identity of classical musicians *as musicians.* In many ways, for Asians in classical music, this musical identity is a more salient factor than socially defined categories such as race or ethnicity; it often functions as a more significant marker of *difference* in American society than race, ethnicity, or nationality, which explains the frequent downplaying of their Asian identity in many of the musicians' narratives about their professional lives.

Whereas Asians in classical music actively claim and perform their identity *as musicians,* other aspects of their identity are highly fluid. Whether it be racial, ethnic, gender, or sexual identity, the particular meanings of these categories come out of dialectical negotiations between the social forces that prescribe the categories onto individuals and the individuals who adopt, maneuver, or transgress those categories. Therefore, the term "Asian" does not have a fixed, singular meaning, but rather is a marker of identity that acquires particular meanings in specific sociohistorical and cultural contexts. Asian identity is constructed through such processes as asserting political alliance in Asian nationalist movements against Western imperialism; claiming shared cultural values in opposition to other groups in the United States; finding one's place in racialized, multicultural America; and affirming the connections of diasporic subjects to their Asian homeland. "Asian" identity also is not performed in isolation from other dimensions of their identity, such as gender and sexuality, which in turn shape the meaning of what it means to be "Asian." For classical musicians, most of whom have spent almost their entire lives practicing music seriously, music is the central site where these constructions and negotiations of identity take place.

Asian and Asian American musicians do not pursue classical music *despite* their Asian background or *because of* their Asian upbringing. Rather, they experience and practice classical music *through* their identity that is partly shaped by their race and ethnicity. At the same time, they come to understand and negotiate their Asian identity *through* their practice of classical music. For these musicians, their Asian identity and their pursuit of classical music are mutually constitutive.

This project bridges several academic fields: Western musicology, ethnomusicology, American studies and cultural studies, and Asian American studies. Seeing this project in relation to each of these fields highlights each field's conceptual and methodological strengths, as well as what we can gain from cross-disciplinary approaches.

First, in the field of Western musicology, two commonly shared premises—the primacy of the composer and the original work and the idea that an abstract, absolute musical form such as classical music transcends issues such as politics and economics—have kept many scholars from asking questions about non-musical factors in the production, performance, and consumption of music. Such elements as the performer's identity have been considered largely irrelevant to the study of the music itself. Yet, as I have tried to show in this book, music is an *embodied* art form; both musicians and their audiences experience music *through* their identities in specific social contexts. This is not to negate or trivialize the power of music to transcend social boundaries, the power that both the performers and the listeners firmly believe in. Yet, by paying closer attention to the non-musical elements of musicians' lives that play a role in shaping their relationship to the music—such as race, gender, class, and language—we come to see classical music not as a fixed *text* produced by the composers of the past but as a cultural *practice* and *process* that are created through a constant, complex, and intense engagement among the composer, the musical text, the performer, and the audience.

On the other hand, the field of ethnomusicology, which has concerned itself with music as a cultural practice and process, has generally paid little attention to Western classical music. Although several scholars—most notably Bruno Nettl, Henry Kingsbury, and Christopher Small—have analyzed the ideologies and cultures of the world of classical music, on the whole Western classical music has been considered the domain of (Western) musicology rather than ethnomusicology, which is primarily interested in the music of the non-Western world or of subcultural groups within the West. Applying ethnomusicological frameworks and methods to classical music, however, enables us to understand classical music as part of, rather than independent of or above, the larger musical culture and society. The seeming isolation of classical music from the rest of society should be a subject of historical, social, and cultural analysis rather than a basis for a re-inscription of such isolation through an academic division of labor. As scholarship in ethnomusicology pays increasing attention to the musical transformations and hybridity accompanying the global flows of capital, media, and migration, it makes sense to direct such inquiry to Western classical music as well.

American studies and cultural studies—which integrate critical theory, historical and structural analysis of social relations, and interdisciplinary readings of cultural texts and practices—do provide frameworks for understanding the ideological, social, and cultural forces that shape Asians' and Asian Americans' pursuit of classical music. However, these fields need to develop a language and framework to analyze *power* in ways other than political, economic, and social to fully understand the ways in which art makes meaning in people's lives and in society at large. As I have demonstrated, the historical and socioeconomic conditions that shape the pro-duction and consumption of classical music are extremely important in understanding its social and cultural functions both in Asia and the United States. Yet, the structural analysis only goes so far in explaining the intensely personal connections that Asian musicians create with the music they per-form or the power of music to cross social boundaries. The political, eco-nomic, and social power that is granted to Asians pursuing classical music is quite limited; yet their pursuit of classical music is also enormously empow-ering for the musicians in ways other social institutions and practices do not allow. Most important, it gives them a voice with which to express their individuality in a society that often ignores it under the cloak of racial and gendered markers. To understand these processes, without attributing them to false consciousness or falling back on decontextualized essentialism or idealist aestheticism, we need to develop a framework for understanding the *language* of music and the arts in its own terms, rather than reducing it to social relations of power. Such concepts as universalism, particularism, and authenticity in music must be theorized not through abstractions but through grounded analysis of how they are understood and practiced by the musicians and their audiences themselves.

Works in Asian American studies generally place primary emphasis on race, ethnicity, and nationality as analytical categories. The very way in which I have chosen to define the subject of this study is in line with this field's tendency to see race as a main, if not exclusive, marker of identity and social relations. The lives and ideas of Asians and Asian Americans in classical music demonstrate, however, that race and ethnicity are not always a defining factor in shaping their lives, especially their musical lives. To analyze their Asian identity independently of their experiences, aspirations, and values *as musicians* would misrepresent the composition of their identi-ties. The field of Asian American studies, therefore, needs to further develop analytical models that seriously consider the articulations of race and eth-nicity in tandem with other elements that shape Asians' lives.

I have also struggled with a larger issue of the tension between academic analysis and the subjective experience of music. As I wrote in the preface, this book is a product of the negotiations between my own identities and interests, one musical and the other scholarly. Both the questions I set out to explore and the arguments I drew in my study are results of the tension between these interrelated but also divided perspectives and investments. I end the book not by resolving this tension but by suggesting what the tension itself might tell us about classical music.

As a researcher, I set out to analyze the relationship between racial identity and music-making and to understand the role of classical music in shaping the social and cultural subjectivities of Asian and Asian American musicians. Yet, what I learned about the lives of classical musicians was often quite removed from such questions. If I had focused my study on the works and careers of star musicians who explicitly engage the themes of East-West relations—Yo-Yo Ma's Silk Road Project and Tan Dun's compositions for film and opera, for instance—I could probably have written a book that addressed such questions more directly and in a more sustained manner. However, in my fieldwork I found that most classical musicians' everyday lives and work do not revolve around their Asian identities or the politics of East-West relations. Their main concerns are not even about their performances, recordings, or auditions (although those events certainly are physically and emotionally consuming). Rather, what occupies them the most is the painstaking work of becoming better musicians. One of the things that I was most struck by in the course of my research was the number of musicians who responded to my question, "What is your main concern as a musician right now?" with a very simple answer, "Playing better." Although my previous musical training had given me some familiarity with the endless process of music-making, I had assumed that the musicians who have managed to become professionals were beyond issues like skills and technique and that their goals were in more subjective areas of individual artistry. I was astonished to learn that the people who were trained at Juilliard or other top-level conservatories and have been performing for many years are still so concerned with their playing skills.

Indeed, the work involved in improving one's playing is truly mind-boggling. A Juilliard-trained Chinese violinist in his late thirties told me that he recently started learning the instrument from scratch after realizing that his way of holding the instrument had been wrong all along; when I asked him to describe his practice method, he told me that on most days he spends almost the entire day just playing individual notes and scales to achieve the right tone. When I observed a recording session for a Japanese marimbist's CD, I was bowled over by the number of takes the musician and the recording engineer assiduously went through with every few measures to get it just right, when almost every one of the 100 takes sounded equally perfect to me. A pianist friend of mine told me of the hours spent in agony having to decide which edition of Chopin's *Grande Polonaise Brillante* to use (Chopin's scores are notorious for the inconsistencies among different editions) as the slight difference in notes had profound implications for the overall effect of the piece. When I met musicians immediately after their performance—whether it be a solo recital or an orchestra concert—they often expressed extremely specific self-criticisms about their playing that, quite honestly, most audiences including myself could not possibly detect, let alone care about. For these musicians, the question that is most urgent and relevant to their identity is that of musicality, and issues such as race and class are secondary to those artistic goals.

Moreover, although I was hoping to understand the practice of classical music in the context of the larger society, I found that, for better or worse, Asian and Asian American musicians' lives indeed do tend to be rather isolated from the outside world. Given that they spend as many as eight to twelve hours every day practicing the tremendous details of musical execution, it is no surprise that most are not particularly engaged politically or socially with the world outside classical music. Still, I was shocked to find out how little many of my informants knew about current affairs. One informant could not distinguish between Palestine and Pakistan; another did not know who Condoleezza Rice was (despite her well-known piano training); yet another had never watched the presidential debates. Although many musicians were quite articulate about their own experiences of racism or sexism, very few of my informants had much understanding of the history or the current state of race relations or gender politics in the United States or Asia. Even in areas that are related much more directly to their profession, their knowledge seemed to be pretty limited. I got the impression that few of my informants had much understanding of, say, Enlightenment philosophy, the ideas behind the German Revolution, the arts and literatures of Romanticism, or the history of Stalinism, all of which have shaped the music they routinely perform. Given such lives and mindsets, the claims—or the charges—of classical music operating outside or above the rest of society seem understandable to an extent.

I learned about the nature of music-making not only by observing my informants but also by returning to my own piano playing. Although the basic techniques of playing had been hammered into my fingers during my childhood years, as I resumed my piano lessons, I could not help but let out a big sigh every time my teacher pointed out the function of each note in the phrase that makes it imperative to hit the key with a particular part of the finger, with particular speed, from a particular angle; the logic of the harmonic progression that should be conveyed through a particular change in dynamics; the interplay between different voices that requires particular shifts in emphasis (those darned middle voices!); the compositional structure that calls for a change in tone color at particular points in the piece; and the musical ideas and emotions that make particular phrasings and pedaling more convincing than others. Although I often felt like crying out of despair, I gained a deeper understanding of the genius expressed in each composition as well as the brilliance of each performance. I also began to understand that musicality lies not in some abstract understanding of the musical text or some innate talent that captures the spirit of each piece but rather in the ability to execute all these incredible details. Despite my hope that my piano playing would give me some epiphany about racial and cultural identity and music-making, for the most part my Japanese upbringing seemed rather irrelevant to my ability on the keyboard.

In addition to my experience as a researcher and a practitioner of classical music, my experience as a listener of classical music brought another dilemma to my project. Although I believed that the ways in which one understands and interprets classical (and any other genre of) music are shaped by the musical language cultivated by one's upbringing and environment, I also found that, at least within the world of classical music, factors like race, ethnicity, and nationality mattered relatively little in terms of performance. There are schools of playing—such as the Russian school or the French school—that reflect the traditions of performance and pedagogy recognizable to trained ears. Beyond that, however, musical rendition is a matter of the performer's individual interpretation and execution, and attributing the characteristics of a musician's playing to his or her ethnicity or nationality often betrays the essentialist construction of the player's identity on the part of the listener more than any substantive analysis of the performance itself. In live performances the performer's visible attributes such as race, gender, and physical appearance as well as his or her facial expressions or bodily movements certainly comprise a part of the musical experience. But when the performance truly moves the audience, such factors quickly recede behind the intense experience of the music itself. Although my scholarly mind always resists such universalist claims about the transcendent power of music, it was also undeniable that my actual experience as a listener often confirmed them.

And yet these experiential aspects of classical music do not unfold in a social vacuum. Nor do the individuals engaged in the often solitary act of honing their musical skills exist outside society, culture, or history. Precisely because music makes meaning through individual as well as collective identities and experiences, we need to see the historical, social, and cultural constitutions of those identities and experiences to understand that meaning-making process. Especially in discussing a group's intense and sustained practice of an art form that does not originate in its own culture, we need to see the structural factors that gave birth to that cultural encounter and engagement. I hope that my scholarly discussion of the historical and social forces that shape Asians' investment in classical music adds to, rather than takes away from, our understanding of the power of music.

This book does not resolve these tensions among my researcher, practitioner, and listener selves. In arguing that music has power because it both expresses and transcends the social and cultural, I have admittedly devoted much more of the discussion to the expression of the social and cultural than on the mechanism of its transcendence. I ultimately chose to focus much more of this book on social and cultural analysis than on more subjective and personal dimensions of musical experience. Yet, my intent is not to reduce the experience of music to social context. In discussing a much different subject matter, Melani McAlister stated eloquently, "The politics of culture is important, not because politics is *only* culture (or because culture is *only* politics), but because where the two meet, political meanings are often made."[1] In a similar vein, I believe that music produces power through the meeting of the performers' and listeners' subjective engagement with the musical text and the social, collective experience of music. Asians' and Asian Americans' realization and performance of identity *in* and *through* music help us see how the subjective and the social meet.

Acknowledgments

First and foremost, I want to express my admiration and respect for all the classical musicians who devote themselves to creating and sharing music. I have been deeply moved and inspired by their dedication and passion, and my interactions with them have renewed my faith in the human spirit.

Like the lives and works of the musicians I discuss in this book, my research has also straddled the Pacific. The staff at the Talent Education Research Institute in Matsumoto and those at Nihon Kindai Ongakukan and Min-on Music Museum in Tokyo were extremely generous in assisting me in my research. The year I spent in New York doing research for this study was filled with stimulating encounters and enriching friendships. I am grateful to Bruce Brubaker and John Davis for helping me make initial contacts for my research, which soon turned into an ever mushrooming pool of informants. Not only were all of my informants quite generous in devoting their time to talking with me between practice, rehearsals, and performances but they were also extremely open, candid, and thoughtful in sharing their experiences and ideas. I am sorry that I could not fit all of their stories into this book, but I was touched by every one of them. Among the amazing group of musicians I befriended, I am particularly indebted to Kimiko Hata, Makiko Hirata, Mina Kusumoto, Makoto Nakura, Satoshi Okamoto, and Shuo Zhang. All the days and nights I spent with them gave me a textured sense of their lives and thoughts far beyond the practice rooms and performance stage. My classmates in the piano performance class at the Juilliard Evening Division formed a nurturing group of adults pursuing music as an avocation, and they reminded me why we invest so much in music when we have so many other things to worry about. Thanks to Julie Jordan for being patient with our fingers and temperaments.

I also encountered many wonderful people who are part of the vibrant and diverse community of the Big Apple. Thanks to Gary Okihiro for hosting me at the Center for the Study of Ethnicity and Race at Columbia University. Attending Sherry Ortner's graduate seminar at Columbia helped me think through the issues for my chapter on class. Timothy Taylor and Elaine Combs-Schilling were both very warm in their expressions of interest in and support for my work. Stacy Hoshino was my great guide in New York, and I am glad that I continue to enjoy his company back in Hawai'i. Much affection and thanks to Andy Erdman for the great times we shared. Joe Vacarello was one of the few people who actually came to listen to my piano performances more than once. The friendships with Andrew Inness, Goro Kusumoto, Daisuke and Yoko Miyao, Yoko Oshima, and Benjamin Schmirler all made my New York life a lot of fun. Thanks to Subramanian Shankar for the unbeatable housing arrangement that made it possible for me to live in the city.

Back in Hawai'i, I am blessed with a community of friends, colleagues, and students who make me miss New York less than I would without them. Scott Anderson and Stephen Dinion are my family, friends, informants, neighbors, readers, students, teachers, and therapists all at once. They have been my most enthusiastic supporters on this project and have read and commented on different sections of the manuscript. To know that these musicians find meaning and value in this project was extremely encouraging for me throughout my writing process. Bravo to the musicians of the Honolulu Symphony for continuing to add their fine performances to the rich and diverse musical culture of Hawai'i. My students in the Department of American Studies and the International Cultural Studies Program at the University of Hawai'i surely have had to hear about this project more than they cared for. I hope that I have shown them a little bit that critical analysis and passion for the arts need not be incompatible. My writing group—Monisha Das Gupta, Cynthia Franklin, Linda Lierheimer, Laura Lyons, Kieko Matteson, and Naoko Shibusawa—helped me untangle my confused brain and sharpen my analysis chapter after chapter while they also supported me warmly and amusedly through the vicissitudes of my (non-) evolving social life. Just like my last book, this one would not have been completed if it were not for this group of smart, strong women who hold high standards both for my writing and my dates. My numerous conversations with Heather Diamond and Frederick Lau, their thoughtful comments on my writing, and all the food we consumed together in numerous cities have greatly enriched this book. Heather also spent many hours helping me with the tedious details of obtaining permissions for the illustrations in this book. I am fortunate to have Robert Perkinson as a friend and colleague who shares a vision and commitment for our workplace, and commiserating with him about writing has eased the pains of the process. Having Theodore Gonzalves, who successfully integrates scholarship and music, as a colleague is a great joy and inspiration. Christine Yano has given me her brilliant comments on many chapters of the manuscript. Pensri Ho's insightful reading and suggestions improved one of my chapters considerably. Ned Davis has shown a great deal of interest and enthusiasm in this book since its very early stages; our conversations and arguments have added much excitement to my life. *Mahalo* to Kevin Miyamura for friendship and conversations and for pushing me through the rough patches. Many thanks to Stewart Kubota for fixing everything.

I was lucky to enjoy the company of David Mozina during my final writing phase. Amidst the pressures of his own work, he generously spent many, many hours, days, weeks, and months reading my drafts, talking ideas through, and looking after me in many other ways. I think he knows how much joy he has brought to my life, but just in case, thanks again for all the love, laughter, understanding, food, wine, hikes, and everything else.

My first ideas for this project were born during my conversations with Robert Lee many years ago. His work on race, culture, and Asian Americans has guided me in many ways over the years. Even though Joanne Melish and I work on different periods and areas, she has always been a big fan of my project, and I have enjoyed and learned greatly from our conversations, which I wish were more frequent. As always, Yujin Yaguchi's friendship and support have a central place in my work and life, and I look forward to more of our collaborations. My friends in other spheres of my life—Masako Ikeda, Akiko Kitagawa, Willamarie Moore, Sanae Nakayama, Makiko Nishikawa, Kazuo Ooka, Yasuko Sato, and Akiko Zama—have been cheerleaders for this project and my life in general, and I hope to be the same for them.

My editor, Janet Francendese, and the entire staff at Temple University Press were overwhelmingly enthusiastic and supportive even before the manuscript was written. I am grateful to Elena Coler for her patience and competence throughout the editing and production process and to Gary Kramer and Ann-Marie Anderson for their faith in the project. Gail Naron Chalew's meticulous copyediting improved my writing tremendously. Many thanks to Timothy Taylor, Judy Tsou, and anonymous readers of the proposal and the manuscript for their thorough and insightful suggestions. In the course of writing this book, I had the opportunity to present pieces of my work at the American Studies Association, Society for Ethnomusicology, Association for Asian Studies, Association for Asian American Studies, Northwestern University, Oberlin Conservatory, and University of Tokyo. The questions and comments from the engaged audiences have helped the book in many ways.

If it were not for all the piano playing I have done over the years, I would not have written this book. Although there have been times when I felt highly ambivalent about my childhood that was consumed by piano, in retrospect I feel privileged to have been given the chance to study and appreciate music. Through my teachers, I have learned the importance of understanding the big picture, paying *lots* of attention to detail, having my own voice, being convinced in my own delivery, enjoying every aspect of the piece, and practicing, practicing, practicing. Having learned the importance of these things has made a difference in my life as a scholar as well. My most recent piano teachers have reminded me why I play music and helped me relate to music in a whole new way. In our lessons, which were simultaneously rigorous and hilarious, Makiko Hirata showed me so much about what I do well and what I do poorly—both on the keyboard and in life—and she has helped me say what I want to say through music. Thomas Yee has helped me see and hear music a lot more clearly. He is quite patient with my agitated nature as it is manifested in my playing, and he has helped me expand my repertoire, both literally and figuratively. These teachers made me remember that music, along with writing, was one of the media with which I first learned to express myself.

Notes

PREFACE

1. On the history of piano in postwar Japan, see Takanori Maema and Yūichi Iwano, *Nihon no Piano 100-nen: Piano Zukuri ni Kaketa Hitobito* (Tokyo: Sōshisha, 2001).

2. The man was sentenced to death in 1975. Although the attorney persuaded the defendant to appeal, the psychiatric examination ordered by the appeals court diagnosed him with paranoia, and the court ruled that he could not be held liable for his actions, the defendant withdrew his appeal without consulting the attorney. The appeals court upheld the death sentence ruling in 1977, but he has not been executed.

3. Maema and Iwano, *Nihon no Piano 100-nen,* Chapter 10.

4. Kirin Narayan, "How Native is a Native Anthropologist?" *American Anthropologist* 95 (1993), 671–686; for recent examples of "native anthropology," see Sherrie B. Ortner, *New Jersey Dreaming: Capital, Culture, and the Class of '58* (Durham: Duke University Press, 2003); Christine R. Yano, *Crowning the Nice Girl: Gender, Ethnicity, and Culture in Hawai'i's Cherry Blossom Festival* (Honolulu: University of Hawai'i Press, 2006).

INTRODUCTION: A RISING SCALE IN RELATIVE MINOR

1. Of the piano contestants, nineteen were from Japan, three from South Korea, two from China, and two from Taiwan; two were Asian Americans, one was Vietnamese, one North Korean, one Japanese Chilean, and one Chinese Canadian. Of the violin contestants, eleven were from Japan, five from China, three from South Korea, and two from Vietnam.

2. Eight were from China, two were from South Korea, and five were Asian Americans.

3. "The Now Dynasty: Exuding Confidence at the Keyboard and Charisma Onstage, China's Posse of Classical Pianists Is Ready to Take the Cliburn by Storm," *Fort Worth Star-Telegram* (March 20, 2005); "Asians Strong Players in Cliburn Competition," *Kansas City Star* [MO] (May 22, 2005); "Far East Makes Inroads into Western Music," *San Diego Union-Tribune* (May 22, 2005); "In the Key of China: Cliburn Showcases New Enthusiasm for Classics," *Dallas Morning News* (June 5, 2005).

4. For example, see "Asian Performers Abound on the American Music Scene," *Christian Science Monitor* (June 18, 1991); "Asian Musicians Face Hurdles in America," *The Times Union* [Albany, NY] (February 13, 1994); "The Sound of New Music Is Often Chinese: A New Contingent of American Composers," *New York Times* (April 1, 2001); "The Next Generation Takes a Bow," *Christian Science Monitor* (November 29, 2001); and "Asians String Together a Classical Profile," *San Francisco Chronicle* (September 19, 2002). Also see Jamie James, "The Rise of a Musical Superpower: A Wave of Top-Class Talent Is Transforming Asia into a Major Player in the World of Classical Music," *Time Asia* 163.26 (July 5, 2004). In 2007, the *New York Times* ran a series of articles about China's embrace of classical music: "Classical Music Looks toward China with Hope," *New York Times* (April 3, 2007); "Increasingly in the West, the Players Are from the East," *Ibid.,* (April 4, 2007); "Pilgrim with an Oboe, Citizen of the World," *Ibid.,* (April 8, 2007).

5. Caucasians comprised approximately 57%, African Americans 9%, and Hispanics 5%. Approximately half of African American and Hispanic students were dance or drama majors, whereas the vast majority of Asians were music majors. Of the 628 music students, 210 were international students, over half of whom were from Asia; another 138 were Asian permanent residents of the United States.

6. Of the international students, 44 came from Korea, 36 from Canada, 28 from Taiwan, 24 from China, 21 from Japan, 12 from Israel, and 8 from Russia. Of the non-citizen permanent U.S. citizens, 57 were from Korea, 42 from Canada, 32 from Taiwan, 27 from China, 27 from Japan, 12 from Israel, and 10 from Russia. "The Juilliard School, Opening Fall Enrollment, College Division," Statistics Prepared by the Office of the Registrar, The Juilliard School, October 6, 2003.

7. Quoted in "Asians Strong Players in Cliburn Competition," *The Kansas City Star* [MO] (May 22, 2005).

8. Quoted in "The Now Dynasty: Exuding Confidence at the Keyboard and Charisma Onstage, China's Posse of Classical Pianists Is Ready to Take the Cliburn by Storm," *Fort Worth Star-Telegram* [TX] (March 20, 2005).

9. Although this study focuses on the United States, a similar trend is apparent in Canada as well. See Denise Lai, "The Rise of Asians in Classical Music," *La Scena Musicale* 9.5 (February 2004), 20–22.

10. Although no further ethnic breakdown of this category, "Asian Americans and Pacific Islanders," is available, it is safe to say that the vast majority of those in this category are East Asian rather than South Asian, Southeast Asian, or Pacific Islander. Roughly 200 of 900 adult orchestras participated in the report. E-mail correspondence, from Amy Yen [American Symphony Orchestra League] to the author, December 6, 2004. Among orchestra musicians, Asian musicians are clearly overrepresented in the

strings, and if one were to count only the string players, the percentage of Asians would clearly be much higher.

11. E-mail correspondence, from Amy Yen to the author, December 6, 2004.

12. Francie Ostrower, *Trustees of Culture: Power, Wealth, and Status on Elite Art Boards* (Chicago and London: University of Chicago Press, 2002).

13. "A Great Cultural Divide: City a Melting Pot, but Top Institutions Lily White," *New York Times* (April 11, 2004).

14. For example, "Opera Singer's Career Came from Risk-Taking," *The Seattle Times* (April 26, 1992); "Violinist Sees Asian Wave as Unifier," *The Commercial Appeal* [Memphis] (January 15, 1993); "Ascending Still: Violinist Chee-Yun Returning to Memphis," *Ibid.* (February 20, 1994); "Music as a Bridge between U.S., Korea," *Fresno Bee* [CA] (August 13, 1995); "Asian Sopranos Highlight 'Butterfly,'" *Times-Picayune* [New Orleans, LA] (November 23, 1995); "From Lieder to Korean Songs," *New York Times* (January 30, 1998); "Soprano to Debut Here," *The Houston Chronicle* (June 20, 1999); "Korean Violinist Has Steller Debut," *Ibid.* (July 3, 2000); "Chinese Soprano Debuts in N.O. Opera," *Times-Picayune* [New Orleans, LA] (April 19, 2001); "Classical Goes Global: Korean Violinist Joins the Wave of Young Asians Making Mark on Western Music," *San Jose Mercury News* [CA] (January 15, 2005).

CHAPTER 1: EARLY LESSONS IN GLOBALIZATION

1. Murray Lerner, dir., *From Mao to Mozart: Isaac Stern in China* (1979).

2. Stern's recollection of his observation of Chinese musicians supports the film's narrative: "As I entered the rehearsal hall in Beijing, I found it jammed with people who, it quickly became apparent, knew music. Also immediately apparent was the rather limited approach of both the conductor and the orchestra to Western music; they were unaccustomed to playing with varieties of color and passion. There was a distinctly stiff, technical, old-fashioned approach to the way they played. . . . In the case of the Central Philharmonic, both the conductor and the players recognized immediately that when I asked them to do this or that, I was not teaching them how to play; I was making them feel individually capable of accomplishing more than they were doing now." Isaac Stern (with Chaim Potok), *My First 79 Years* (New York: Knopf, 1999), 246.

3. Bonnie C. Wade, *Music in Japan: Experiencing Music, Expressing Culture* (New York: Oxford University Press, 2005), 12; Ury Eppstein, *The Beginnings of Western Music in Meiji Era Japan* (Lewiston, NY: Edwin Mellen Press, 1994).

4. Sheila Melvin and Jindong Cai, *Rhapsody in Red: How Western Classical Music Became Chinese* (New York: Algora Publishing, 2004), 84–86.

5. Okon Hwang, "Western Art Music in Korea: Everyday Experience and Cultural Critique," (PhD diss., Wesleyan University, 2001), 75; Young-Min Lee, "The Development of Western-Style Orchestral Music in Korea," (PhD diss., Catholic University of America, 1988), 15–16.

6. Melvin and Cai, *Rhapsody in Red,* 45–83.

7. Hwang, "Western Art Music in Korea," 76–78; Lee, "The Development of Western-Style Orchestral Music in Korea," 10–11.

8. Wade, *Music in Japan,* 14–15.

9. Melvin and Cai, *Rhapsody in Red,* 83.

10. Wade, *Music in Japan,* 12–14.

11. Melvin and Cai, *Rhapsody in Red,* 86–88.

12. Lee, "The Development of Western-Style Orchestral Music in Korea," 12–13.

13. Eppstein, *The Beginnings of Western Music in Meiji Era Japan,* 28–30.

14. Lee, "The Development of Western-Style Orchestral Music in Korea," 14–15; Hwang, "Western Art Music in Korea," 84–85.

15. Melvin and Cai, *Rhapsody in Red,* 99–100,189.

16. *Ibid.,* 92–95.

17. Lee, "The Development of Western-style Orchestral Music in Korea," 15.

18. Andrew F. Jones, *Yellow Music: Media Culture and Colonial Modernity in the Chinese Jazz Age* (Durham: Duke University Press, 2001).

19. Melvin and Cai, *Rhapsody in Red,* 126.

20. *Ibid.,*100–106.

21. Quoted in Tatsuhide Akiyama, ed., *Nihon no Yōgaku Hyakunen-shi* (Tokyo: Dai-ichi Hōki Shuppan, 1976), 409.

22. *Ibid.,* 410.

23. *Ibid.,* 554–56.

24. Kuniharu Akiyama, *Shōwa no Sakkyokuka tachi: Taiheiyō Sensō to Ongaku* (Tokyo: Misuzu Shobō, 2003).

25. Melvin and Cai, *Rhapsody in Red,* 225–64.

26. On the cultural climate of Japan during this period, see Stephen Vlastos, *Mirror of Modernity: Invented Traditions of Modern Japan* (Berkeley: University of California Press, 1998); Harry Harootunian, *Overcome by Modernity: History, Culture, and Community in Interwar Japan* (Princeton: Princeton University Press, 2000); Sharon A. Minichiello, "Greater Taishō: Japan 1900–1930," in *Taishō Chic: Japanese Modernity, Nostalgia, and Deco* (Honolulu: Honolulu Academy of Arts, 2001), 9–15.

27. The most comprehensive biography of Miura is Hisayuki Tanabe, *Kōshō Miura Tamaki* (Tokyo: Kindai Bungei-sha, 1995).

28. Akemitsu Yoshimoto, ed., *Ochō Fujin: Denki Miura Tamaki* (Tokyo: Ubunsha, 1947), 285.

29. *The New York World* [n.d., n.p.], quoted in the *Musical Courier* (February 12, 1920), 9.

30. On the gender ideology of "good wife, wise mother" and the challenges posed by the "Modern Girl," see Sharon H. Nolte and Sally Ann Hastings, "The Meiji State's Policy toward Women, 1890–1910," in *Recreating Japanese Women, 1600–1945,* ed. Gail Lee Bernstein (Berkeley: University of California Press, 1991), 151–74; Miriam Silverberg, "The Modern Girl as Militant," in *Ibid.,* 239–66; Kendall H. Brown, "Flowers of Taishō: Images of Women in Japanese Society and Art, 1915–1935," in *Taishō Chic,* 17–28.

31. Tamaki Shibata, *Sekai no Opera* ([Tokyo]: Kyōeki Shōsha, 1912).

32. *Ibid.,* 467.

33. *Ibid.,* 469.

34. Yoshimoto, *Ochō Fujin,* 58–59.

35. Tanabe, *Kōshō Miura Tamaki*, 189–207.

36. For example, see *Ibid.*, 358–362.

37. Tamaki Miura, *Kageki Ochō Fujin* ([Tokyo]: Ongaku Sekai-sha, 1937), 141.

38. Tamaki Miura, "Watashi no Ochō Fujin 5," *Jiji Shinpō* (December 25, 1935).

39. Yoshimoto, *Ochō Fujin,* 58.

40. On the story about the Japanese woman after whom Madame Butterfly was presumably modeled, see Yoshiaki Kusudo, *Mou Hitori no Chō-Chō-Fujin: Nagasaki Gurabaa-tei no Onna Shujin Tsuru* (Tokyo: Mainichi Shinbun-sha, 1997).

41. Miura Tamaki, "Watashi no Ochō Fujin 4," *Jiji Shinpō* (December 24, 1935).

42. Yoshimoto, *Ochō Fujin,* 58.

43. Ayako Kano, *Acting Like a Woman in Modern Japan: Theater, Gender, and Nationalism* (New York: Palgrave Macmillan, 2001), 6, 15–16, 92–93.

44. Silverberg, "The Modern Girl as Militant."

45. Shūichi Takaori, "Sokoku Seinen Gakka wa Ikanishite Shin-tenchi ni Hatten Subeki ka 2," *Ongakkai,* 179 (September 1916): 17.

46. "Nihon ni Kaeru madeno Miura Tamaki san to sono Uramen no Kushin," *Yomiuri Shinbun* (May 1, 1922).

47. *Tokyo Mainichi Shinbun* (March 26, 1909); *Tokyo Nichinichi Shinbun* (March 27, 1909); *Yomiuri Shinbun* (April 2, 1909); *Yomiuri Shinbun* (April 3, 1909).

48. "Geijutsu to Kekkon tono Mondai," *Ongakkai* 2.5 (May 1909): 9–11; Ikuta Aoi, "Matsui Sumako to Shibata Tamaki," *Chūō Kōron* 27.7 (July 1912): 140–141.

49. "Fujii Tamaki shi ni," *Ongakkai* 2.5 (May 1909): 29

50. *Yomiuri Shinbun* (May 28, 1932); *Tokyo Asahi Shinbun* (May 28, 1932).

51. *Nihon Shinbun* (May 28, 1932).

52. On the contradictory nature of government sanctions on "Western" music during the war years, see Akiyama, *Nihon no Yōgaku Hyakunen-shi,* 409–10.

53. Miura Tamaki, "Nihon no Uta wo," *Ongaku Bunka* 1.1 (1943): 42.

54. Keizō Horiuchi, "Kageki 'Madamu Batafurai' Jōen ni tsuki," n.t., [1930], 76. Yamada Kōsaku Collection, Microfilm 90, Scrapbook 16, frame 290. Nihon Kindai Ongakukan.

55. "Katakoto majiri de Kokujoku Kaifuku no Iki [With Smattering of English, Actress Determined to Rectify National Humiliation]," n.t., [1930], n.p. Yamada Kosaku Collection, Microfilm 90, Scrapbook 16, frame 285.

56. Horiuchi, "Kageki 'Madamu Batafurai' Jōen ni tsuki," 77–79.

57. "'Ochō Fujin' wo Miru," n.t., [1930], n.p. Yamada Kōsaku Collection, Microfilm 90, Scrapbook 16, frame 288.

58. Atsuko Hirai, "Government by Piano: An Early History of the Piano in Japan," in James Parakilas, et al., *Piano Roles: Three Hundred Years of Life with the Piano* (New Haven: Yale University Press, 2000), 312–314.

59. Takanori Maema and Yūichi Iwano, *Nihon no Piano 100-nen: Piano Zukuri ni Kaketa Hitobito* (Tokyo: Sōshisha, 2001), 245.

60. Minoru Nishihara, *Piano no Tanjō: Gakki no Mukou ni "Kindai" ga Mieru* (Tokyo: Kodansha, 1995), 249–54; Maema and Iwano, *Nihon no Piano 100-nen,* 195–261.

61. Minoru Nishihara, *Piano no Tanjō,* 253.

62. Melvin and Cai, *Rhapsody in Red,* 308.

63. See http://english.people.com.cn/english/200101/03/eng20010103_59532.html

64. Maema and Iwano, *Nihon no Piano 100-nen,* 245.

65. *Ibid.,* 244–48.

66. *Ibid.,* 238–41.

67. Hwang, "Western Art Music in Korea," 95–99.

68. Melvin and Cai, *Rhapsody in Red,* 308.

69. Maema and Iwano, *Nihon no Piano 100-nen,* 248–258.

70. See http://www.bluebookofpianos.com/basics.htm

71. Maema and Iwano, *Nihon no Piano 100-nen,* 259–260.

72. *New York Times* (November 13, 1977); *Asahi Shinbun* (June 25, 1979); *Asahi Shinbun* (June 27, 1979); Masami Kojima, *"Suzuki mesoddo" Sekai ni Yōji Kakumei wo: Suzuki Shinichi no Ai to Kyōiku* ([Tokyo]: Kyōdō Ongaku Shuppansha, 1985), 4.

73. *Time* (August 1, 1983): 88.

74. Akio Mizuno, "Suzuki Chirudoren Kaigai Ensō Tsuaa no Seika: Sainō Kyōiku Kaigai Haken no 20-nen" [1984], reprinted in *Suzuki Shinichi Zenshū* Vol. 7 ([Tokyo]: Sōhaisha, 1989), 375.

75. Shinichi Suzuki, "Chikara Zuyoki Kyōiku " [1941], reprinted in *Suzuki Shinichi Zenshū* Vol. 1 ([Tokyo]: Sōhaisha, 1989), 11, 12, 15. My translation.

76. Quoted in Masaaki Honda, *Ai no Hito Suzuki Shinichi Sensei* ([Tokyo]: Zen-on Gakufu Shuppansha, 1978), 59.

77. Shinichi Suzuki, *Ai ni Ikiru: Sainō wa Umaretsuki dewa Nai* ([Tokyo]: Kōdansha, 1966).

78. Shinichi Suzuki, "Yōji no Sainō Kyōiku to Sono Hōhō" [1946], reprinted in *Suzuki Shinichi Zenshū* Vol. 1 ([Tokyo]: Sōhaisha, 1985), 68–69, 71.

79. Jeff Magee, "25th Anniversary of Suzuki Ties Celebrated at Oberlin," *Oberlin Alumni Magazine* (Spring 1984):12; Interview with Kenji Mochizuki, June 4, 2003.

80. "Shinichi Suzuki 'Talent Education Tour' to Appear in Carnegie Hall: 'East Meets West,'" [press release] Sheldon Soffer Management, Inc., September 14, 1972.

81. "Young Violinists Play with Ease: 10 Japanese Pupils Display Success of Suzuki System," *New York Times* (October 10, 1966).

82. "Concert: Violin Students of Suzuki Method," *New York Times* (May 29, 1984).

83. "Playing by Ear," *Time* (August 24, 1959): 36.

84. Alfred Garson, "Learning with Suzuki: Seven Questions Answered," *Music Educators Journal* 56 (January 1, 1970): 64–66, 153–154

85. Ronarudo Kavaie [Ronald Cavaye] and Shifu Nishiyama, *Nihonjin no Ongaku Kyōiku* (Tokyo: Shinchō Sensho, 1987), 93–109.

86. Lois Peak, "The Suzuki Method of Music Instruction," in Thomas P. Rohlen and Gerald K. LeTendre, eds., *Teaching and Learning in Japan* (New York: Cambridge University Press, 1996), 358.

87. For example, see "Fiddling Legions," *Newsweek* (March 23, 1964): 73; "Instrumentalists: Invasion from the Orient," *Time* (November 3, 1967): 46; "'Like a Flower on a Pond': The Classics Flourish in Japan, but How Deep Are Their Roots?" *Time* (August 1, 1983): 77.

88. "Fiddling Legions," 73.

89. "Instrumentalists: Invasion from the Orient," 46.

90. Fumiyo Kuramochi interview, June 2, 2003; Toshio Takahashi interview, June 2, 2003; Kōji Toyoda interview, June 2, 2003.

91. Kōji Toyoda interview, June 2, 2003.

92. Toshio Takahashi interview, June 2, 2003.

93. Wes Craven, dir., *Music of the Heart* (1999); Allan Miller and Lana Miller, dirs., *Small Wonders* (1995).

94. Kenji Mochizuki, "Bei-eiga 'Myuujikku obu za Haato' Zenkoku Kōkai ni yosete," [Matsumoto] *Shimin Taimusu* (October 5, 2000).

95. *Ibid.,* 10.

CHAPTER 2: ROOTS AND ROUTES OF ASIAN MUSICIANS

1. Junah Chung interview, May 14, 2004.

2. Jennifer Koh interview, March 3, 2004.

3. Henry Kingsbury, *Music, Talent, and Performance: A Conservatory Cultural System* (Philadelphia: Temple University Press, 1988); Bruno Nettl, *Heartland Excursions: Ethnomusicological Reflections on Schools of Music* (Urbana and Chicago: University of Illinois Press, 1995).

4. This includes the number of dance and drama majors as well as part-time students, but those three categories combined include only 11 of 106 Asian American students. "The Juilliard School, Opening Fall Enrollment, College Division," Statistics prepared by the Office of the Registrar, the Juilliard School, October 6, 2003.

5. Andrew Le interview, September 30, 2003.

6. Sarah Chang telephone interview, January 22, 2004.

7. Conway Kuo interview, June 22, 2004.

8. Hiroko Yajima interview, December 10, 2003.

9. Kōichirō Yamamoto interview, April 28, 2004.

10. I-Bei Lin interview, September 9, 2004.

11. Duoming Ba interview, June 25, 2004.

12. *New York Times* (July 28, 1986).

13. "Unpretentious Prodigy Puzzled by All the Fuss," *New York Times* (July 29, 1986); "The Prodigy Factor," *Boston Globe* (August 4, 1986); "Musical Prodigies Strive for Harmony Onstage and Off," *New York Times* (July 24, 1987).

14. Akinori Okuda, *Haha to Shindō: Gotō Setsu Monogatari* (Tokyo: Shōgakukan, 1998).

15. Makoto Nakura interview, November 5, 2003.

16. Aihwa Ong, *Flexible Citizenship: The Cultural Logics of Transnationality* (Durham: Duke University Press, 1999). Also see Arjun Appadurai, "Disjuncture and Difference in the Global Economy," in *Modernity at Large: Cultural Dimensions of Globalization* (Minneapolis: University of Minnesota Press, 1996), 27–47.

17. Soyeon Lee interview, September 26, 2003. Tiffany Kuo, "Petschek Winner Plays for the 'Home Crowd,'" *The Juilliard Journal* 19.7 (April 2004): 5.

18. Ju-Ying Song interview, September 28, 2003.

19. Ignace Jang interview, September 15, 2004.

20. Henry Wong Doe interview, September 16, 2003.

21. Thomas Yee interview, September 3, 2004.

22. Jennifer Shyu interview, October 21, 2003.

23. Makiko Hirata interview, April 21, 2004.

24. Selina Miyazaki interview, February 11, 2004.

25. Junah Chung interview, May 14, 2004.

26. Myra Huang interview, September 29, 2003.

27. Makiko Hirata, personal communication, 2004.

28. Jennifer Koh interview, March 3, 2004.

29. Junah Chung interview, May 14, 2004.

30. Hiroko Yajima interview, December 10, 2003.

31. Muneko Otani interview, January 19, 2004.

32. Joel Tse, personal communication, 2004.

33. Kimiko Hata interview, January 18, 2004.

34. Kent Nagano interview, June 3, 2005.

35. October 21, 2002, Neal Blaisdell Concert Hall, Honolulu.

36. See www.ny.us.emb-japan.go.jp/en/n/report_27.html

37. Kimiko Hata, personal communication, 2004.

38. See, for example, Deborah Wong, *Speak it Louder: Asian Americans Making Music* (New York: Routledge, 2004); Adelaida Reyes, *Songs of the Caged, Songs of the Free: Music and the Vietnamese Refugee Experience* (Philadelphia: Temple University Press, 1999).

39. Warren Mok interview, February 7, 2005.

40. Helen Huang interview, September 12, 2003.

41. See, for example, Andrea Louie, *Chineseness across Borders: Renegotiating Chinese Identities in China and the United States* (Durham: Duke University Press, 2004); Ien Ang, *On Not Speaking Chinese: Living between Asia and the West* (London and New York: Routledge, 2001); Aihwa Ong, *Flexible Citizenship*; Aihwa Ong and Donald Nonini, eds., *Ungrounded Empires: The Cultural Politics of Modern Chinese Transnationalism* (New York and London: Routledge, 1996); Rey Chow, *Writing Diaspora: Tactics of Intervention in Contemporary Cultural Studies* (Indianapolis: Indiana University Press, 1993).

CHAPTER 3: PLAYING GENDER

1. *Fort Worth Star-Telegram* [TX] (March 20, 2005).

2. *Dallas Morning News* (June 12, 2005).

3. Ruth A. Solie, "'Girling' at the Parlor Piano," in *Music in Other Words: Victorian Conversations* (Berkeley: University of California Press, 2004), 85–117. Also see Richard Leppert, *Music and Image: Domesticity, Ideology and Socio-cultural Formation in Eighteenth-Century England* (Cambridge: Cambridge University Press, 1988) and *The Sight of Sound:*

Music, Representation, and the History of the Body (Berkeley: University of California Press, 1993); Judith Tick, "'Passed Away Is the Piano Girl': Changes in American Musical Life, 1870–1900," in *Women Making Music: The Western Art Tradition, 1150–1950,* eds. Jane Bowers and Judith Tick (Urbana: University of Illinois Press, 1986), 325–348.

4. Atsuko Hirai, "Government by Piano: An Early History of the Piano in Japan," in *Piano Roles: Three Hundred Years of Life with the Piano,* eds. James Parakilas, et al. (New Haven: Yale University Press, 2000), 303–316.

5. Geijutsu Kenkyū Shinkō Zaidan, Tokyo Geijutsu Daigaku Hyakunen-shi Henshū Iinkai, *Tokyo Geijutsu Daigaku Hyakunen-shi Daigaku-hen* ([Tokyo]: Gyōsei, 2003), 660–661.

6. Okon Hwang, "Western Art Music in Korea: Everyday Experience and Cultural Critique," (PhD diss., Wesleyan University, 2001), 206.

7. Tony Cho interview, February 9, 2005.

8. Warren Mok interview, February 7, 2005.

9. Frederick Lau interview, June 15, 2005.

10. Conway Kuo interview, June 22, 2004.

11. Satoshi Okamoto, personal communication.

12. Helen Huang interview, September 12, 2003.

13. Jennifer Koh interview, March 3, 2004.

14. Myra Huang interview, September 29, 2003.

15. Miori Sugiyama, September 23, 2003.

16. Anne Akiko Meyers telephone interview, September 20, 2005.

17. Soyeon Lee interview, September 26, 2003.

18. Makiko Hirata, personal communication, 2004.

19. Sachiko Kato interview, April 7, 2004.

20. See http://www.vanessamae.com

21. See http://www.anneakikomeyers.com

22. Sarah Chang telephone interview, January 22, 2004.

23. For examples of queer studies approaches to musicology, see Ruth A. Solie, ed., *Musicology and Difference: Gender and Sexuality in Music Scholarship* (Berkeley: University of California Press, 1993); Philip Brett, et al., eds., *Queering the Pitch: The New Gay and Lesbian Musicology* (New York & London: Routledge, 1994); Nadine Hubbs, *The Queer Composition of America's Sound: Gay Modernists, American Music, and National Identity* (Berkeley: University of California Press, 2004).

24. Tony Cho interview, February 9, 2005.

25. Anthony Tommasini, a music critic for the *New York Times* who has identified himself as gay in his articles, was also unconvinced by Nadine Hubbs's argument about a gay sensibility in music by American modernists, such as Aaron Copland, Virgil Thomson, Paul Bowles, and Ned Rorem:

> Ms. Hubbs's treatise, which focuses mostly on Copland and Thomson, is enriched by her keen sensitivity to traces of coded gay sexuality, veiled homophobia and cultural anxieties in American music and life during the early decades of the 20th century. The book will rightly provoke heated discussion in musicological and queer-history

circles. My gay brothers and sisters should welcome Ms. Hubbs's account of the pivotal role played by gay composers in the development of a musical idiom that as the book argues, still signifies 'America,' not just in the concert hall but also in movies, television and commercial culture.

Yet, I suspect that many musicians, however fascinated by Ms. Hubbs's treatise, will share my discomfort over the notion of trying to identify anything as elusive as a gay sensibility in music. It's significant, I think, that most of the advance praise for the book . . . comes from cultural historians, not musicians. My aim here is not to review the book but to raise the stakes for the debate Ms. Hubbs's work is sure to provoke . . .

Ultimately, what we may most value about music is that it moves us in powerful but indistinct ways. It's the one thing that cannot be analyzed or deconstructed for its expressive content, and thank goodness for that.

New York Times (October 24, 2004).

26. Hubbs, *Queer Composition,* 177.

CHAPTER 4: CLASS NOTES

1. See, for instance, Paul DiMaggio and Francie Ostrower, *Race, Ethnicity, and Participation in the Arts: Patterns of Participation by Hispanics, Whites, and African-Americans in Selected Activities from the 1982 and 1985 Surveys of Public Participation in the Arts* (Washington, DC: Seven Locks Press, 1992); Richard A. Peterson and Albert Simkus, "How Musical Tastes Mark Occupational Status Groups," in Michèle Lamont and Marcel Fournier, eds., *Cultivating Differences: Symbolic Boundaries and the Making of Inequality* (Chicago and London: University of Chicago Press, 1992), 152–186.

2. Pierre Bourdieu, *Distinction: A Social Critique of the Judgement of Taste,* trans. Richard Nice (Cambridge: Harvard University Press, 1984), 18.

3. William J. Baumol and William G. Bowen, *Performing Art—The Economic Dilemma: A Study of Problems Common to Theater, Opera, Music and Dance* (New York: Twentieth Century Fund, 1966). Baumol painted a somewhat more hopeful picture in a more recent study, "Children of Performing Arts, The Economic Dilemma: The Climbing Costs of Health Care and Education," *Journal of Cultural Economics* 20.3 (1996): 183–206.

4. On the history of state funding for the arts through the National Endowment for the Arts, see Donna M. Binkiewicz, *Federalizing the Muse: United States Arts Policy and the National Endowment for the Arts, 1965–1980* (Chapel Hill: University of North Carolina Press, 2004).

5. "The Juilliard Effect: Ten Years Later," *New York Times* (December 12, 2004).

6. Blair Tindall, *Mozart in the Jungle: Sex, Drugs, and Classical Music* (New York: Atlantic Monthly Press, 2005).

7. On mediated class locations, see Erik Olin Wright, *Class Counts: Comparative Studies in Class Analysis* (Cambridge: Cambridge University Press, 1997), 26–27, 257–260.

8. The national differences in symbolic boundaries of cultural capital are discussed in Michèle Lamont, *Money, Morals, and Manners: The Culture of the French and American Upper-Middle Class* (Chicago and London: University of Chicago Press, 1992).

9. On middle-class locations, see Wright, *Class Counts,* 19–26.

10. Some sociological studies that use cultural capital as a primary theoretical framework include Michèle Lamont and Annette Lareau, "Cultural Capital: Allusions, Gaps and Glissandos in Recent Theoretical Developments," *Sociological Theory* 6 (Fall 1988): 153–168; Michèle Lamont, *Money, Morals, and Manners*; John R. Hall, "The Capital(s) of Cultures: A Nonholistic Approach to Status Situations, Class, Gender, and Ethnicity," in *Cultivating Differences: Symbolic Boundaries and the Making of Inequality,* eds. Michèle Lamont and Marcel Fournier (Chicago: University of Chicago Press, 1992), 257–285; and Jan C. C. Rupp, "Rethinking Cultural and Economic Capital," in *Reworking Class,* ed. John R. Hall (Ithaca: Cornell University Press, 1997), 221–241.

11. For instance, see Bourdieu, *Distinction*; DiMaggio and Ostrower, *Race, Ethnicity, and Participation in the Arts*; Peterson and Simkus, "How Musical Tastes Mark Occupational Status Groups"; David Halle, "The Audience for Abstract Art: Class, Culture, and Power," in *Cultivating Differences,* eds. Lamont and Fournier, 131–151; and Vera L. Zolberg, "Barrier or Leveler: The Case of the Art Museum," in *Ibid,* 187–209.

12. Paul DiMaggio, *Managers of the Arts: Careers and Opinions of Senior Administrators of U.S. Art Museums, Symphony Orchestras, Resident Theaters, and Local Arts Agencies* (Washington, DC: Seven Locks Press, 1988); Francie Ostrower, *Trustees of Culture: Power, Wealth, and Status on Elite Art Boards* (Chicago and London: University of Chicago Press, 2002).

13. Jennifer Shyu interview, October 21, 2003.

14. Ju-Ying Song interview, September 28, 2003.

15. Sherry B. Ortner, *New Jersey Dreaming: Capital, Culture, and the Class of '58* (Durham: Duke University Press, 2003), 270. On the "professional managerial class," see also Barbara Ehrenreich, *Fear of Falling: The Inner Life of the Middle Class* (New York: Pantheon Books, 1989); Barbara Ehrenreich and John Ehrenreich, "The Professional-Managerial Class," Reprinted in *Between Labour and Capital*, ed. Pat Walker (Hassocks, Sussex: Harvester Press, 1979 [1977]), 5–45.

16. Myra Huang interview, September 29, 2003.

17. Frederick Lau interview, June 15, 2005.

18. Richard Curt Kraus, *Pianos and Politics in China: Middle-Class Ambitions and the Struggle over Western Music* (New York: Oxford University Press, 1989), viii. Also see Kraus's *The Party and the Arty in China: The New Politics of Culture* (Lanham, MD: Rowman & Littlefield, 2004).

19. Bichuan Li interview, November 27, 2004.

20. William W. Kelly, "Finding a Place in Metropolitan Japan: Ideologies, Institutions, and Everyday Life," in *Postwar Japan as History,* ed. Andrew Gordon (Berkeley: University of California Press, 1993), 189–216.

21. Charles Yuji Horioka, "Consuming and Saving," in *Ibid.,* 259–92.

22. Denise Potrzeba Lett, *In Pursuit of Status: The Making of South Korea's "New" Urban Middle Class* (Cambridge, MA: Harvard University Asia Center, 1998).

23. For instance, see Pyong Gap Min, *Caught in the Middle: Korean Communities in New York and Los Angeles* (Berkeley: University of California Press, 1996).

24. Wen Qian interview, June 20, 2004.

25. David Kim interview, January 13, 2004.

26. Jihea Hong interview, September 23, 2003.

27. Yi-Heng Yang interview, September 11, 2003.

28. On Jews in American popular music and film, see Jeffrey Melnick, *A Right to Sing the Blues: African Americans, Jews, and American Popular Song* (Cambridge, MA: Harvard University Press, 1999) and Michael Rogin, *Blackface, White Noise: Jewish Immigrants in the Hollywood Melting Pot* (Berkeley: University of California Press, 1996).

29. Liuh Wen Ting interview, September 4, 2003; Sachiko Kato interview, April 7, 2004.

30. Grace Wang, "Soundtracks of Asian American Identity: Music, Race, and National Belonging," (PhD diss., University of Michigan, 2005).

31. Chee-Yun [Kim] interview, January 19, 2004.

32. Lamont, *Money, Morals, and Manners.*

33. Aihwa Ong, *Flexible Citizenship: The Cultural Logics of Transnationality* (Durham: Duke University Press, 1999), 90–91.

34. *Ibid.,* 91–92.

35. "The Facts about Orchestra Salaries," http://www.orchestrafacts.org

36. "Analysis: Comparing Political Office to Auditioning for an Orchestra," *NPR Morning Edition,* February 18, 2004.

37. "Four Major Orchestras Facing Contract Issues," *New York Times* (September 16, 2004).

38. "The Facts about Orchestra Salaries."

39. Conway Kuo interview, June 22, 2004.

40. On class structure and the "middle class" in contemporary capitalist societies, see, for example, Erik Olin Wright, "Rethinking, Once Again, the Concept of Class Structure," in *Reworking Class,* ed. John R. Hall (Ithaca: Cornell University Press, 1997), 41–71.

41. On the cultural performance of the middle class, see Mark Liechty, *Suitably Modern: Making Middle-Class Culture in a New Consumer Society* (Princeton: Princeton University Press, 2003).

42. Mari Kimura interview, August 28, 2003.

43. Sidney Yin interview, October 8, 2003.

44. Ayako Watanabe interview, December 30, 2004.

45. Kurt Muroki telephone interview, December 15, 2004.

46. A large-scale organizational study of seventy-eight professional symphony orchestras in four nations showed that, in terms of the level of internal motivation, symphony musicians are at the top of the scale. The researchers, J. Richard Hackman and Jutta Allmendinger, concluded that "orchestra players are, indeed, fueled by their own pride and professionalism." Paul R. Judy, "Life and Work in Symphony Orchestras: An Interview with J. Richard Hackman," *Harmony* 2 (April 1996): 1–12.

47. Pierre Bourdieu, *The Field of Cultural Production* (New York: Columbia University Press, 1993), 35.

48. *Ibid.,* 79.

49. *Ibid.,* 115.

50. Julian Johnson, *Who Needs Classical Music? Cultural Choice and Musical Value* (Oxford: Oxford University Press, 2002), 8–9.

51. Bourdieu, *Distinction,* 317.

CHAPTER 5: A VOICE OF ONE'S OWN

1. Hiroko Yajima interview, December 10, 2003.

2. *West Essex Tribune* [Livingston, NJ] (November 24, 1999).

3. Walter Benjamin, "The Work of Art in the Age of Mechanical Reproduction," [1936] in *Illuminations* (New York: Harcourt, Brace, & World, 1968), 217–252.

4. Roy Wagner, *The Invention of Culture* (Chicago: University of Chicago Press, 1981); Eric Hobsbawm and Terence Ranger, eds., *The Invention of Tradition* (Cambridge: Cambridge University Press, 1983).

5. James Clifford and George Marcus, eds., *Writing Culture* (Berkeley: University of California Press, 1988); James Clifford, *The Predicament of Culture* (Cambridge, MA: Harvard University Press, 1988).

6. On the politics of Asian and Asian American bodies and performance, see Karen Shimakawa, *National Abjection: The Asian American Body on Stage* (Durham: Duke University Press, 2002); Josephine Lee, *Performing Asian American: Race and Ethnicity on the Contemporary Stage* (Philadelphia: Temple University Press, 1998); and Dorinne Kondo, *About Face: Performing Race in Fashion and Theater* (New York: Routledge, 1997).

7. Bruno Nettl, *The Western Impact on World Music: Change, Adaptation, and Survival* (New York: Schirmer Books, 1985); Ury Eppstein, *The Beginnings of Western Music in Meiji Era Japan* (Lewiston, NY: Edwin Mellen Press, 1995); Young-Min Lee, "The Development of Western-Style Orchestral Music in Korea," (PhD diss., Catholic University of America, 1988); Okon Hwang, "Western Art Music in Korea: Everyday Experience and Cultural Critique," (PhD diss., Wesleyan University, 2001).

8. Deborah Wong, *Speak It Louder: Asian Americans Making Music* (New York: Routledge, 2004); Adelaida Reyes, *Songs of the Caged, Songs of the Free: Music and the Vietnamese Refugee Experience* (Philadelphia: Temple University Press, 1999); Susan Miyo Asai, "Transformations of Tradition: Three Generations of Japanese American Music Making," *The Musical Quarterly* 79.3 (1995): 429–453.

9. Frederick Lau interview, June 15, 2005.

10. Pei-Chun Tsai interview, August 29, 2003.

11. Siu Yan Luk interview, October 10, 2003.

12. Duoming Ba interview, June 25, 2004.

13. Bruno Nettl, *Heartland Excursions: Ethnomusicologica Reflections on Schools of Music* (Urbana and Chicago: University of Illinois Press, 1995), 107.

14. Sachiko Kato interview, April 7, 2004.

15. Helen Huang interview, September 12, 2003.

16. Han-Na Chang interview, March 20, 2004.

17. Ayako Watanabe interview, December 30, 2004.

18. Jennifer Koh interview, March 3, 2004.

19. Kent Nagano interview, June 3, 2005.

20. Joel Tse interview, August 8, 2005.

21. The issue of authenticity is important in other musical genres as well, but the issue is manifested differently. See, for instance, Shuhei Hosokawa, "'Salsa no tiene frontera': Orquesta de la Luz and the Globalization of Popular Music," *Cultural Studies* 3.3 (1999): 509–534 and E. Taylor Atkins, *Blue Nippon: Authenticating Jazz in Japan* (Durham: Duke University Press, 2001).

22. Nettl, *Heartland Excursions*, 106.

23. *Ibid.,* 100.

24. Kent Nagano interview, June 3, 2005.

25. Chee-Yun [Kim] interview, January 19, 2004.

26. Sachiko Kato interview, April 7, 2004.

27. Pheng Cheah and Bruce Robbins, eds., *Cosmopolitics: Thinking and Feeling beyond the Nation* (Minneapolis: University of Minnesota Press, 1998); Timothy Brennan, *At Home in the World: Cosmopolitanism Now* (Cambridge: Harvard University Press, 1997).

28. Nettl, *Heartland Excursions,* 102.

29. Satoshi Okamoto interview, April 16, 2004.

30. I make a similar argument in my article, "The Flight of the Japanese Butterfly: Orientalism, Nationalism, and Performances of Japanese Womanhood," *American Quarterly* 56.4 (2004): 975–1001.

31. Angela Ahn telephone interview, October 22, 2002.

32. Kōichirō Yamamoto interview, April 28, 2004.

33. Mariko Furukawa interview, January 25, 2004.

34. Mari Kimura interview, August 28, 2003.

35. Hiromi Fukuda interview, March 8, 2004.

36. Kaori Kato interview, March 11, 2004.

37. Ju-Ying Song interview, September 28, 2003.

38. Kurt Muroki telephone interview, December 15, 2004.

39. Conway Kuo interview, June 22, 2004.

40. Anne Akiko Meyers phone interview, September 20, 2005.

41. Mari Kimura interview, August 28, 2003.

42. Ayako Watanabe interview, December 30, 2004.

43. Yoshihara, "The Flight of the Japanese Butterfly."

44. Kimiko Hata interview, January 18, 2004.

45. Lea Woods Friedman interview, January 25, 2005.

46. Hawaii Opera Theatre, *The Mikado,* Blaisdell Concert Hall, Honolulu, HI, August 6–15, 2004. "'Mikado' Revels as Un-PC," *Honolulu Star-Bulletin* (August 6, 2004); "Taiko Drums and Gag Lines," *Honolulu Star-Bulletin* (August 9, 2004).

47. Henry Akina interview, January 9, 2005.

48. Warren Mok interview, February 7, 2005.

49. Nettl, *Heartland Excursions,* 101.

50. Akemi Naito, *Strings & Time* (Composers Recordings, Inc., 1997).

51. Akemi Naito interview, December 20, 2003.

52. Moto Osada interview, February 13, 2004.

53. Frederick Lau, "Fusion or Fission: The Paradox and Politics of Contemporary Chinese Avant-Garde Music," in *Locating East Asia in Western Art Music,* eds. Yayoi Uno Everett and Frederick Lau (Middletown: Wesleyan University Press, 2004), 28.

54. *Ibid.,* 35–36.

55. Sheila Melvin and Jindong Cai, *Rhapsody in Red: How Western Classical Music Became Chinese* (New York: Algora Publishing, 2004), 332.

56. On different methods of "using" Asian music in post-1945 Western art music, see Yayoi Uno Everett, "Intercultural Synthesis in Postwar Western Art Music: Historical Contexts, Perspectives, and Taxonomy," in *Locating East Asia in Western Art Music,* eds. Yayoi Uno Everett and Frederick Lau (Middletown, CT: Wesleyan University Press, 2004), 1–21.

57. Ge Ganru interview, November 21, 2003.

58. Lau makes this point in "Fusion or Fission," 36.

59. Regina Bendix, *In Search of Authenticity: The Formation of Folklore Studies* (Madison: University of Wisconsin Press, 1997), 17.

CONCLUSION: MUSICIANS FIRST

1. Melani McAlister, *Epic Encounters: Culture, Media, and U.S. Interests in the Middle East since 1945,* updated edition (Berkeley: University of California Press, 2005), xviii.

Selected Bibliography

ENGLISH-LANGUAGE SOURCES

Adorno, Theodor. *Essays on Music*. Ed. Richard Leppert. Trans. Susan H. Gillespie. Berkeley: University of California Press, 2002.

Ang, Ien. *On Not Speaking Chinese: Living Between Asia and the West*. London: Routledge, 2001.

Appadurai, Arjun. "Disjuncture and Difference in the Global Economy." In *Modernity at Large: Cultural Dimensions of Globalization*. Minneapolis: University of Minnesota Press, 1996. 27–47.

Asai, Susan Miyo. "Transformations of Tradition: Three Generations of Japanese American Music Making." *The Musical Quarterly* 79.3 (1995): 429–453.

Atkins, E. Taylor. *Blue Nippon: Authenticating Jazz in Japan*. Durham: Duke University Press, 2001.

Attali, Jacques. *Noise: The Political Economy of Music*. Trans. Brian Massumi. Minneapolis: University of Minnesota Press, [1977] 1985.

Ayer, Julie. *More than Meets the Ear: How Symphony Musicians Made Labor History*. Minneapolis: Syren Book Company, 2005.

Bakhle, Janaki. *Two Men and Music: Nationalism in the Making of an Indian Classical Tradition*. New York: Oxford University Press, 2005.

Barenboim, Daniel and Edward W. Said. *Parallels and Paradoxes: Explorations in Music and Society*. New York: Pantheon Books, 2002.

Barz, Gregory F. and Timothy J. Cooley, eds. *Shadows in the Field: New Perspectives for Fieldwork in Ethnomusicology*. New York: Oxford University Press, 1997.

Baumol, William J. "Children of Performing Arts, The Economic Dilemma: The Climbing Costs of Health Care and Education." *Journal of Cultural Economics* 20.3 (1996): 183–206.

Baumol, William J. and William G. Bowen. *Performing Art—The Economic Dilemma: A Study of Problems Common to Theater, Opera, Music and Dance.* New York: Twentieth Century Fund, 1966.

Becker, Howard S. *Art Worlds.* Berkeley: University of California Press, 1982.

Bellman, Jonathan. *The Exotic in Western Music.* Boston: Northeastern University Press, 1998.

Bendix, Regina. *In Search of Authenticity: The Formation of Folklore Studies.* Madison: University of Wisconsin Press, 1997.

Benjamin, Walter. "The Work of Art in the Age of Mechanical Reproduction." In *Illuminations.* New York: Harcourt, Brace, & World, [1936] 1968. 217–252.

Binkiewicz, Donna M. *Federalizing the Muse: United States Arts Policy and the National Endowment for the Arts, 1965–1980.* Chapel Hill: University of North Carolina Press, 2004.

Born, Georgina and David Hesmondhalgh, eds. *Western Music and Its Others: Difference, Representation, and Appropriation in Music.* Berkeley: University of California Press, 2000.

Bourdieu, Pierre. *Distinction: A Social Critique of the Judgment of Taste.* Trans. Richard Nice. Cambridge, MA: Harvard University Press, 1984.

———. *The Field of Cultural Production.* New York: Columbia University Press, 1993.

Brennan, Timothy. *At Home in the World: Cosmopolitanism Now.* Cambridge, MA: Harvard University Press, 1997.

Brett, Philip, et al. eds. *Queering the Pitch: The New Gay and Lesbian Musicology.* New York: Routledge, 1994.

Brodine, Russell V. *Fiddle and Fight: A Memoir.* New York: International Publishers, 2001.

Brown, Kendall H. "Flowers of Taishō: Images of Women in Japanese Society and Art, 1915–1935." In *Taishō Chic: Japanese Modernity, Nostalgia, and Deco.* Honolulu: Honolulu Academy of Arts, 2001. 17–28.

Cheah, Pheng and Bruce Robbins, eds. *Cosmopolitics: Thinking and Feeling Beyond the Nation.* Minneapolis: University of Minnesota Press, 1998.

Chow, Rey. *Writing Diaspora: Tactics of Intervention in Contemporary Cultural Studies.* Indianapolis: Indiana University Press, 1993.

Chuh, Kandice and Karen Shimakawa, eds. *Orientations: Mapping Studies in the Asian Diaspora.* Durham: Duke University Press, 2001.

Clifford, James. *The Predicament of Culture.* Cambridge, MA: Harvard University Press, 1988.

———. *Routes: Travel and Translation in the Twentieth Century.* Cambridge, MA: Harvard University Press, 1997.

——— and George Marcus, eds. *Writing Culture.* Berkeley: University of California Press, 1988.

Cook, Nicholas and Mark Everist, eds. *Rethinking Music.* New York: Oxford University Press, 1999.

Cook, Susan S. and Judy S. Tsou, eds. *Cecilia Reclaimed: Feminist Perspectives on Gender and Music.* Champaign: University of Illinois Press, 1994.

DiMaggio, Paul. *Managers of the Arts: Careers and Opinions of Senior Administrators of U.S. Art Museums, Symphony Orchestras, Resident Theaters, and Local Arts Agencies.* Washington, DC: Seven Locks Press, 1988.

——— and Francie Ostrower. *Race, Ethnicity, and Participation in the Arts: Patterns of Participation by Hispanics, Whites, and African-Americans in Selected Activities from the 1982 and 1985 Surveys of Public Participation in the Arts.* Washington, DC: Seven Locks Press, 1992.

Ehrenreich, Barbara. *Fear of Falling: The Inner Life of the Middle Class.* New York: Pantheon Books, 1989.

——— and John Ehrenreich. "The Professional-Managerial Class." Reprinted in *Between Labour and Capital* Ed. Pat Walker. Hassocks, Sussex: Harvester Press, [1977] 1979. 5–45.

Eppstein, Ury. *The Beginnings of Western Music in Meiji Era Japan.* Lewiston, NY: Edwin Mellen Press, 1994.

Espiritu, Yen Le. *Asian American Panethnicity: Bridging Institutions and Identities.* Philadelphia: Temple University Press, 1992.

Everett, Yayoi Uno. "Intercultural Synthesis in Postwar Western Art Music: Historical Contexts, Perspectives, and Taxonomy." In *Locating East Asia in Western Art Music.* Eds. Yayoi Uno Everett and Frederick Lau. Middletown, CT: Wesleyan University Press, 2004. 1–21.

Hall, John R. "The Capital(s) of Cultures: A Nonholistic Approach to Status Situations, Class, Gender, and Ethnicity." In *Cultivating Differences: Symbolic Boundaries and the Making of Inequality.* Eds. Michèle Lamont and Marcel Fournier. Chicago: University of Chicago Press, 1992. 257–285.

Hall, Stuart. "Notes on Deconstructing 'The Popular.'" In *People's History and Socialist Theory.* Ed. Raphael Samuel. London: Routledge, 1981. 227–249.

——— and Paul Du Gay, eds. *Questions of Cultural Identity.* London: Sage, 1996.

Halle, David. "The Audience for Abstract Art: Class, Culture, and Power." In *Cultivating Differences: Symbolic Boundaries and the Making of Inequality.* Eds. Michèle Lamont and Marcel Fournier. Chicago: University of Chicago Press, 1992. 131–151.

Harootunian, Harry. *Overcome by Modernity: History, Culture, and Community in Interwar Japan.* Princeton: Princeton University Press, 2000.

Hirai, Atsuko. "Government by Piano: An Early History of the Piano in Japan." In *Piano Roles: Three Hundred Years of Life with the Piano.* Eds. James Parakilas, et al. New Haven: Yale University Press, 2000. 312–314.

Hobsbawm, Eric and Terence Ranger, eds. *The Invention of Tradition.* Cambridge: Cambridge University Press, 1983.

Horioka, Charles Yuji. "Consuming and Saving." In *Postwar Japan as History.* Ed. Andrew Gordon. Berkeley: University of California Press, 1993. 259–292.

Hosokawa, Shuhei. "'Salsa no tiene frontera': Orquesta de la Luz and the Globalization of Popular Music." *Cultural Studies* 3.3 (1999): 509–534.

Hubbs, Nadine. *The Queer Composition of America's Sound: Gay Modernists, American Music, and National Identity.* Berkeley: University of California Press, 2004.

Hwang, Okon. "Western Art Music in Korea: Everyday Experience and Cultural Critique." PhD diss. Wesleyan University, 2001.

Johnson, Julian. *Who Needs Classical Music? Cultural Choice and Musical Value.* Oxford: Oxford University Press, 2002.

Jones, Andrew F. *Yellow Music: Media Culture and Colonial Modernity in the Chinese Jazz Age.* Durham: Duke University Press, 2001.

Kano, Ayako. *Acting like a Woman in Modern Japan: Theater, Gender, and Nationalism.* New York: Palgrave Macmillan, 2001.

Kelly, William W. "Finding a Place in Metropolitan Japan: Ideologies, Institutions, and Everyday Life." In *Postwar Japan as History.* Ed. Andrew Gordon. Berkeley: University of California Press, 1993. 189–216.

Kingsbury, Henry. *Music, Talent, and Performance: A Conservatory Cultural System.* Philadelphia: Temple University Press, 1988.

Kogan, Judith. *Nothing but the Best: The Struggle for Perfection at the Juilliard School.* New York: Random House, 1987.

Kondo, Dorinne. *About Face: Performing Race in Fashion and Theater.* New York: Routledge, 1997.

Kraus, Richard Curt. *Pianos and Politics in China: Middle-Class Ambitions and the Struggle over Western Music.* New York: Oxford University Press, 1989.

———. *The Party and the Arty in China: The New Politics of Culture.* Lanham, MD: Rowman & Littlefield, 2004.

Lamont, Michèle. *Money, Morals, and Manners: The Culture of the French and American Upper-Middle Class.* Chicago: University of Chicago Press, 1992.

——— and Annette Lareau. "Cultural Capital: Allusions, Gaps and Glissandos in Recent Theoretical Developments." *Sociological Theory* 6 (1988): 153–168.

Lau, Frederick. "Fusion or Fission: The Paradox and Politics of Contemporary Chinese Avant-Garde Music." In *Locating East Asia in Western Art Music.* Eds. Yayoi Uno Everett and Frederick Lau. Middletown: Wesleyan University Press, 2004. 22–39.

Lee, Josephine. *Performing Asian American: Race and Ethnicity on the Contemporary Stage.* Philadelphia: Temple University Press, 1998.

Lee, Young-Min. "The Development of Western-Style Orchestral Music in Korea." PhD diss. Catholic University of America, 1988.

Leppert, Richard. *Music and Image: Domesticity, Ideology and Socio-cultural Formation in Eighteenth-Century England.* Cambridge: Cambridge University Press, 1988.

———. *The Sight of Sound: Music, Representation, and the History of the Body.* Berkeley: University of California Press, 1993.

Lett, Denise Potrzeba. *In Pursuit of Status: The Making of South Korea's "New" Urban Middle Class.* Cambridge, MA: Harvard University Asia Center, 1998.

Liechty, Mark. *Suitably Modern: Making Middle-Class Culture in a New Consumer Society.* Princeton: Princeton University Press, 2003.

Lipsitz, George. *Dangerous Crossroads: Popular Music, Postmodernism and the Poetics of Place.* London: Verso, 1994.

Louie, Andrea. *Chineseness Across Borders: Renegotiating Chinese Identities in China and the United States.* Durham: Duke University Press, 2004.

Lowe, Lisa. *Immigrant Acts: On Asian American Cultural Politics.* Durham: Duke University Press, 1996.

Maira, Sunaina Marr. *Desis in the House: Indian American Youth Culture in New York City.* Philadelphia: Temple University Press, 2002.

Manalansan, Martin F. IV, ed. *Ethnic Compass: Ethnographic Explorations of Asian America.* Philadelphia: Temple University Press, 2000.

McAlister, Melani. *Epic Encounters: Culture, Media, and U.S. Interests in the Middle East since 1945.* Berkeley: University of California Press, 2005.

McClary, Susan. *Feminine Endings: Music, Gender, and Sexuality.* Minneapolis: University of Minnesota Press, 1991.

Melnick, Jeffrey. *A Right to Sing the Blues: African Americans, Jews, and American Popular Song.* Cambridge, MA: Harvard University Press, 1999.

Melvin, Sheila and Jindong Cai. *Rhapsody in Red: How Western Classical Music Became Chinese.* New York: Algora Publishing, 2004.

Min, Pyong Gap. *Caught in the Middle: Korean Communities in New York and Los Angeles.* Berkeley: University of California Press, 1996.

Minichiello, Sharon A. "Greater Taishō: Japan 1900–1930." In *Taishō Chic: Japanese Modernity, Nostalgia, and Deco.* Honolulu: Honolulu Academy of Arts, 2001. 9–15.

Morley, David and Kuan-Hsing Chen, eds. *Stuart Hall: Critical Dialogues in Cultural Studies.* London: Routledge, 1996.

Narayan, Kirin. "How Native is a Native Anthropologist?" *American Anthropologist* 95 (1993): 671–686.

Nettl, Bruno. *The Western Impact on World Music: Change, Adaptation, and Survival.* New York: Schirmer Books, 1985.

———. *Heartland Excursions: Ethnomusicological Reflections on Schools of Music.* Urbana: University of Illinois Press, 1995.

Nolte, Sharon H. and Sally Ann Hastings. "The Meiji State's Policy toward Women, 1890–1910." In *Recreating Japanese Women, 1600–1945.* Ed. Gail Lee Bernstein. Berkeley: University of California Press, 1991. 151–174.

Omi, Michael and Howard Winant. *Racial Formation in the United States.* 2nd ed. New York: Routledge, 1994.

Ong, Aihwa. *Flexible Citizenship: The Cultural Logics of Transnationality.* Durham: Duke University Press, 1999.

——— and Donald Nonini, eds. *Ungrounded Empires: The Cultural Politics of Modern Chinese Transnationalism.* New York: Routledge, 1996.

Ortner, Sherrie B. *New Jersey Dreaming: Capital, Culture, and the Class of '58.* Durham: Duke University Press, 2003.

Ostrower, Francie. *Trustees of Culture: Power, Wealth, and Status on Elite Art Boards.* Chicago: University of Chicago Press, 2002.

Peak, Lois. "The Suzuki Method of Music Instruction." In *Teaching and Learning in Japan.* Eds. Thomas P. Rohlen and Gerald K. LeTendre. New York: Cambridge University Press, 1996. 345–368.

Peterson, Richard A. and Albert Simkus. "How Musical Tastes Mark Occupational Status Groups." In *Cultivating Differences: Symbolic Boundaries and the Making of Inequality.* Eds. Michèle Lamont and Marcel Fournier. Chicago: University of Chicago Press, 1992. 152–186.

Radano, Ronald and Philip V. Bohlman, eds. *Music and the Racial Imagination.* Chicago: University of Chicago Press, 2000.

Reyes, Adelaida. *Songs of the Caged, Songs of the Free: Music and the Vietnamese Refugee Experience.* Philadelphia: Temple University Press, 1999.

Rogin, Michael. *Blackface, White Noise: Jewish Immigrants in the Hollywood Melting Pot.* Berkeley: University of California Press, 1996.

Rupp, Jan C. "Rethinking Cultural and Economic Capital." In *Reworking Class.* Ed. John R. Hall. Ithaca: Cornell University Press, 1997. 221–241.

Said, Edward W. *Orientalism.* New York: Random House, 1978.

———. *Musical Elaborations.* New York: Columbia University Press, 1991.

———. *Culture and Imperialism.* New York: Vintage, 1994.

Sand, Barbara Lourie. *Teaching Genius: Dorothy DeLay and the Making of a Musician.* Portland, OR: Amadeus Press, 2000.

Shimakawa, Karen. *National Abjection: The Asian American Body on Stage.* Durham: Duke University Press, 2002.

Silverberg, Miriam. "The Modern Girl as Militant." In *Recreating Japanese Women, 1600–1945.* Ed. Gail Lee Bernstein. Berkeley: University of California Press, 1991. 239–266.

Small, Christopher. *Music of the Common Tongue: Survival and Celebration in African American Music.* Hanover: Wesleyan University Press, 1987.

———. *Music, Society, Education.* Hanover: Wesleyan University Press, 1996.

———. *Musicking: The Meanings of Performing and Listening.* Hanover: Wesleyan University Press, 1998.

Solie, Ruth A. "'Girling' at the Parlor Piano." In *Music in Other Words: Victorian Conversations.* Berkeley: University of California Press, 2004. 85–117.

———, ed. *Musicology and Difference: Gender and Sexuality in Music Scholarship.* Berkeley: University of California Press, 1993.

Stern, Isaac (with Chaim Potok). *My First 79 Years.* New York: Knopf, 1999.

Taylor, Timothy. *Global Pop: Capitalism and Contemporary World Music.* New York: Routledge, 1997.

———. *Beyond Exoticism: Western Music and the World.* Durham: Duke University Press, 2007.

Tick, Judith. "'Passed Away Is the Piano Girl': Changes in American Musical Life, 1870–1900." In *Women Making Music: The Western Art Tradition, 1150–1950.* Eds. Jane Bowers and Judith Tick. Urbana: University of Illinois Press, 1986. 325–348.

Tindall, Blair. *Mozart in the Jungle: Sex, Drugs, and Classical Music.* New York: Atlantic Monthly Press, 2005.

Vlastos, Stephen. *Mirror of Modernity: Invented Traditions of Modern Japan.* Berkeley: University of California Press, 1998.

Vo, Linda Trinh and Rick Bonus. *Contemporary Asian American Communities: Intersections and Divergences.* Philadelphia: Temple University Press, 2002.

Wade, Bonnie C. *Music in Japan: Experiencing Music, Expressing Culture.* New York: Oxford University Press, 2005.

Wagner, Roy. *The Invention of Culture.* Chicago: University of Chicago Press, 1981.

Wang, Grace. "Soundtracks of Asian American Identity: Music, Race, and National Belonging." PhD diss. University of Michigan, 2005.

Wong, Deborah. *Speak It Louder: Asian Americans Making Music.* New York: Routledge, 2004.

Wright, Erik Olin. *Class Counts: Comparative Studies in Class Analysis.* Cambridge: Cambridge University Press, 1997.

———. "Rethinking, Once Again, the Concept of Class Structure." In *Reworking Class* Ed. John R. Hall. Ithaca: Cornell University Press, 1997. 41–71.

Yano, Christine R. *Tears of Longing: Nostalgia and the Nation in Japanese Popular Song.* Cambridge, MA: Harvard University Press, 2002.

———. *Crowning the Nice Girl: Gender, Ethnicity, and Culture in Hawai'i's Cherry Blossom Festival.* Honolulu: University of Hawai'i Press, 2006.

Yoshihara, Mari. *Embracing the East: White Women and American Orientalism.* New York: Oxford University Press, 2003.

———. "The Flight of the Japanese Butterfly: Orientalism, Nationalism, and Performances of Japanese Womanhood." *American Quarterly* 56.4 (2004): 975–1001.

Zheng, Su. "Immigrant Music and Transnational Discourse: Chinese American Music Culture in New York City." PhD diss. Wesleyan University, 1993.

———. "Music Making in Cultural Displacement: The Chinese-American Odyssey." *Diaspora* 3.3 (1994): 273–288.

———. *Claiming Diaspora: Music, Transnationalism, and Cultural Politics in Asian/ Chinese America.* New York: Oxford University Press, 2006.

Zolberg, Vera L. "Barrier or Leveler: The Case of the Art Museum." In *Cultivating Differences: Symbolic Boundaries and the Making of Inequality.* Eds. Michèle Lamont and Marcel Fournier. Chicago: University of Chicago Press, 1992. 187–209.

JAPANESE-LANGUAGE SOURCES

Akemitsu, Yoshimoto, ed. *Ochō Fujin: Denki Miura Tamaki.* Tokyo: Ubunsha, 1947.

Akiyama, Kuniharu. *Shōwa no Sakkyokuka tachi: Taiheiyō Sensō to Ongaku.* Tokyo: Misuzu Shobō, 2003.

Akiyama, Tatsuhide, ed. *Nihon no Yōgaku Hyakunen-shi.* Tokyo: Dai-ichi Hōki Shuppan, 1976.

Geijutsu Kenkyū Shinkō Zaidan Tokyo Geijutsu Daigaku Hyakunen-shi Henshū Iinkai, ed. *Tokyo Geijutsu Daigaku Hyakunen-shi Daigaku-hen.* [Tokyo]: Gyōsei, 2003.

Honda, Masaaki. *Ai no Hito Suzuki Shinichi Sensei.* [Tokyo]: Zen-on Gakufu Shuppansha, 1978.

Kavaie, Ronarudo [Ronald Cavaye] and Shifu Nishiyama. *Nihonjin no Ongaku Kyōiku.* Tokyo: Shinchō Sensho, 1987.

Kojima, Masami. *"Suzuki mesoddo" Sekai ni Yōji Kakumei wo: Suzuki Shinichi no Ai to Kyōiku.* [Tokyo]: Kyōdō Ongaku Shuppansha, 1985.

Kusudo, Yoshiaki. *Mou Hitori no Chō-Chō-Fujin: Nagasaki Gurabaa-tei no Onna Shujin Tsuru.* Tokyo: Mainichi Shinbun-sha, 1997.

Maema, Takanori and Yūichi Iwano. *Nihon no Piano 100-nen: Piano Zukuri ni Kaketa Hitobito.* Tokyo: Sōshisha, 2001.

Miura, Tamaki. *Kageki Ochō Fujin.* [Tokyo]: Ongaku Sekai-sha, 1937.

Nishihara, Minoru. *Piano no Tanjō: Gakki no Mukou ni "Kindai" ga Mieru.* Tokyo: Kōdansha, 1995.

Okuda, Akinori. *Haha to Shindō: Gotō Setsu Monogatari.* Tokyo: Shōgakukan, 1998.

Ozawa, Seiji. *Boku no Ongaku Musha Shugyō.* Tokyo: Shinchōsha, 1980.

———— and Toru Takemitsu. *Ongaku.* Tokyo: Shinchōsha, 1984.

Shibata, Tamaki. *Sekai no Opera.* [Tokyo]: Kyōeki Shōsha, 1912.

Suzuki, Shinichi. *Ai ni Ikiru: Sainō wa Umaretsuki dewa Nai.* [Tokyo]: Kōdansha, 1966.

Suzuki Shinichi Zenshū. 9 Vols. [Tokyo]: Sōhaisha, 1985.

Tanabe, Hisayuki. *Kōshō Miura Tamaki.* Tokyo: Kindai Bungei-sha, 1995.

Watanabe, Hiroshi. *Nihon Bunka Modan Rapusodi.* Tokyo: Shunjūsha, 2002.

Index

African Americans, 46, 89, 92–93
Ahn, Angella. *See* Ahn Trio
Ahn Trio, 95, 121–122, 181–183, 202
Akina, Henry, 212–213
American music, 196–197
American studies, 228–230
Anthony, Lifen, 52–55
anti-commercialism, 7, 157–165
anti-materialism, 7, 157–165
Appenzeller, Henry G., 17
Asian American studies, 65, 228, 230
Asian Americans: assertions of American
  identity, 196–197; class background
  of, 142–143; communities and groups,
  84–85, 104, 193; diversity among, 7–8,
  65–69; musicians' sense of racial identity,
  63, 66–69. *See also* Chinese Americans;
  immigrants; *individual musicians*; Japanese
  Americans; Korean Americans
Asian music, 83, 167–170, 175, 192–196,
  217, 221
Aspen Music Festival, 87, 183
assimilation, 3, 84–85, 147, 172, 193
auditions, 64, 106, 153
authenticity: academic debates over notions
  of, 189–190, 223–224; Asian musicians'
  playing being questioned of, 90, 187–189;

Asian musicians seen as authentic Asians,
  24–25; 192, 211; in composition, 214–215;
  creating authentic representations of Asian
  culture, 26, 31–33; debates about cultural
  authenticity and music, 6, 179–181,
  190–191, 197–199; in instrumental
  performance, 197–199; in opera, 210–211
avant-garde music, 219–221, 227

Ba, Duoming, 71, 194
Baumol, William and William Bowen, 132
Beijing opera, 65, 175, 193
Beijing Piano Company, 36
Bendix, Regina, 223
Benjamin, Walter, 189
Bourdieu, Pierre, 132, 135–136, 148–150,
  157, 161–164, 227. *See also* cultural capital;
  field
Bunch, Kenji, 80, 181–186
Butterfly Lovers Concerto, The, 120, 174

Cage, John, 166–170, 221
Cai, Jindong. *See* Melvin, Sheila and Jindong
  Cai
Calaf. See *Turandot*
Cavaye, Ronald, 43
Central Conservatory of Music (Beijing), 18

Central Philharmonic (Beijing), 11, 12
Chang, Han-Na, 74–75, 119, 195
Chang, Sarah, 38, 65, 67, 119, 122–125, 152
ch'anggas, 18
Chee-Yun (Kim), 149, 199
Chen, Sa, 2, 101
Chen Yi, 219
China (People's Republic of): Chinese
    composers studying and working in the
    United States, 37, 219–222; the Cultural
    Revolution, 12, 22–23, 52–54, 140–141,
    226; *From Mao to Mozart,* 11–14;
    introduction of Western music to, 16–20;
    manufacturing of musical instruments
    in, 34, 37; musical culture in, 193; rise of
    classical musicians from, 100–101. *See also
    individual musicians*
Chinese Americans, 68. *See also individual
    musicians*
Cho, Tony, 104, 126–127
Chosun Institute of Classical Music, 18
Chou Wen-Chung, 220
Chung, Junah, 62, 88–91
Chung, Kyung-Wha, 36, 113, 122
Chung, Myung-Wha, 36
Chung, Myung-Whun, 36
church, 16. *See also* missionaries
Cio-Cio-San. See *Madama Butterfly*
class: background of classical musicians, 66,
    75, 137–143; class-based gender norms,
    102–106; classical music as a marker
    of, 33–34, 102–103, 131–132, 226;
    consciousness among musicians, 137,
    157–158, 164–165; downward mobility
    among Asians, 148–150; economic lives
    of classical musicians, 131, 133, 151–156;
    theories of, 134–136. *See also* Bourdieu,
    Pierre; cultural capital; middle class;
    professional middle class; working class
Cliburn, Van: International Piano
    Competition, 2, 100–102, 152
colonialism: Japanese colonialism in Asia, 14,
    18, 20, 31. *See also* imperialism
Communist Party (China), 19, 22. *See also*
    Cultural Revolution
competitions: Asians' success in major, 2;
    cost of entering, 145; as a path to a career,

69, 76, 151–152. *See also* Cliburn, Van;
    Tchaikovsky Competition, International
composers: Chinese composers in the United
    States, 37; collaborations with performers,
    75, 169, 175, 178–180, 195; meaning
    of authenticity for, 214–222; place of in
    musicology, 191, 197–198, 225, 228. *See
    also individual composers*
conductors, 110, 133
conservatories (of music): cost of attending,
    143–144; culture of, 64, 72, 87, 88, 146,
    214–215; founding of, 18; jobs in, 155;
    social symbolism of, 103; training at, 35,
    53–54; 64, 133, 193. *See also individual
    conservatories*
Cook, Clifford, 40
Cooper, Kristina Reiko, 80
cost: of musical instruments, 143, 152; of
    musical training, 72, 143–145
cultural capital, 33–34, 47–48, 75, 87, 132,
    133, 136, 138 147–150, 157–165. *See also*
    Bourdieu, Pierre; middle class
Cultural Revolution (China), 11, 12, 14,
    22–23, 37, 53, 65, 140–141, 162, 220, 226
cultural studies, 228–230
Curtis Institute of Music, 3

DeLay, Dorothy, 49–50, 60, 73, 174
Doe, Henry Wong, 79–80
Dong Bei Piano Company, 36

East Asia: attitude toward homosexuality,
    126; dominance of East Asians in classical
    music, 7; gender norms in, 102–106;
    introduction of Western music to, 15–23;
    musical culture in, 193, 223; number of
    musicians from, 3; role of classical music
    in, 33–36, 150, 193, 226. *See also* China;
    Japan; Korea
Eastman School of Music, 3
Eckert, Franz, 16
Ehwa Women's College (Ehwa Women's
    University), 18
elite: classical music as a form of elite culture,
    132, 133, 135; elite intellectuals' role in
    promoting classical music in Asia, 6, 15,
    47; ownership of musical instruments, 33

empire. *See* imperialism
essentialism, 190–192, 202, 233
ethnicity: and class, 136; ethnic
    communities, 93–99, 193, 223; ethnic
    composition of Asian musicians in the
    United States, 7; ethnic identity of Asian
    musicians, 62–69, 76–99; marketing of
    identity, 162, 177, 215, 218, 222
ethnomusicology, 194, 228, 229
Europe: Asian musicians living and studying
    in, 69, 70, 75, 78–79, 90–91, 177–178,
    206; perceptions of Asian musicians in,
    61, 90–91; social significance of domestic
    music-making in, 102

feminism, 107
field, 157, 162–165, 227. *See also* Bourdieu,
    Pierre
flute, 56–57
Frautschi, Jennifer and Laura, 80
freelance, 88, 155–156
Friedman, Lea Woods, 211–212
From Mao to Mozart, 11–14, 23. *See also*
    Stern, Isaac
Fukuda, Hiromi, 204
Furukawa, Mariko, 203

Galimir, Felix, 187
gay musicians, 109, 125–129. *See also*
    sexuality
Ge Ganru, 167, 169, 220–222
gender: Asian musicians' feminist
    consciousness, 107, 111; gendered portrayals
    of Asian musicians, 100–102, 116–125;
    gender norms in classical music practice,
    40, 102–103, 148; impact of gender norms
    on female musicians, 29–31, 106–116,
    129, 210; impact of gender norms on male
    musicians, 104–106, 129, 210; sexism in
    classical music, 55, 106–107, 110, 112–113.
Gilbert, Alan, 80
Gilbert, William. See *Mikado, The*
globalization, 6, 75, 76–78, 190, 200, 229
Goto, Midori. *See* Midori
government: Asian governments' role in
    promoting classical music, 6, 15, 17, 18, 47,
    201; funding for the arts, 132–133

Griffes, Charles, 168–169
Guaspari-Tzavaras, Roberta, 46

Harlem (New York), 46, 92–93
Harbin (China), 20
Hata, Kimiko, 92, 96, 211
Hawai'i, 79, 82–83, 212–213
Hawaii Opera Theatre, 212–213
He Luting, 22
high culture, 3–4, 6, 47, 131–132. *See also*
    elite
Hirata, Makiko, 86–87, 89, 113–114,
    188–189
homophobia, 126–129
homosexuality. *See* gay musicians;
    homosexuality; sexuality
Hong, Hei-Kyung, 211
Hong, Jihea, 147
Horiuchi, Keizō, 31–32
Huang, Helen, 97–99, 107, 119, 195
Huang, Myra, 88–89, 108, 138–139
Hubbs, Nadine, 128–129
"hybrid Asians," 78–81
hymns, 16–17, 21. *See also* church

"immigrant geniuses," 72–75, 148–149
immigrants, 66, 72, 74–75, 142–143, 147,
    150
Immigration Act of 1965, 66, 75, 142
imperialism: classical music seen as a tool of
    Western imperialism, 11, 22, 47; Western
    imperialism as context for the introduction
    of classical music to Asia, 6, 14, 15, 18, 47.
    See also colonialism
instruction methods, 33, 35, 37–48. *See also*
    Suzuki Method
instruments: Asian musicians' choice of,
    3, 103, 172, 183, 226; cost of, 143, 152;
    manufacturing of, 33–36
international students, 69–72, 88, 144
Izawa, Shūji, 17

Jang, Ignace, 79
Japan: attitude toward homosexuality in, 126;
    censorship of Western music in, 20–22;
    gender norms in, 29–30, 102, 116, 148;
    introduction of Western music to, 15–18,

102; Japanese musicians studying and working in the West, 36; manufacturing of musical instruments in, 33–36; middle class in, 141–142; musical culture in, 193, 216; spread of classical music among the middle class in, 33–37; Suzuki Method, 37–48. *See also individual musicians*

Japanese Americans, 93–95, 142. *See also individual musicians*

jazz, 84–85, 94, 196

Jews: 1, 21, 50, 147, 174, 217; European Jews in China, 20; Russian Jews in China, 20

Jo, Sumi, 211

Johnson, Julian, 163–164

Juilliard School, the: careers of the graduates from, 133; culture of, 68, 87, 108, 139, 184; gender dynamics at, 108, 112–113; musicians' recollections of the time at, 61, 77, 89, 139, 172, 184; Pre-College, 1, 50–51, 72–74, 86–87, 89, 112, 139, 144, 146, 147–148, 159, 183; racial and ethnic composition of the student body at, 2–3, 4, 66, 69; racial and ethnic dynamics at, 1, 68, 77, 89, 108, 172, 50–51; training at, 60, 174, 184; tuition at, 143

Kato, Kaori, 204–205

Kato, Sachiko, 114–116, 195, 199–200

Kawai Piano Company, 33, 35

Kawakubo, Tamaki, 2

Kim, Chee-Yun. *See* Chee-Yun (Kim)

Kim, David, 1, 49–52, 144

Kim, Young-Whan, 19

Kimura, Mari, 158–159, 203, 208–209

Kingsbury, Henry, 64, 229

Koh, Jennifer, 38, 62–63, 90, 107, 160, 196

Korea (Republic of): gender composition of musicians trained in, 103; gender norms in, 148; introduction of Western music to, 15–19, 193; Korean musicians studying and working in the West, 36–37, 74–75; manufacturing of musical instruments in, 34; middle class in, 142; musical culture in, 193; spread of classical music among the middle class in, 33–37; stereotypes of musicians from, 108. *See also individual musicians*

Korean Americans, 77, 95. *See also individual musicians*

Korean National University of the Arts, 18

Korean War, 34, 142

Kraus, Richard Curt, 140

Kuo, Conway, 67–68, 105, 207

labor: as basis for class position, 134–135, 164; classical music as a form of, 131–134, 151–156, 164; musicians' union, 153–154

Lamont, Michèle, 150

language: Asian musicians' English language skills, 72, 86–87, 88; music as a language, 87, 88, 205–207, 230

Latino Americans, 46

Lau, Frederick, 83, 105, 139, 194, 219–220

Le, Andrew, 67

Lee, Soyeon, 77–78, 111–113

lessons: cost of, 143–144; cultural differences in, 60; group, 35, 38, 43–44; private, 35, 37, 102, 109, 155, 193; teacher–student relations in, 109

Li, Bichuan, 140–141

Li Delun, 11–12

Li Shutong, 17

Li, Yundi, 117–118

Lim, Anna, 138

Lin, Cho-Liang, 98, 170–175

Lin, I-Bei, 71, 83

Liu Shikun Piano Arts School (Hong Kong), 35

Lu Hongen, 22

Luk, Siu Yan, 194

Ma Sicong, 22–23

Ma, Yo-Yo. *See* Yo-Yo Ma

Madama Butterfly, 23–33, 96, 210–211

Mae, Vanessa, 120

management (booking agencies), 75, 110, 149, 151, 152

Manchuria, 20

Manhattan School of Music, 143

Manzanaar: An American Story, 93–95. *See also* Nagano, Kent; Sekiya, Naomi

marimba, 75, 175–181

marketing: of musical instruments, 34; of musicians, 116–125; of racial and ethnic identity, 162, 177, 215, 218, 222

marriage, 103, 108, 109, 112, 115, 148
Marx, Karl. *See* Marxism
Marxism, 134–135, 164
Matsudaira, Satoko, 31
May Fourth Movement (China), 19
media: dependence of musicians' labor on, 135; portrayal of Asian musicians, 2, 5, 94, 100–102; portrayal of the Suzuki Method, 41–42, 44
Melvin, Sheila and Jindong Cai, 19, 34, 220
Meyers, Anne Akiko, 80, 110, 121, 208
middle class: Asian middle class's aspiration for classical music, 39, 47, 193, 226; background of Asian musicians, 66, 75, 78, 137–138, 157–161; in East Asia, 140–142; gender norms among, 102–106; in postindustrial economy, 134–136; spread of classical music among the Asian middle class, 15, 33–37, 47, 75. *See also* cultural capital; professional middle class
Midori (Goto), 72–73, 119, 152, 160
"migrant professionals," 75–76
Mikado, The, 210, 212–213
militarism: Japan, 21, 31
military band, 15–16
mission schools, 16–17
missionaries, 16–17
Miura, Tamaki, 23–31, 48, 210
mixed race, 8, 80–81, 181, 185, 211
Miyazaki, Selina, 88, 92–93, 96
Mochizuki, Kenji, 40
model minority, 3–4, 42, 84, 125, 142
modernization, 6, 15–20, 226
Mok, Warren, 97, 104, 137, 213
mothers: role in music training, 38, 40, 49–50, 72–73, 139, 183. *See also* parents
"mother tongue approach," 38. *See also* Suzuki Method
Muroki, Kurt, 1, 161, 207
Music Investigation Committee (Japan), 18
Music of the Heart, 46. *See also* Guaspari-Tzavaras, Roberta
musicology, 125–126, 164, 198, 228–229
music therapy, 204–205
Nagano, Kent, 65, 93–95, 118, 196, 198
Naito, Akemi, 215–217
Nakamatsu, Jon, 152

Nakamura, Hiroko, 36, 116
Nakura, Makoto, 75–76, 175–181
nationalism: China, 14, 19; East Asia, 15, 20, 47, 227, 228; Europe, 90; Japan, 20–22, 28–30, 39; Korea, 14
Nettl, Bruno, 64, 197, 198, 214, 229
New York (City), 8, 9, 46–47, 178, 215–216
New York Philharmonic, 2
NHK Symphony Orchestra (Tokyo), 36
Nie Er, 19

Okamoto, Satoshi, 105–106, 201–202
Ong, Aihwa, 150
opera, 23–33, 97, 110, 210–214, 226
Opus 118 Music Center, 46. *See also* Guaspari-Tzavaras, Roberta
orchestras: auditions for, 64, 106, 131, 153; financial conditions of, 132, 153–154; jobs in, 49, 51–52, 71, 72, 131, 133, 135, 153–154, 161
Orientalism, 24–27, 29, 31–32, 44, 168, 210, 213
Osada, Moto, 217–219
Otani, Muneko, 91–92
Out of Peking Opera (Tan Dun), 175
Ozawa, Seiji, 36, 65, 69, 80, 93

Pacific War, 30. *See also* World War II
parents: attitude toward homosexuality, 126; background of musicians' parents, 137–139; motivations for giving music lessons to children, 147–148; role in music training, 38, 72–75, 105, 184; role in marketing musicians, 117, 119, 125, 145–148
particularism, 191, 202–209, 227, 230
patronage: of classical music, 132; of musicians, 69, 110, 143, 144
Peak, Lois, 43
Pearl River (Piano Company), 34, 36
pedagogy. *See* instruction methods
Peking opera. *See* Beijing opera
piano: manufacturing of, 33–34; social symbolism of, 33–34, 102; training in, 63, 102, 103, 112, 226
politics: musicians' involvement in, 68, 232; political culture in conservatories, 68, 107; political discourse of classical music,

64; political language for expressions of identity, 107

prodigy, 73, 82, 119

professional managerial class. *See* professional middle class

professional middle class, 66, 75, 78, 80, 135, 137–138. *See also* middle class

proletarian movement: Japan, 21

Puccini, Giacomo, 23, 27, 32. See also *Madama Butterfly*; *Turandot*

Qian, Wen, 144

queer studies, 125–126, 128–129

race: Asian musicians' experience of racism in America, 66–67, 84, 92; in casting (in opera), 210–214; and class, 136, 149, 165; crossing of racial boundaries through music, 92–93; racial identity of Asian musicians, 62–69, 76–77, 78–99; racialization, 63, 81, 223, 228; racism in classical music, 64, 90–91; relevance of in music-making, 187–192, 199–224; and sexuality, 126

"reverse flow," 8, 15, 35–37, 40–48, 56–57, 58, 80, 227

Ricci, Mateo, 16

Russian Revolution, 14, 20

Russians, 20. *See also* Jews

Saitō, Hideo, 69, 80

Samick (Piano), 34, 36

Satoh, Somei, 167, 208

school songs, 17, 19, 193, 226

schools: music education in mission schools, 17; music education in public schools, 17, 34–35, 160; classical musicians' experience in high school, 84, 86, 87–88, 183. *See also* conservatories; mission schools; universities

Sekiya, Naomi, 93–95. See also *Manzanaar: An American Story*

sexism, 55, 106–107, 112–113

sexuality, 30, 109–111, 119–122, 125–129, 162. *See also* gay musicians

Shanghai, 18, 19, 20

Shanghai Conservatory of Music, 12, 18, 22, 220

Shanghai Municipal Orchestra, 18

Sheng, Bright, 170, 219

Shen Xingong, 17

Shin, Heejin, 138

Shyu, Jennifer, 84–85, 137

Singapore, 166–168

Sino-Japanese War: of 1894, 95, 16, 17; of 1937, 41, 22

Small Wonders, 46. *See also* Guaspari-Tvaras, Roberta

Solie, Ruth A., 102, 104

solo: career as a soloist, 49, 51, 71, 110, 131, 133, 151–153

Song, Ju-Ying, 78–79, 137, 205

sponsors. *See* patronage

stereotypes: of Asian musicians, 61, 82, 108–109, 185; of Asians, 84, 210; gender, 112, 115–116, 210; of parents of Asian musicians, 145

Stern, Isaac, 11–14, 46, 48, 170, 174. See also *From Mao to Mozart*

style (of playing), 54–55, 173–175, 179–181

Sugiyama, Miori, 108–109

Sullivan, Arthur. See *Mikado, The*

Suzuki Method, 8, 37–48, 56–61, 144, 227. *See also* Suzuki, Shinichi

Suzuki, Shinichi, 8, 37–39, 41, 44–45, 56–57, 59

Taiwan, 170–173. *See also individual musicians*

Takahashi, Toshio, 45, 56–57

Takaori, Shūichi, 28

Takebe, Yoko, 80

Takemitsu, Toru, 175, 195, 208, 221

Takezawa, Kyoko, 38, 57–61, 97, 151–152, 173

Talent Education Research Institute. *See* Suzuki Method

Tan Dun, 65, 84, 166, 169, 170, 175, 195, 196, 218, 219, 231

Tan, Margaret Leng, 166–170

Tan Shuzhen, 12, 22

Tchaikovsky Competition, International, 2

teaching: career in, 72, 102, 131; teacher-student relationships, 109, 184

Tindall, Blair, 133

Tokyo University of Fine Arts and Music (Tokyo Music School), 18, 103

Toyoda, Kōji, 44
"transnational offspring," 76–78
Trio Xia, 83
Tsai, Pei-Chun, 194
Tse, Joel, 92, 196
Turandot, 120, 210, 212, 214

Uchida, Mitsuko, 113, 116, 122, 173
Uehara, Ayako, 2
umak hakwon, 35
Underwood, Horace G., 17
union (musicians'), 154
universalism, 5–6, 7, 180–181, 191, 199–202, 205, 207–209, 227, 230
universities: jobs in, 155

Wang Xilin, 22
Watanabe, Ayako and Haruka, 161, 195, 209
Weber, Max, 135
working class, 134–135, 138, 160
World War I, 24
World War II, 39, 80, 93

Xi, Chen, 2
Xiao Youmei, 19

Yajima, Hiroko, 69–70, 91, 187–188
Yamada, Kōsaku, 31–32, 96
Yamaha, 33, 35–37
Yamamoto, Kōichirō, 70, 202–203
Yang, Joyce, 2, 101
Yang, Yi-Heng, 138, 147
Yee, Thomas, 81–83, 85
yellow peril, 44
Yin, Sidney, 160
Yonsei University, 19
Yotsuya, Fumiko, 21
Young Chang (Piano), 34, 36
Yo-Yo Ma, 65, 118, 152, 170, 231
Yuan Shikai, 16

Zeng, Zhimin, 17
Zhang, Xian, 2
Zhang, Zhidong, 16
Zhou Long, 219

About the Author

Mari Yoshihara is Associate Professor of American Studies at the University of Hawaii at Manoa. She is the author of *Embracing the East: White Women and American Orientalism.*